BOYD'S HANDBOOK OF PRACTICAL APOLOGETICS

*Scientific Facts, Fulfilled Prophecies,
and Archaeological Discoveries
That Confirm the Bible*

Robert T. Boyd

kregel
PUBLICATIONS

Grand Rapids, MI 49501

Boyd's Handbook of Practical Apologetics

Copyright © 1997 by Robert T. Boyd

Published by Kregel Publications, a division of Kregel, Inc., P.O. Box 2607, Grand Rapids, MI 49501. Kregel Publications provides trusted, biblical publications for Christian growth and service. Your comments and suggestions are valued.

Cover and book design: Alan G. Hartman

Library of Congress Cataloging-in-Publication Data
Boyd, Robert T.
     Boyd's handbook of practical apologetics / by Robert T. Boyd.
          p.   cm.
          Includes indexes.
     1. Bible—Evidences, authority, etc.—Handbooks, manuals, etc. 2. Creationism—Handbooks, manuals, etc. 3. Bible—Antiquities—Handbooks, manuals, etc. 4. Bible—History of Biblical events—Handbooks, manuals, etc. 5. Bible—History of contemporary events—Handbooks, manuals, etc. 6. Apologetics—Handbooks, manuals, etc. I. Title.
BS480.B633   1997   220.1—dc20   95-18159
                                                                    CIP
ISBN 0-8254-2161-6

          1 2 3 4 5 printing / year 01 00 99 98 97
                    Printed in the United States of America

BOYD'S HANDBOOK OF PRACTICAL APOLOGETICS

Books by Robert T. Boyd

The Acts of the Apostle Paul

World's Bible Handbook

To my sister, Helen McConnell, and
to my brother, Ernest L. Boyd

Contents

Charts and Figures

Charts

Figures

Foreword

I am honored to write a foreword to Bob Boyd's *Handbook of Practical Apologetics.* Dr. Boyd has, throughout his lifetime of fruitful ministry, written a great number of tracts, pamphlets, and books. This work is the quintessence of them all.

Bob Boyd, in all his activities, has consistently upheld the Bible as inerrant, absolute truth in a day when we see some evangelical leaders getting "soft" on such a position. Or, if they claim that they still hold to it, they have weakened people's faith in the Bible by stretching plain and simple passages to fit the latest fads in so-called science (actually, a philosophy of science) and liberal interpretations of archaeological finds. Not Bob Boyd.

With his practical teaching and writing he has encouraged untold numbers of the Lord's people. And to those who know him personally, his upbeat, victorious view of life is truly inspiring. He not only is victorious, but in the midst of infirmity, he makes light of it. The readers of this *Handbook,* therefore, are availing themselves of a work by an author who has been "through the mill" and come out on top.

The *Handbook's* purpose is not only to confirm the Scriptures through science, prophecy, and archaeology, but to cast new light on obscure or hard-to-understand passages. It answers many questions most often asked about the Bible. In the Appendix one finds some of the latest archaeological finds. And, fortunately, the book is written so anyone can understand it.

This *Handbook* will be helpful for Sunday school and youth teachers; for pastors in sermon preparation; for homeschoolers, especially, because it is almost an encyclopedia in itself; for families to use in devotions (many items are short nuggets); for personal Bible study; and for many other uses.

God loves "encouragers" (*parakletos,* John 14:26). This highly important activity is performed by the Holy Spirit when He comes to live in believers. Maybe this is why "encouraging the brethren" is emphasized in Hebrews 10:25. We read there that the brethren are told to "exhort" (KJV) one another, but the word really means "encourage" from the same root (*parakalountes*). This has been the hallmark of Bob Boyd's ministry.

—David Livingston
Associates for Bible Research

Acknowledgments

T he author wishes to express his appreciation to the following people for their help, suggestions, and encouragement in making this volume possible: my wife, Peggy; Darlene Stambaugh for proofreading; Dr. Henry M. Morris; Dr. David Livingston; Dr. Harry Rimmer; and Dr. Joseph P. Free.

Scripture references are from the King James Version (KJV) unless otherwise noted.

Introduction

The Bible is an interesting book that contains history, literature, philosophy, poetry, and science. It appeals not only to religious leaders, educators, parents, and students, but to people in general. It has also become the most hated book in all the world—in spite of the fact that it is the most loved as well as the best seller. Although it is loved and hated, it is first and foremost a book of spiritual assertions—a book that contains the very heart and mind of God Himself—a book of great value that meets the need of everyone.

Reasons for Believing the Bible

The Bible is a nameless book. The word "Bible" comes from the Greek *biblia*, which means "the book." Names are used to distinguish one book or person from another. Since the Bible is *the* supreme book in all the world, it does not need a name; it is enough to simply say, "The Bible—The Book."

The Bible is a timeless book. Other books come and go because they no longer fit the thoughts of different ages or meet the needs of human hearts. They all have their day. Not so with the Bible. It is timeless, ageless. People are different, but this book alone interests all races and classes, no matter what their cultural or educational background. Beginning with the Septuagint ca. 250 B.C. and continuing through the present day, the Book of Books called the Bible has been translated into thousands of languages all over the earth.

The Bible has an Architect, not an author. The unity of this book, while it too had authors, shows that Someone besides humans had a part in it. Who else but God could have put together these sixty-six books with one theme, one self-authenticating message fortified with spiritual power, and one purpose?

There are many who bring the structure of a building to completion, and each knows there was an architect. Although the some forty writers of the Bible were separated by some 1,500 years were from vastly different classes and cultures, from a king on his throne to humble and unlearned fishermen, the Bible has an uncanny unity. Portions were written during Israel's wilderness wanderings, some in Babylon, Persia, Asia Minor, in a Roman prison, in Jerusalem, and in scattered parts of Palestine. When we think of the unity of this book, we must conclude that each book was written according to the Architect's design.

There are other reasons for believing the Bible to be God's Word. Though there are sixty-six separate books, it is *one* book. It tells one continuous story; it gives one progressive unfolding of Truth; it speaks of one redemption, and it has but one theme—the person and work of the Lord Jesus Christ. There was perfect oneness and harmony among these writers over these many centuries and the only answer for this can be that "holy men spake as they were moved by the Holy Ghost" (2 Peter 1:21).

Think for a moment of its miraculous preservation, its complete triumph over its enemies who down through the centuries have sought to destroy it. The story is told of persecution of Christians in Ireland. As Bibles were being burned, an enemy took a little boy's New Testament. The boy told them, "You can burn my copy, but you can't take the Word of God out of my heart!" Only God can guard, protect, preserve, secure, and make safe such a book, even giving us assurance that His Word shall not pass away, that it is forever settled in heaven (Matt. 24:35; Ps. 119:89).

The integrity of copies (translations) in various languages through human hands reveals God's hand in preserving His Word. Language barriers are very difficult to overcome and have at times caused different spellings and pronunciations of words, but the cardinal truths of His Word still stand as shown by the discovery of the Dead Sea Scrolls containing the whole Scroll (book) of Isaiah and other manuscripts. The exact copying of the text through many centuries is a phenomenon unequaled in history. [See "Dead Sea Scrolls."]

Though the stories in the Bible are old, the freshness of the Bible's message is always new. Its promises have given spirit, life, courage, and confidence to those who have sought and still seek the deeper things of God (John 6:63; Ps. 92:5). God's mercies are new every morning and He daily loads all His benefits on those who have experienced His so great salvation through the Lord Jesus Christ (Lam. 3:23; Ps. 68:19). It is wonderful how this aged book helps and encourages the saints of God but also how it comes to the aid of those who have become discouraged and troubled in mind and heart.

God has a wonderful diet in His Word.

1. Milk (1 Peter 2:2)
2. Bread (Matt. 4:4)
3. Meat (Heb. 5:12–14)
4. Honey (Ps. 119:103)

Jeremiah said: "[God's] words were found, and I did eat them" (15:16). Job said: "I have esteemed the words of his mouth more than my necessary food" (23:12). People keep trying to find what their hearts need with their own prescription, but the only remedy can be found by tasting the Word of God and finding that He is good (Ps. 34:8).

The testimony of a transformed life by the influence of the Bible upon character and conduct demonstrates the Bible's power. The purpose of God in redemption as revealed in the Scriptures is to restore fallen humankind to God from whom they became estranged through sin—to redeem people "from all iniquity, and purify unto himself a peculiar people, zealous of good works" (Titus 2:14).

Has this been done? The history of the Christian church replies in the affirmative! Peter, the impetuous Christ-denier, became a powerful preacher and leader of early Christians. Saul of Tarsus, the persecutor of the church, became the theologian and establisher of the church. Early New Testament saints, John Bunyan, Martin Luther, the Wesley brothers, Charles Spurgeon, Dwight L. Moody, and Billy Sunday have been transformed by grace divine and attested to the avowed purpose of the Scriptures.

A mechanic was ridiculed by an engineer for his above-board conduct and for reading his well-worn Bible during lunchtime. Because the mechanic could not prove who wrote each book, the engineer made a nuisance of himself by discrediting God's Word.

After several days of harassment the mechanic asked the engineer who wrote the multiplication table. "I don't know but it is a necessity in my field." He was then asked why he relied on something whose author was unknown to him, and he heatedly replied, "It works in my profession." And so the humble mechanic said, "For that same reason I believe the Bible. It works in my life."

What about those who reject the claims of the Bible? English teachers will use it, particularly the King James Version, but only for its literary value. They sees no importance in its message. Historians will refer to it, but too often with a critical view in regard to what they call "historical inaccura-

cies." (This will be discussed in section 3.) Modern philosophers ignore its spiritual value because they think that humans have sufficiently elevated themselves from their primitive views of religious myths and can now control their own destiny. Humanism has been enthroned so now faith in a prayer-hearing God assumed to love, care, understand, and help people is an unproved, outmoded, and outdated faith. Humanism begins with humans, not God. Humans alone save themselves. This makes humanism a religion, a religion of evolution.

Some religious leaders are guilty of not accepting the Bible for its true intent. Liberal and modernistic preachers who rebel at the truth of a blood-bought redemption by Jesus Christ call it a "slaughter-house" religion. They do so because they believe they are good within themselves, that they have a "spark of the divine" within, that everybody is a child of God. The supernatural is not compatible with natural reasoning, and so believing, no one is a sinner; there is, therefore, no need for a Savior. Such critics will attack the Bible, and all that does not appeal to their reasoning (such as miracles) is not seen as inspired. That which does appeal to them, of course, is inspired, in spite of the fact that the Bible they use teaches that "*All* Scripture is given by inspiration of God" (2 Tim. 3:16). They grasp at straws to belittle those who believe in the inerrancy of the Scriptures.

Since it is difficult for these liberal critics to disprove what they do not believe, they employ subtle attacks on the Bible by charging that the accepted authors did not write the portions attributed to them. As a result, they have concluded that the first book of the Bible, Genesis, is the work of more than one author, basing their conclusions on what they say are repetitious statements and contradictions in the text.

One "contradiction" cited in Genesis is the claim that there are two different accounts of creation in chapters 1 and 2. One of the "inconsistencies" mentioned is the use of two different words for Supreme Deity— "J" for *Jahweh* and "E" for *Elohim*.

Actually, these two chapters come under the heading of the "Law of Recurrence," which means that what chapter 1 did not mention, chapter 2 did. In no way are there two creation accounts in this Book. These scholars also attribute the remaining portion of Genesis to a "priestly" writer designated "P." According to these liberals, Deuteronomy was written by "D."

Some time ago a very liberal scholar was interviewed on a morning talk show and said he believed a woman wrote portions of the Scriptures.

The theory of multiple authorship is widely taught in liberal seminaries throughout our land and has been labeled the "Documentary Hypothesis."

A bit of scientific news came to light in 1982. A team of researchers in Israel's Institute of Technology has concluded, after feeding the over 20,000-word book of Genesis into a computer for analysis, that there were not several authors, but a *single* author. The team said it found the "J" and "E" narratives difficult to distinguish linguistically. They found *no* evidence that there were separate authors. It was also found that the two separate accounts of creation in the first two chapters of Genesis were linguistically identical.

Interesting, is it not, to find that in our computer/scientific age such a device goes along with Bible-believers in their acceptance that Genesis has but *one* author, whom we believe was none other than Moses, who was inspired by the Holy Spirit.

Scholarly critics have also said there were two Isaiahs who wrote the book under that name. They claimed that two different linguistic styles indicated this, but they have overlooked the fact that Isaiah used one style when addressing Israel's spiritual condition and another when prophesying future events. The discovery of the "Isaiah Scroll" in the Dead Sea caves put a stop to this argument.

Since the Bible has a divine Architect, its message is from God. It is His message to man—an authoritative message, a self-authenticating message, one that is fortified with spiritual power. As God's Word it is

1. Indestructible (Matt. 24:35)
2. Incorruptible (1 Peter 1:23–25)
3. Indispensable (Deut. 8:3; Job 23:12)
4. Infallible (Matt. 5:18)
5. Inexhaustible (Ps. 92:5)

Its Design, Subject, and Purpose

The design of the Bible is to testify of Christ (John 5:39).

The subject of the Bible is redemption (Eph. 1:3–14). It was purposed and planned by the Father (1 John 4:9–10), accomplished by the Son (Matt. 20:28), and revealed by the Holy Spirit (John 16:7–9, 13–14). God thought it, Christ wrought it, the Holy Spirit brought it, the Devil fought it, and I got it!

The purpose of the Bible is to provide a foundation for our faith (Rom. 1:17; 10:17), to make us wise unto salvation, and for doctrine, reproof, correction, and instruction in righteousness for the man of God to produce good works (2 Tim. 3:15–17).

Strange as it may seem, when considering the subject, design, and purpose of this wonderful book, the world in general does not accept its true intent. In every generation Christians have battled to uphold the truthfulness of the Scriptures, and ours is no exception. This author stands unashamedly for biblical inerrancy.

In this volume we will deal with three subjects that will confirm the accuracy of the Bible.

1. Science. The question is often raised as to the scientific accuracy of the Bible, and it is often answered by saying that the Word of God is not a scientific textbook. True, it is not, but it does make some scientific statements. When rightly interpreted, these statements harmonize with the known facts relating to the physical constitution of the earth, planetary, and stellar worlds; people and their complex nature; and animals, plant, and vegetable life. There is no discrepancy between true science and the Scriptures. In science nothing is a fact until it is first a theory that can be proven. Many scientific facts from the Bible will show its opposition to evolution.

2. Fulfilled prophecy. No one but God can foretell or predict the future; therefore, if it can be shown that the Bible contains numerous predictions that have been literally fulfilled, we cannot doubt that this book came from God. The Bible says that it was inspired by God, and history has confirmed it. Fulfilled prophecy provides undeniable evidence that the Bible is a supernatural book written with more than mere human knowledge. In this section we will list when many of these prophecies were made, and how and when they were fulfilled.

3. Archaeology. The Bible is not a history textbook, but it does contain history from the creation of the world through the first century A.D. Archaeological discoveries have confirmed the accuracy of many events recorded in the Scriptures. The Bible has also been helpful in illuminating many customs of antiquity. A long list of such discoveries will be given in this section, from the beginning of such discoveries to the present time. You will see almost one hundred illustrations concerning these findings that relate them specifically to biblical authenticity.

SECTION ONE

Science in the Bible

1

Creation and Modern Science

Creation and evolution will be discussed in this first section. In the minds of evolutionists, humanists, atheists, and many scientists, there is no room for creation, no room for a Creator/Designer. To those who deny that creation is a result of a direct act by a Creator, everything about planet earth and the universe around us happened by chance of an evolutionary process.

Christians hold an entirely different view. In addition to believing in the finished work of the Lord Jesus Christ on the cross for salvation from sin, the Christian believes in and confesses God as the Creator. His trust is in the Person of creation, who "in the beginning . . . created" (Gen. 1:1). The Bible reveals not only that God created all things, but also that as Creator He is independent of creation in that He is personal and capable of relating to His creatures. To the Christian He is the Cause and Designer of everything— our very lives. Both the will to *create* and the will to *relate* are inherent in Him. His personhood guarantees life's structure, purpose, and order. "In Him we live, and move, and have our being" (Acts 17:28). The Genesis proclamation, "Let us make man in our image" (1:26), and the attendant details of the Creator's involvement in the shaping of human life make it clear that the Creator of the cosmos is not a distant, impersonal force or idea.

Why is the continual affirmation of God as Creator so important to the Christian faith? To confess God as Creator is to acknowledge Him as the one and only sovereign Lord of all things. "Know therefore this day, and consider it in thine heart, that the LORD he is God in heaven above, and upon the earth beneath: there is none else" (Deut. 4:39). "By the word of the LORD were the heavens made; and all the host of them by the breath of his mouth. . . . Let all the earth fear the LORD: let all the inhabitants of the world stand in awe of him. For he spake, and it was done; he commanded, and it stood fast" (Ps. 33:6, 8–9).

Since Christians believe that God is the Creator, they accept the fact that it is not possible for them to become their own god. Any pretension to such authority is foreign to a believer's perspective of life, and hence

Christians are always called upon to reflect their limitations.

This is what makes the difference between the Christian and the evolutionist or humanist who thinks he or she can become or is his own god. The child of God's confession of God as Creator carries the implication that the world is totally a revelation of His majesty and self-sufficient power. The doctrine of creation denies the error of the naturalist who, by regarding evolution as the principle of beginnings, is forced to reduce people to the level of nature.

What thrills Christians is that this Creator became their Savior. God was incarnate in Christ (2 Cor. 5:19; John 17:21–22). It was God who brought to the world the everlasting Gospel and in so doing, the angel of the Lord said, "Fear God, and give glory to him . . . and worship him that made heaven, and earth, and the sea, and the fountains of waters" (Rev. 14:7). By our fearing, worshiping, and giving Him glory, we are not only obligated to openly confess Christ as our own personal Savior but also to confess God as the Creator.

Can one truly be Christian without such a confession? An agnostic could dismiss the Genesis record as a fable that requires no particular response. An evolutionist could look to an accidental arrangement or the placing together of atoms for the origin of things and life. A philosopher might turn to a first cause. Agnostics, who doubt the existence of God, don't care how they got here, or even where they are going.

The Christian, however, must begin with a faith affirmation in a Person—a firm committal to and a confession of the biblical account of creation as found in Genesis 1:1 and John 1:3: "In the beginning God created . . . all things were made by him and without him was not anything made that was made."

Science: Yesterday and Today

From about A.D. 400 to 1500, theology dominated western European countries. Such subjects as creation were controlled by a belief in a sovereign God. Although there was scientific progress in other areas, notably agriculture, anyone who dabbled in the science of creation, the solar system, or the planet earth became a heretic in the eyes of the Roman Catholic Church. Such men as Galileo and Copernicus, whose calculations and theories continued for several centuries, and even the famous Monkey Trial in Tennessee in 1925, brought about many clashes between theology and science.

In days gone by science was thought to search for truth. Objective scientists honestly tried to get to the bottom of things to obtain knowledge. It is quite different in our day. Science has been reclassified as naturalism, and it is nearly impossible in general science to include the supernatural.

It seems the job of science now is to find an explanation that excludes a cause of effect and a Designer with a supernatural ability to create. Simply put, to the believer in divine creation and the supernatural, the naturalistic scientists are professing themselves to be wise but have become fools (Rom. 1:22). Science as we know it today chose this path over one hundred years ago with the popularity of Charles Darwin, one of the founders of modern evolutionary thinking.

In his denial of biblical truth, Darwin turned to a nonscientific, naturalistic explanation. If there is no Creator, he reasoned, then only naturalistic origin is possible, namely *evolution*. A naturalistic explanation, no matter how irrational, must be favored over the supernatural. And what are believers to expect from such minds, since they are blind to truth? Their minds are like cement—thoroughly mixed and permanently set. Their cry is, "Don't confuse me with facts." They permit their preexisting bias to rule their thinking and decisions.

The Bible: True Today

No matter what honest science was in the past, scientists whose theories control our educational system and our textbooks today claim that the Bible is antiquated when considered scientifically. True, the Bible is not meant to be considered from a scientific viewpoint, or as a scientific textbook, although there are numerous scientific statements made therein. Critics have ridiculed the Scriptures for centuries because of so-called false scientific statements. The cry today seems to be, "Which will you have—science or religion? You must make a choice. They are fundamentally opposed. You cannot have both." Science all but claims it has become the truth to meet people's needs—all of them—spiritual, physical, and mental. The science of naturalistic evolution, according to most of the scientific world, has the upper hand. The two (science and theology) are at odds over the issue of *truth*. Science says it is arriving at truth, while proponents of the Bible claim to already have it. We must, however, keep in mind that science is limited—it can tell us how or what a thing is, but it is unable to

tell us why. Any projection of a *why* is purely theoretical. Christians believe the Bible gives the answers to the why of things.

If the Bible were a textbook of science, it would have to be revised every decade or so. A textbook of science written ten years ago is obsolete. The purpose of science is to develop a knowledge of all the facts, the laws, and the processes of nature. It is an objective study of the world around us to gain knowledge and truth, whether one is a Christian or not.

Science has no answer for humankind's dilemma. The important task of the Bible is to let people know who and what they are, what their needs are, and how they can be whole. The Bible, having the insight of God, is free from constant change and correction. The Bible *is* the Word of God. Since the Scripture is true and its revelations are indeed from almighty God, we need not fear to test it by any standard that is honest and established. It has remained unchanged for centuries.

When science began to become uppermost in the minds of the learned, a suggestion was made that the Bible should be rewritten to conform to scientific conclusions. Had scientists tampered with its sacred pages to bring it into harmony with what they dogmatically believed to be undisputed facts, they would have found many of those "undisputed facts" to have been proven false. And had the Bible been rewritten to suit these "learned" professors, within twenty-five years after the first change the world would be ridiculing this new Bible. Yet the Bible and *true* science are in harmony.

If science as it is presented today is truth, then we have nothing to lose so far as life and destiny are concerned. We die just like animals, and in keeping with the worshipers of idols at Thessalonica, after death there is no life, and in the grave, there is no recognition. If, however, the Bible is right, one has everything to lose if its truths are not received and applied.

To reiterate, the Bible is not a textbook on science even though it does contain scientific facts and makes some scientific statements, often in nonscientific language.

Someone has asked why these scientific facts of Scripture are not couched in scientific language. If they had been, the Bible would be missing the purpose of its message. For example, in 2 Kings 2:23 we note that Elisha had no hair on top of his head. In other words, he was bald. If we put this in scientific language, it would read, "He had no follicle appendages posterior to the sagital suture and anterior to the lomdoidal suture where the follicle appendages habitually germinate." How would you like to read a Bible with that kind of language?

Keep in mind that most of the scientific statements recorded in the Bible were made centuries before Christ. It is amazing how true science today has confirmed their accuracy. It involves a willingness to cast aside preconceived notions and a commitment to search for truth wherever it might lead.

Christians are of the opinion that when the Bible is honestly and correctly interpreted and when science itself arrives at truth, the two will harmonize.

It is possible for someone with an honest conscience to be both a Christian and a scientist, believing in both the inspiration of the Bible and in the substantiated findings of scientific experiments, for one will not contradict the other.

This is one reason why Christians such as Dr. Henry M. Morris of the Institute for Creation Research and Dr. David Livingston of the Associates for Biblical Research and organizations such as Creation-Life Publishers are proclaiming that the Bible and true science are compatible, especially in matters of creation and evolution. *

---

* Dr. Henry M. Morris is the Director of the Institute for Creation Research. This organization specializes in the promotion of creation science—teaching in our public schools the creation verses the evolution of all things known to us. They have films, cassettes, books, and other resources on this subject, and the staff members are available for speaking engagements and debates in high schools, colleges, and churches. For more information write to: Institute for Creation Research, P.O. Box 2667, El Cajon, CA 92021-0667

Dr. David Livingston is the Director of Associates for Biblical Research, an organization which not only specializes in creationism, but also in biblical archaeology, the occult, and comparative religions. Staff members are available for speaking engagements in churches and schools. For more information write to: Associates for Biblical Research, P.O. Box 125, Ephrata, PA 17522

Creation-Life Publishers has a wide variety of books and video material available for the general public. Materials are suited for schools and churches as well. For more information write to: Creation-Life Publishers, P.O. Box 15666, San Diego, CA 92115

2

Creation—Fact or Fable

The first verse in the Bible is a scientific statement: "In the beginning God created the heaven and the earth" (Gen. 1:1). Though Christians believes this statement by faith, it is true that they have a hard time proving their belief. Evolutionists, however, have a harder time trying to prove their theory about the origin of things. Those of the evolutionists' school who criticize the Bible and those who believe in creation by God's direct acts or works are poles apart in their beliefs. Those who believe in direct creation by God are beginning to make headway in presenting their claims in spite of the fact that evolutionists appear to be in the majority.

Evolutionists often insist that evolution is a proven fact of science. This, of course, is nothing but wishful thinking. Evolution is not a scientific hypothesis because there is absolutely no way to test it.

True science deals with facts that are observable, testable, and reproducible under controlled conditions. Since creation is not observable, not testable, and not reproducible, this will place the question of origins outside of science. What, then, does science have? It has some facts or data. These belong to all of us. We have a considerable amount of facts and more are being accumulated each year. Evolution is one way of looking at the facts science has; creation is another way of looking at them. Since we know the origin of things is an unobservable, untestable, nonreproducible event of the past, the only way we can know about it is by guesswork or by divine revelation. Here creationists have the decided advantage. We have "inside" information from the Creator. This places the fact of creation *above* science but not *against* it.

True science must work with that which already exists. It does not offer any explanation as to the origin of life or the universe. It may talk about a big bang theory that happened 15 billion years ago or it may talk about some little cell that over a period of hundreds of millions of years became what we are today, but the problem of origin is a stubborn one. Science has solved questions and secrets of this universe, but the simple fact of life seems to

31

resist every effort of the man of research. Life's origin is as much a scientific mystery today as it has ever been.

How then did the heavens and the earth get here? Science says they evolved, that evolution is the answer. The Bible says that God created them. Both cannot be right. The Christian accepts God's statement by faith. Evolutionists also accept their view by faith. Believing in the theory of evolution is the same as believing in special creation. Evolution is an interpretation of nature that requires faith.

Some scientists have called evolution a metaphysical belief. They have come to recognize the essentially "religious" nature of evolutionism. They acknowledge the fact that they *believe* in evolution! Science, however, is not supposed to be something one just believes in. It is knowledge that can be demonstrated and observed and repeated. Evolution cannot be proved or tested. Like creation, it can only be believed.

Evolution is more than a theoretical explanation for the origin of things. It is a philosophy of life! It does away with the supernatural, unless one allows for a theistic evolution. Theistic evolution is a theory held by some evangelicals who say that God created matter but left it up to itself to evolve. They agree with evolutionists in the matter of hundreds of millions of years for things to develop.

But Darwin's evolutionary hypothesis has pushed God completely out of the picture. With creation simply a myth to them, Darwinists credit the Bible as merely a record of evolution from primitive superstitions to exalted ideas about some vague God and a code of ethics. This eliminates any

authority the Word of God would have over people's lives.

Evolution has created a faith all its own—a religion of its own! Evolution has shifted from "evolution as knowledge" to "evolution as faith." Evolution has become a scientific religion. This theory *omits* God, while Christian belief admits Him as the focal point of our being, our origin, and our destiny.

One might say that it takes more faith to believe in the theory of evolution than it does to believe what the Bible says about creation. This seems to point to the absurdity of banning creationist teaching from schools on the basis that it is a religion. The schools are already saturated with the teaching of religion in the guise of evolutionary science. In the modern school this teaching mostly takes the form of secular humanism.

The concept of evolution did not originate with Darwin. It has been the essential ingredient of all pagan religions and philosophies such as atomism, pantheism, and gnosticism.

Darwin simply added fuel to a fire that was already burning. It would seem reasonable that if creationism is not permitted in our public schools, should not the theory of evolution be excluded as well? Why teach one religion and ban another?

Moses and the Big Bang Theory

When Moses was found by Pharaoh's daughter, he was taken to the palace. For the next forty years he was schooled in all the wisdom and sciences of the Egyptians (Acts 7:20–23). He knew their beliefs concerning the existence of things. They taught that the earth was hatched out of a huge flying egg that now rests on pillars. Yet when Moses penned the account of the beginning of things under the inspiration of God, he simply said, "In the beginning, God created the heaven and the earth" (Gen. 1:1). He brushed aside all of the theories and speculations.

A proponent of the Big Bang theory, Carl Sagan presents it as a fact and says that the entire universe resulted from a cosmic explosion over 15 billion years ago involving all of the matter and energy in the universe. He believes that our marvelous complex and organized universe evolved from the explosion of a cosmic "egg." In it living systems have somehow evolved and developed. Of course his story is based on the speculations of evolutionary scientists. There is absolutely no scientific proof for this theory.

It is interesting that evolutionary theories *evolve!* Something new is discovered and different statements begin to appear. One evolutionist will question another, and a discussion follows as to just how all the stars and galaxies came to be there.

On January 18, 1990, NASA's Cosmic Background Explorer (COBE) satellite was sent into orbit to gather data on an event they believe happened billions of years ago. The result was the exact opposite of what the proponents of the Big Bang expected. Instead of the satellite instruments showing evidence of a scattering explosion, it allegedly showed that the primordial fireball that spawned the universe was a completely *smooth explosion.*

Has anyone ever heard of a *smooth* explosion? What the multi-million-dollar experiment showed was that there wasn't actually anything there. What was originally believed to have

been a violent explosion resulting in irregular disturbances and "lumps" that somehow formed the galaxies turned out to be something completely different.

No wonder the Bible says that when people turn from the Creator to themselves, they become vain in their imaginations and their foolish hearts are darkened (Rom. 1:21). Let's face it—scientists are smart. What a tragedy they use their minds to explore only the natural. Because they refuse to recognize a Creator, the apostle Paul tells us that not many "mighty" people—those of natural power—are called, but "God hath chosen the foolish things of the world to confound the wise; and God hath chosen the weak things of the world to confound the things which are mighty; And the base things of the world, things which are despised, has God chosen, yea, and things which are not, to bring to naught things that are: That no flesh should glory in his presence" (1 Cor. 1:27–29). I would rather fit in with those who know the Creator who became Savior than with those whose Big Bang theory deafened them to the call of God.

Creation vs. Evolution

The Bible tells us that God created man (Gen. 1:26–27). Science tells us that humans evolved. Which is right?

When Moses penned these words of our creation by God, here again we must consider what he had been taught by Egyptian scholars. Egyptians taught that people came from white worms that inhabited the flood lands of the Nile (this river being one of their gods). Darwin said we originated from an ape.

One can describe the theory of evolution simply and humorously as follows: One day a little cell was washed ashore during a terrible storm at sea. (Never mind how the sea got there or how the cell originated.) All alone and under the blazing sun on the burning sand (this is not the time to ask where the sun or sand of the earth came from), this cell had to move somewhere in the shade to survive. In its struggle to move inland it had no means with which to navigate. Of itself it was not mobile. Trying to squirm (?) inland, suddenly, to its surprise (and after 200 million years!), two objects began to sprout from its hind-side, and movement progressed. (The evolutionist calls these sprouts "legs.")

Pleased with the advancement of these two sprouts, the cell began to reason (in spite of the fact that sufficient time had not elapsed for it to evolve a brain) that if it could move only so fast with two sprouts, it could double its time with two more. (What mathematical ability it had at this stage of its development!) Lo and behold, in no time flat (just 100 million years or so), the cell had so evolved that it was walking around on four sprouts/legs.

By this time, enjoying the shade of the forest, which in over one billion years time had grown and come to the rescue of this little half-grown cell, the cell began to wonder what was in the trees, having noticed some objects the evolutionists later labeled "fruit and nuts." Yes, by this time the cell had eyes (at least one). So, experimenting with its legs (no longer sprouts), it soon learned to climb a tree, go out on the branches, and enjoy the goodies that evolution had provided for this now movable, growing, changing, beautiful cell.

Out on a limb one day, Mr. Cell (we assume it was a male—no females were anywhere to be found yet) saw an unusual species of fruit (or was it a nut?) it had never seen before. It was on another tree. How could he get to that bit of morsel without going back down the tree and climbing the other?

He had an idea. Why not swing from one tree to another. But how? To the surprise and delight of this cell (and another 90 million years later), before he realized it, a long, curved, movable object had shot out from the base of his spine (The cell now has bones!). For some strange reason, known only to researchers in this field, this movable offshoot was called a "tail." This name probably originated from some unknown or forgotten gibberish 300,000 years earlier, which was interpreted—"hang in there, buddy, or down you fall." Now that we have the root meaning of the word "tail," Mr. Cell began to go—swing is a better word—from limb to limb, enjoying his fling through the air and eating all the food that "mother nature" had provided for him.

One day while swinging in trees from limb to limb, he missed his grip (tail grip, that is) and fell to the ground. Upon impact, his tail was completely knocked off. Puzzled, he stood erect on his two hind sprouts—oops, pardon me—its "legs," and you and I have been walking around ever since!

This is evolution in a nutshell. This is the theory the evolutionists would have us believe regarding the origin of humankind.

It is amazing that the human race continues to reject its divine origin, believing fiction rather than fact. If you thought the fictitious illustration just given was humorous, consider this true story. A recent article from London, England, has this headline: "Scientist: Early Humans Walked Erect to Stay Cool." Peter Wheeler, Director of Biological and Earth Sciences at Liverpool Polytechnic, believes that the human race first began to walk erect when they moved from forests into the open and found it was too hot to stay down on all fours. He went on to say: "Between four and seven million years ago they began walking upright to keep cool because an upright animal exposes only one third of its surface to the sun's rays compared to a four-legged animal. Many anthropologists have said our human ancestors rose to two legs to make it easy to hunt, scavenge, use tools, and to see prey."

Wheeler disagrees with this theory, saying, "I believe 'heat' was the key to evolution. It appears that because of global climate change, the rain forest covering Africa began to fragment and shrink in size when temperatures rose and caused increasing aridity; out on these African tropical grasslands a four-legged animal must often have been on the verge of a sun or heatstroke, so heat regulation was the reason why early man evolved." If this article and the illustration on evolution were not so pathetic, they might have been humorous.

A recent wire report titled "New Theory of Evolution" says this: "Climate changes that depleted tropical forests millions of years ago were a major force in spurring the advance of human intelligence, according to a new theory of evolution. Only after they were forced to abandon life in the trees, did large primates evolve into the large-brained creatures who were ancestors to humans, a Johns Hopkins professor of earth sciences believes."

Malcolm Ritter, an Associated Press science writer, recently wrote that "Scientists say that 'Comet Dust' may have seeded life here" (11/91). The chemical seeds for life on earth may have arrived on dust that fell from some disintegrating comets. Some ancient soil on earth, according to this theory, contained amino acids that apparently came from outer space.

In the late 1950s a Ph.D. from Texas A&M University said that humans evolved from brown seaweed and that vegetation came from green seaweed. He believed that all animals are in reality a type of highly modified plant life, derived a billion years ago from a common ancestry with the brown seaweed. From new evidence (he doesn't tell us what this new evidence is), all life belongs to only one kingdom, which must be recognized as the kingdom of plants. Complex animals *apparently* evolved from this branch of brown seaweed by some *unknown* process. This, generally, is the type of weak argument of an evolutionist.

Moses did not tell of our metamorphosis from worms or apes into human beings. He said we came from God. What a contrast between believing Moses' lofty, dignified statements and the crude statements of our day.

Ethnology

True science involves a willingness to cast aside preconceived notions, to stand up to peer pressure with a commitment to follow the search for truth wherever it might lead. The science of ethnology and the science of archaeology both follow this rule. As ethnology is a science of records and customs of the living races, so archaeology is the science of races that are dead and gone. What do these living and dead records say about our origin?

Ethnologists agree on two basic principles. One principle states when widely isolated peoples have in common a body of traditions and beliefs, that common possession establishes a relationship or common ancestry.

The other principle states that when widely separated peoples all have a common tradition or belief in a certain past event, common tradition establishes a historical occurrence as the basis of this belief.

The science of archaeology teams up with the science of ethnology in this matter of a common belief. There are no fewer than thirty-three separate records from distinctly different people groups that tell of a worldwide flood. The similarities between these accounts and Moses' description of the flood in Noah's time (Gen. 6–11) are remarkable.

There is one law in the matter of evidence that should always be kept in mind: Anything in the theory stage is not fact; it will remain a theory until proven to be fact!

One great fault of some evolutionists is their biased reasoning. Where is their proof? Their theory is taught as fact with *no proof* whatsoever!

The Creation Tablets

The science of archaeology, which does not distort evidence to suit preconceived theories, has come up with some solid evidence of early thinking and beliefs to support creation. At least three "creation tablets" dating back thousands of years have been discovered.

One is called the Creation Epic, another is called the Babylonian Creation account, and still another was a recent find (1950s) at Tel Mardikh (Ebla) in northern Syria. The first two were found in ancient Mesopotamia. These records must be taken at face value, no matter what is written on them. They should convince biased minds of the facts of early beliefs concerning creation. [See "Creation, Biblical" in Index.]

Amazingly, these creation tablets, especially the Creation Epic account, correspond to the seven days mentioned in Genesis chapter 1—six days of creation and one of rest. Actually, this epic is on seven tablets—one for each day. The first tablet relates a time when heaven and earth did not exist, when a watery deep, or chaos, existed, and when gods who represented order and system were born. There is certainly no similarity here between the God of Genesis 1:1 and these "gods," yet there is some similarity of a time when the heaven and the earth were not in existence and when there was a watery deep and chaos (Gen. 1:2).

Another tablet of the Creation Epic tells of the creation of the stars to mark existing time and the moon to give a specific time for each day. It is implied in this tablet that heavenly bodies precede any creative work of plant, animal, or human life. This corresponds to our fourth day (Gen. 1:14–19).

On the sixth tablet is a record of man's creation, and the seventh tablet refers to a special day. This corresponds to the creation of man on the sixth day (Gen. 1:26–31) and to a special seventh day of rest (Gen. 2:1–3).

The Babylonian Creation account relates to a gruesome story of gods who assembled themselves in a holy conclave in a drunken stupor and killed one another in jealousy. As in the Creation Epic, there is no similarity of these gods to the God of the Bible, yet there is a striking phenomenon in the outline of these two accounts. It is simply amazing—and no one can change either record—to find that the Word of God and the Babylonian account have the following order:

1. Primeval chaos
2. Beginning of light
3. Creation of the firmament
4. Appearance of dry land
5. Creation of luminaries
6. Creation of man
7. Deity rests

People, so the Bible tells us, had a beginning, and at their creation by God, they began as people who were intelligent, capable of decisions, and who could replenish the earth with offspring *after their kind.*

People, so the evolutionist tells us, evolved from a mess of slimy goo. Darwin's idea was to replace creation with a family tree of the history of any plant or animal species. None has ever been produced. Regrettably, they have shaken the faith of many weak believers in their attempt to discredit the authority of the Bible. Their guesses, inferences, and so-called evidence of evolutionary processes have not amounted to even a demonstration! They are not sufficiently agreed even to meet in a council and formulate a creed as to the origin of the world or man. Nor are they likely to. There are many more evolutionists than there are bits of evidence to support the theory they seek to uphold.

What the discovered creation tablets do show is that early humans had no concept of any theory of evolution, but they did believe the origin of life or being, as well as that of heaven and earth and plant and animal life, came as a result of *direct creation* by their deities. No discovery to date even hints that they believed they came from some lower stage or form of life, or that they evolved into what they were, when they left their record of creation. The records they left in the Creation Epic must have been handed down from one generation to another.

Why did they not leave a record that would support the evolutionist? Why has no record been found with a tradition that humans descended from any of the lower forms of life? Biblical and archaeological records do not show any such tradition. Early people, like all evolutionists and even creationists, never witnessed any evolutionary changes. To date, no one has discovered the one thing needed to prove otherwise—the missing link.

The Word of God tells us that God formed man from the dust of the earth (Gen. 2:7; 3:19; Ps. 103:14). The same sixteen or seventeen elements found in the dust of the earth's surface are the very same elements found in the human body. God breathed into man's nostrils and man became a living soul (Gen. 2:7). He was created in God's image and likeness.

This gave people something animals do not have—a spirit, which enables us to reach out toward God, to submit to worship. Why is there no semblance of a spirit or soul in animals from whence people supposedly came? If evolution is true, how many millions of years did it take for a spirit of worship to evolve in the transition from animal to person? Has anyone ever seen an animal build an altar and worship a higher being? Why do even the most primitive of people acknowledge a supreme being? The only answer I know is that we were *created* by God with a soul and a spirit—created differently from animals, a fact that is not found in the annals of evolution.

It is also interesting to note that science itself confirms a difference between the flesh of people, the flesh of beasts, the flesh of fish, and the flesh of birds (1 Cor. 15:39). We were reminded at the start of our study that religion seemed to hold sway over science for several centuries, and we noted that the theology of the Roman Catholic Church said that eating meat on Friday was wrong. But according to them, fish is not meat, so fish was acceptable on that day. It was a speculative theory that Paul's statement of different kinds of flesh was scientifically wrong.

Today scientists are aware of the cytoplasm and the nuclei of cells by which four kinds of flesh can be distinguished, and Paul mentions all four—all meat. Even though he had nothing scientific in mind at all, his statement is perfectly correct, and "meat" can be eaten today on Fridays. Also, in distinguishing different kinds of flesh, even though each is meat, why is our flesh different from our ancestor the ape if we evolved from it?

The Monkeys' Viewpoint

The Bible teaches us that plant and animal life, including people, reproduces "after its kind" (Gen. 1:11–12, 21, 25; 4:1–2; 5:3). What evolutionist can refute this scientific principle? "After its kind" leaves absolutely no room for the process of evolution. What is true in one kingdom is true in the other. If a person and an ape are so related as evolutionists say, why is it that the person cannot take a blood transfusion from an ape? Isn't a person, according to the evolutionist, "after its [the ape's] kind"? The species of apes and the species of humankind are so vastly different, even flesh-wise, that to give a person a blood transfusion from an ape would kill them—the blood would coagulate. And, if we are so "akin to an ape," why haven't there been any successful results in cross-breeding one with a human being? If anything would ever convince me that evolution were true, it would be the fact that people, at times, act like monkeys! Did you ever wonder how a monkey feels about the evolutionary theory?

Three Monkeys

Three Monkeys once dining in a
    coconut tree,
Were discussing some things they
    heard true to be.
What do you think? Now listen you
    two—
Here, Monkeys, is something that
    cannot be true,
That Humans descended from our
    pure race;
Why, it's simply shocking—a
    terrible disgrace!

Who ever heard of a Monkey
    deserting his wife?
Let a baby starve and ruin its life?
And have you ever known of a
    mother monk
To leave her darling with a stranger
    to bunk?
Their babies are handed from one to
    another
And scarce even know the love of a
    mother!

And, I've never known a Monkey so
selfish to be
As to build a big fence around his
tree
So other Monkeys can't get a wee
taste,
But would let all the coconuts there
go to waste
Why, if I'd put a fence around this
coconut tree,
Starvation would force you to steal
from me.

And here is another thing a Monkey
won't do—
Seek a bootlegger's shanty, and get
in a stew;
Carouse and go on a whoopee,
disgracing his life,
Then reel madly home and beat up
his wife!
They call this all a pleasure and
make a big fuss,
They descended from something, but
not from us!

—Author Unknown

In the matter of God telling the first parents to be fruitful and multiply (Gen.1:28), the Bible gives scientific information to us about conception between male and female and the reproduction of human life. In the matter of embryonic development the psalmist says this: "For thou [God] has possessed my reins [inward parts]: thou hast covered me in my mother's womb. I will praise thee; for I am fearfully and wonderfully made . . . My substance was not hid from thee, when I was made in secret, and curiously wrought in the lowest parts of the earth. Thine eyes did see my substance . . ." (139:13–16).

There is absolutely nothing in this portion of God's Word that would contradict modern medical science. Science confirms that in embryonic development there *is* life, otherwise how could there be any development or growth of bones (Eccl. 11:5)? How does the U.S. Supreme Court and proabortionist groups answer this?

Not only is the Bible scientifically accurate in the matter of birth, it is also scientifically accurate in the matter of death. Life came when God breathed the breath of life (Gen. 2:7). Death is defined as cessation or withdrawal—a recalling of this God-breathed breath (Ps. 104:29). God has so wondrously made us (Ps. 139:14) that even in death, nature takes over with "minute undertakers" whose function is to start decomposition immediately (in spite of embalming). "The worm shall feed sweetly on him" (Job 24:20), and "then shall dust [of man] return to the earth as it was" (Eccl. 12:7).

People vs. Animals

If the hypothesis of evolution is true, then living matter originated from nonliving matter. But evolution itself cannot contradict this one scientific fact: Life cannot reproduce except by life because it reproduces after its own kind. This makes people different and presents to the evolutionist some scientific realities that are difficult to refute. Science can dissect a person and an animal and find some similarities between the two, but how can we account for the following differences unless humans were created differently by God?

1. Articulate speech. If we did come from apes (or seaweed), how is it that we can frame words—that we have the ability of intelligent speech? Speech is the vocalization of thoughts. Animals may communicate through

sound, but none can spell, write, translate, or deliver addresses. Only people can do this.

2. Invention. Technology is a science that belongs only to our inventive genius. Animals and birds have dens and nests, but their structure is always the same. It is people who invent, change, and improve.

God says this about people: "Nothing will be restrained from them, which they have imagined to do" (Gen. 11:6). When God gave Adam instructions to till the Garden of Eden and have dominion over other creatures (Gen. 1:26; 2:15), this was the beginning of applied science. This can be seen in archaeological discoveries as humans advanced from one period to another, just as we advance today in technology. Adam's early descendants were skilled in music and metallurgy (Gen. 4:21–22). Cats meow and dogs can bark on TV commercials, but neither could have invented the microphone or the TV. The world of modern science is due to our inventive ability.

3. The human body. The human race is of one blood (Acts 17:26). True science confirms this. Blood plasma teaches the same thing. We *are* different in flesh from animals, fish, and fowl (1 Cor. 15:39). The posture (structure or form) of humans versus animals, or the science of morphology, shows humans to be vastly different. The science of anthropology, which has to do with our early development, physical facts, ethnology, geographical distribution, and culture, comes from the word *anthropos* meaning "the one with the upward look."

People stand erect with their eyes on the horizon. They were made to *look up*—"I will lift up mine eyes"

(Ps. 121:1). Animals look down and around. People looks *up* to God in worship. People can bend their knees for prayer, as opposed to the hind legs of most animals. People also have an opposable thumb for grasping. As the Bible states, we are "fearfully and wonderfully made" (Ps. 139:14). Animals are wonderfully made, but they were not made for the same purpose.

4. Moral beauty. Only humans can know moral beauty—only humans can break moral law. God's moral laws are as real as His physical laws. Animals do not sin, neither do they practice virtue. They are not immoral; they are amoral. They do not stoop to the level of the perverted nor do they rise to the heights of godly people.

Humans are the only ones of God's creatures who can display moral courage. When they break or disobey moral laws, they bring to themselves degradation and misery. Yes, this is an indictment against humans, but they have freedom of choice; animals do not. People can behave as they please—either good or bad. Animals can only follow instinct.

5. Conscience. Because people can know moral beauty and can break moral law, no one can deny that we are distinguished from animals in that we have a conscience. Conscience serves as a guilt mechanism in our moral nature. We can repent, break habits, start anew in the betterment of society (that is, if their conscience hasn't been seared with a hot iron [1 Tim. 4:2]). Animals can only do the same thing over and over—neither right nor wrong.

6. Influence. The writer of Hebrews says: "Abel . . . being dead yet speaketh" (11:4). Animals die, and

may be remembered by their owners for a short period of time, but they do not speak and leave no lasting memorial. People do. Great religious movements exist because of the influence of their leaders. History records the influence of such great leaders as Moses, the apostles Peter and Paul, Alexander the Great, Martin Luther, George Washington, Abraham Lincoln, and others. The influence of Jesus Christ, who lived almost 2,000 years ago, still knows no bounds.

Because evolutionists are unable to refute many scientific facts that distinguish people from animals, they then grasp at straws, such as asking, "If all things were created by God, who created Him? Where did He come from? If things did not evolve, if God made them, then He had to have a beginning. Who created Him?"

Christians believe that God is life *inherent*, life within Himself. There are two types of life: *creature* life is life that is transmitted and *deity* life is life that is inherent. The Creator is self-existent, and there is no other term for infinity more expressive than Inherent Being. God always was, for there could be no beginning to deity.

In the Bible (Genesis in particular), questions concerning the creation of heaven, earth, light, vegetation, animal, and human life, which were written about 3,500 years ago, are presented and answered in a simple and rational way: "In the beginning God created . . ." (Gen. 1:1). When one truly believes this verse, one will have little difficulty believing the rest of the 31,172 verses! This single verse refutes false theories about the origin of humankind. Thus, atheism is false because God is a fact—reality. Materialism is false because matter had

a beginning. Pantheism is false because God was outside of His creation. Polytheism is false because there was only one God creating. Evolution is false because heaven and earth and all things in it were *created*.

All these philosophies are essentially the same. They all teach us that the present cosmos came into existence by the operation of the "gods" or the forces of nature acting upon the previously existing material matter that already existed.

The Logic of Biblical Creation

It is a generally accepted fact that there are two explanations for the origin of the universe and human life—evolution and creation. Either the origin of things can be understood in terms of *continuing natural processes* (evolution), or they cannot. If they cannot, then we must resort to *completed supernatural processes* (creation) to explain the origin of at least the basic symptoms of the cosmos. Evolution and creation thus exhaust the possibilities, as far as origins are concerned. It must be one or the other. There is *no* other option.

Evolution

By definition, evolution should still be occurring *now*, since it is explained by *present processes*. There is *no* evidence whatsoever that evolution is occurring today—that is, true vertical evolution from some simpler form to a more complex form. No one has ever observed a star evolve from hydrogen, life evolve from chemicals, a higher species evolve from a lower species, a man from an ape, or anything else of this sort. Not only has no one ever observed true evolution in action, no one has ever observed how it *might* work. Since no one has ever seen it happen (despite thousands of experiments that have tried) and no one has come up with a workable mechanism to explain it, it would seem that it has been falsified. The evolutionist should recognize that this means their theory is not scientific, since it is not observable.

Since there are no *present* processes, what about the past? Actually, there is no evidence that evolution took place in the past either. In all of recorded history extending back nearly 7,000 years, no one has ever recorded the natural evolution of any kind of creature (living or non-living) into a more complex kind. Furthermore, all known vertical changes seem to go in the wrong direction. No new species have evolved during that time. Stars explode, comets and meteorites disintegrate, life deteriorates, and eventually everything dies, so far as all historical observations go. Nothing has ever evolved into a higher complexity.

What about *prehistoric* changes? The only real records we have of the prehistoric period are presumably to be found in the sedimentary rocks of the earth's crust, where billions of fossils of former living creatures have been preserved for our observation. Again, however, the story is one of *extinction*, not *evolution*. Numerous kinds of extinct animals are found (e.g., dinosaurs), but *never*, in all of these numberless fossils, is a truly incipient or transitional form found. No fossils has ever been found with half-scales, half-feathers, half-legs, half-wings, or any other such thing.

If evolution were true, there should be millions of transitional types among these multiplied numberless fossils. In fact, *everything* should show transitional features. But they do not! If one were to rely strictly on the observed evidence, one would have to agree that past evolution has also been falsified. No matter what the evolutionist believes, it is accepted by faith, *not* fact.

Creation

If evolution did not occur in the past and does not occur in the present, then it is entirely imaginary. This leaves only *creation* as the necessary explanation of origins. This fact is also confirmed by the best proved laws of science—the First and Second Laws of Thermodynamics.

The first law notes that *nothing* is being created or is evolving by present processes. Matter and/or energy are remaining constant, even though they are frequently changing form. "Like begets like"—dogs are always dogs, though they may occur in many varieties.

The second law notes that the quality of any system—its usefulness, its complexity, its information value—*always* tends to decrease. In living organisms, true vertical changes go *down*, not up. Mutations cause deterioration, individuals die, species become extinct, such laws drive us to the logical necessity of a primal creation—a creation that was accomplished not by present natural processes, but by past supernatural processes.

This implies that there is a Creator. Being the Creator of the infinitely complex, highly energized cosmos, that Creator necessarily must be omniscient and omnipotent. Having created life, as well as human personalities, He must also be a living Person. *No effect can be greater than its cause.* Therefore, He is capable of revealing to us knowledge about His creation—knowledge that could never be learned through studying present processes (evolution). This He has done in the first book of the Bible. Only Genesis (chaps. 1–2) attempts to tell us how the universe and living organisms came to be.

Whether most people believe it or not, the creation account in Genesis is God's record of His creation. Jesus Christ also taught this truth, so surely any true Christian should believe it. This account does not allow even the possibility of evolution, since everything was created separately and reproduces "after its kind" (Gen. 1:24), and since, after six days of creating and making things, God "rested from all his work" (Gen. 2:3) and so is no longer using processes which create things, as theistic evolutionists believe. Instead, He is now "upholding all things" (Heb. 1:3) through His law of conservation—the First Law.

The entrance of sin into the world brought a disordering principle into the Creator's perfect creation in the form of God's curse on the *whole* creation—the principle of decay and death—the Second Law (Gen. 3:17–19; Rom. 8:22). Thus, the natural laws now governing the processes of the universe are not laws of origins and development, as evolution requires, but of conservation and decay, in accordance with the truth of primeval special creation.

When the Bible is banned as a sectarian book, the field is left wide open for the purely unscientific theory of evolution. If scientific methods of experimentation and documentation were applied to evolution, it would die.

The Bible account of creation is constantly ridiculed by atheists, patronized by liberals, and often allegorized even by conservatives. The fact is, however, that it is God's own account of creation, corroborated by Jesus Christ Himself, *who was there* (Mark 10:6)! We are well advised to take this issue seriously, for God says what He means and will someday hold us accountable for believing what He says. Furthermore, the scriptural account is reasonable and logical, fully in accord with all science and history.

Paul tells us that people, if they refuse to retain a knowledge of God in their hearts and minds, will change natural law into that which is contrary to nature and will do that which is unseemly (unnatural). Read Romans 1:18–31 for a sordid picture of a man who leaves God out of his life and goes his own way where anything goes.

People are *not* going upward. What evolution has done has caused humans to become animalistic. If purebred cattle, for example, are left alone, cross-breeding results and the animals degenerate or revert to common stock. All nature bears evidence to the fact that creatures (including human beings) naturally gravitate to a lower level. Evolution has deceived people into believing they are their god, that they can lift themselves by their bootstraps and control their own destiny. By attacking the creationist and fighting against the truth of the Bible, they are fighting a losing battle and will be like the rich man in Luke 16:19–31 who lifted up his eyes from hell, desirous that someone back on earth would warn others to heed the truth.

Changing Opinions Among Scientists

In spite of the fact that the vast majority of scientists cling to the theory of evolution, there is a movement today among teachers who realize that presenting only evolutionary ideas is not good education. An increasing number of teachers, parents, and students are beginning to realize that true academic teaching must involve not only the freedom to discuss *how* evolution occurred but also *whether* evolution occured. Nothing is more crucial to good science and good education than the ability to compare critically two sets of assumptions. Students compare assumptions in social studies, literature, and day-to-day life, so why not science? Comparing facts and assumptions ought to be the backbone of the open-ended approach to problem solving.

Some good reports are beginning to surface indicating there are many scientists, as well as some in the medical profession, who are having second thoughts about the validity of evolution. An ad in the Jewish Press was organized and signed by forty-nine Jewish medical doctors stating their belief in the divine origin of human beings. The declaration sought to express opposition to certain ideas prevalent in the scientific community in which the origin of the world and life is ascribed to random events and chance occurrences. On the contrary, these doctors believe that form and function of every organ of the human body testifies to the handiwork of a Divine Creator.

Alexander Paltera, at the recent Second International Torah-Science Conference in Florida, raised two good questions pertinent to the cosmos: "If the cosmos runs on *cause and effect*, what got it rolling? And if matter were simply of quantum bundles of energy, what held the bundles together?" What was his answer? "I consider that there must have been a creator. Things just didn't happen by themselves."

The *Capitol Voice* lists "Confessions of Scientists," which certainly does not sound like the thinking of evolutionists and which should encourage believers as they face the unbelief of the critics of divine creation.

President Eliot of Harvard said, "Evolution is an hypothesis, and not a science at all."

Agassiz of Harvard said, "Any man who accepted the doctrine of evolution ceased thereby to be a scientist."

Darwin confessed, "Not one change of species into another is on record."

Professor Dawson says, "Evolution existed in the oldest days of philosophy and poetry. It is destitute of any shadow of proof. To believe it again shows that the world has fallen into a state of senility and dotage again."

Wallace confessed that "There is a gulf between matter and nothing; one between life and the non-living; and a third between man and the lower creation, and science cannot bridge any of them."

President Leavitt of Lehigh said, "Protoplasm evolving a universe is a superstition more pitiable than paganism."

Virchow, the world's greatest physiologist, anthropologist, paleontologist, and chemist of his day, said, "It cannot be proved by science that man descends from the ape or any other animal. The midlink has never been found and never will be."

Etheridge, fossilologist of the British Museum, says, "In all this great museum there is not a particle of evidence of evolution. It is sheer nonsense, not founded on observation, and unsupported by fact. This museum is full of proofs of the utter falsity of evolution."

Professor Fleishman of Germany writes, "Evolution is purely the product of the imagination. It spins theories and twists facts."

St. George Mivert of England says, "Evolution is but a Puerile [childish, immature] hypothesis."

Robin, a French infidel, in the French *Encyclopaedia of Science* writes, "Evolution is a fiction, a poetical accumulation of probabilities without proof, and of attractive explanations without demonstrations."

Professor Millikan says, "The pathetic thing is that we have scientists who are trying to prove evolution, which no scientist can ever prove."

Professor Hyatt says, "A scientist who has a theory to support is as stubbornly difficult to convince, even on clear evidence, than any other man."

3

The Universes of the Heavens

"The heavens declare the glory of God; and the firmament sheweth his handiwork" (Ps. 19:1). We stand in awe every time we look into the heavens and see the expanse of the heavenly bodies. We see ourselves as a tiny speck of dust as we consider the works of God's hand (see Ps. 8:3). On a clear, dark night we can see much of the Milky Way with the naked eye. What lies beyond our galaxy staggers the imagination.

In 1982, a supercluster of stars was discovered beyond known space. It was estimated to contain 50,000 galaxies and 100 billion times that many stars. The *Science* journal, the Associated Press, and the United Press International gave reports about the discovery of a "Great Wall" of galaxies. Astronomers say it is the biggest structure seen in the universe. Its size is so difficult to explain that it raises new questions about the theories of origin and the structure of the universe.

Astronomers Margaret Geller and John Huchra of the Harvard-Smithsonian Center for Astrophysics in Cambridge were able to estimate the dimensions of the newly discovered galaxies. We should first note that one *year* is the distance light travels—about 5.88 trillion miles. The speed of light is 186,000 miles per second. The galaxies that make up this newly discovered wall form a sheet that is at least 500 million light years long, or 3,000 billion miles, and it is 200 million light years wide, 15 million light years thick, and between 200 to 300 million light years from the earth!

Galaxies are collections of stars, intercellular gas, and dust. Our own Milky Way contains about 100,000 billion stars and is at least 100,000 light years across. Some astronomers think the entire universe is between 10 billion and 20 billion light years across.

Giving astronomers and scientists due credit for calculating such vital information, it still amazes us why, in view of such a systematic order in the heavens, so many astronomers and scientists still refer to the evolutionary Big Bang theory. It is no wonder that, as Edwin Turner of Princeton University said, "we keep being surprised that we keep seeing something bigger as we go out further." Gellar said, "In my opinion we have a real problem. I think when taken all together, these observations indicate there is something important missing in our understanding of the way structures form in the universe." Maybe such discoveries will be the straw that breaks the camel's back, and they will blast evolutionary theories into dust. "The heavens declare the glory of God; and the firmament sheweth his handiwork" (Ps. 19:1).

The Solar System

When we consider the vastness of the heavens and the order of our galaxy, the Milky Way, there must be an admission that it didn't just happen or evolve. There must have been a Designer. The probability of such a complex universe originating by accident or by evolution is comparable to the probability of a luxury sedan resulting from an explosion in a junk yard!

Ordinances of Heaven

The book of Job contains a large number of scientific questions and statements. God asks Job some forty questions concerning creation and the universe. One of the questions God asked was if Job knew "the ordinances of heaven" (38:33).

This expression has to do with the physical laws that control the billions of heavenly, or solar, bodies. Nothing in the universe is as exact as their fixed motion. Mariners through the centuries have depended on these "ordinances of heaven" for safe passage on the high seas, but it wasn't until the use of the telescope that their scientific accuracy could be proved.

The psalmist refers to the moon and stars being ordained, or "fixed." In the book of Jeremiah (31:35–36), we are assured that these ordinances are obeying their laws—the sun shining and the moon going through its phases. God put these ordinances in the firmament of the heavens as signs (Gen. 1:4–18). They *have been* signs, not only to navigators, but also to the agriculturist, meteorologist, and astronomer.

The prophet Amos (5:8) mentions order, or scientific accuracy, in the matter of stars. According to evolutionists, what (or who) could have even devised the mathematical structure of the universe, including our solar system and the exact proportions of chemical elements that compose matter. We believe that God, the Designer of the whole universe, created such perfection.

According to the Bible, our solar system was created by God (Gen. 1:14–19). The lights—sun, moon, and stars—are in the heavens as signs. The *greater* light, or sun, rules the day, and the lesser light, or moon, rules the night. Moses was scientifically correct not to refer to the sun as the *greatest* light, for there are numerous stars far greater than our sun. Job was scientifically correct when he made a statement about light: "the *way* [not *place*] where light dwelleth" (38:19). *Place* would not have been scientifically correct, since light travels 186,000 miles per second. It could not, therefore, dwell in any one place. How scientifically accurate is the Word of God in such matters as these!

The Sun

There are many scientific facts about the sun in God's Word. Not only is it the greater light in our orbit to give us day, but its gravitational pull on the earth makes it possible, as the earth rotates on its axis, for us to have night and day. Night and day are mentioned in Genesis 1:4–5 and 14–19. Amos 5:8 states that God "turneth the shadow of death [darkness of night] into morning, and maketh the day dark with night."

Nothing here is in scientific language, but by simple deduction one can easily conclude that the Bible is saying that the earth is rotating on its axis to give us night and day. True science admits this to be true.

The record in Genesis was made around 1500 B.C., and the reference by Amos was from 785 B.C. Around A.D. 1500 (3,000 years after Moses and 2,285 years after Amos), Copernicus discovered that the earth not only revolved on its axis, but it also revolved around the sun. Before this discovery, the sun was thought to revolve around the earth. Job made this claim more than 3,750 years before Copernicus. He said "*It* [the earth, not the sun] is turned as clay to the seal [sun] . . ." (38:14).

James (1:17) used an expression relating to science to establish the unchangeableness of God—"shadow of turning." This reference refers to the sundial, an ancient method of telling time. The sundial was common throughout the world during biblical times. This expression is also mentioned twice in the Old Testament (2 Kings 20:11 and Isa. 38:8). "Shadow of turning" refers to the fact that there is less and less light on the base of the sundial until it is covered in darkness. This illustration also refers to the earth turning on its axis. James, referring to a sundial, is stating that with the Lord, there is no "shadow of turning"—the light does not dissipate. God is unchangeable (1 John 1:5).

Moses makes mention of the "precious things of heaven . . . brought forth by the sun" (Deut. 33:13–14). It was proven in 1804 (3,300 years after Moses' statement) that carbon in plants came from carbon dioxide, a result of the sun's rays. In 1844, a scientist found out that the metabolic energy of plants came from the energy of the sun by means of photosynthesis. We know today that this is a scientific fact—that the light of the sun influences the production of plant life. God, not chance, "causeth the grass to grow for the cattle, and herb for the service of man: that he may bring forth food out of the earth" (Ps. 104:14).

Science has established that the earth's source of energy is the sun. The psalmist hints at this in Psalm 19:4–6. Just as the sun is the earth's source of energy, so the *Sun* of Righteousness, Jesus Christ, is the source of energy for the Christian (Mal. 4:2; John 15:5).

The sun is also the source of wind systems—another established scientific fact. Job 38:24 says: "By what way is the light parted [energy of the sun distributed], which scattereth the east wind upon the earth?"

It was not until Galileo (A.D. 1630) that wind circuits were discovered. Wind systems are due to the earth's rotation and the sun's radiation on the earth's surface. Coupled with Galileo's discovery, it was discovered in the mid-1800s that the circulating winds of the northern hemisphere deflect to the right, and those of the southern hemisphere deflect to the left. This same principle applies to water drainage. Water in the northern hemisphere drains clockwise in a sink or tub, and it drains counter-clockwise in the southern hemisphere. These examples show a pole-to-equator pattern of circulation. How wise Solomon was when he mentioned this fact of science in

Ecclesiastes 1:6: "The wind goeth toward the south, and turneth about unto the north."

It is a scientific fact that the sun helps to produce rain. Amos said (5:8; 9:6) that God "calleth for the waters of the sea [evaporation by the sun's heat], and poureth them out [rain] on the face of the earth." It's no wonder that Moses said precious things come from the sun. The sun

a. rules the day (Ps. 136:8)
b. divides seasons (Gen. 1:14)
c. has its own glory (1 Cor. 15:41)
d. diffuses light and heat (Ps. 19:6; Eccl. 11:7)
e. produces fruit (Deut. 33:14)
f. is frequently destructive (Ps. 121:6; 2 Kings 4:18–20)

The sun is illustrative of

a. God's favor (Ps. 84:11)
b. Christ's coming (Mal. 4:2)
c. Christ's glory (Matt. 17:2)
d. future glory of saints (Matt. 13:43)
e. praise (Ps. 148:3)
f. a bridegroom (Ps. 19:4b, 5a)
g. a strong man (Ps. 19:4b, 5b)
h. power for saints (Judg. 5:31)
i. supreme rulers (Gen. 37:9)
j. clearness; Christ's purity (Song of Sol. 6:10)
k. judgment and calamities (Ezek. 32:7–8)
l. wickedness and righteousness (Eccl. 3:16)

The Moon

In Old Testament times the moon, which controls the seasons, was thought to mark months and years rather than the sun, as we know today (Gen. 1:14; Ps. 104:19; Exod. 12:2; Num. 28:14).

The gravitational pull of the moon governs the oceanic tides, permitting oceans to "come in" just so far. Job 38:8–11 describes the tides and how the Lord ordained a "decreed place" where the tides come in. It's no wonder Moses said that "precious things [are] put forth by the moon" (Deut. 33:14). The moon

a. rules the night (Ps. 136:9)
b. is the lesser light compared to the sun (Gen. 1:16; Job 31:26)
c. has its own glory (1 Cor. 15:41)
d. divides night from day (Gen. 1:14; Jer. 31:35)
e. is a sign for seasons (Gen. 1:14; Ps. 104:19)
f. influences vegetation (Deut. 33:14)
g. has no light of its own (Job 25:5)
h. affects gravitational pull of the tides (Job 26:10; 38:8–11)

The moon is illustrative of

a. Christ's glory in His bride (Isa. 60:19)
b. the Church's light, or clearness, reflecting the Son's light (Song of Sol. 6:10)
c. Church in subjection to Christ (Rev. 12:1)
d. peace (Ps. 72:7)
e. changeableness of kingdoms (Rev. 12:1–5)
f. judgment and calamities (Jer. 8:2; Joel 2:10)

The word *lunar* refers to the moon. It should be pointed out that *lunacy* is superstitiously attributed to the influence of the moon. In Roman mythology Luna is the goddess of the moon. It is her name that gave us *lunatic* because she was thought to create madness. Superstition also attributed blindness, death to newborn animals, insanity, spoilage of meat, and facial distortions to a full moon. Some based this on Psalm 121:6: "The sun shall not smite thee by day, nor the moon by night." None of these things is a result of creation. They can only be accounted for by the presence of sin in the world.

The Stars

Numberless. Is the Bible scientifically correct in speaking of the number of stars? Yes! God told Abraham to look toward heaven and count the stars "if thou be able to number them" (Gen. 15:5). This would imply that the stars are numberless. Hipparchus, who lived several hundred years after Jeremiah (ca. 150 B.C.), stated that there were exactly 1,026 stars in the universe. Ptolemy, the Roman scientist who lived in the time of Christ, said there were 1,056.

It was not until the time of Galileo's telescope that scientists began to realize the heavens contained a vast number of stars. It has been estimated that there are about 10 billion galaxies that are within range of the two hundred-inch telescope. Einstein estimated that the totality of space is at least 100,000 times greater than observable space. With this deduction, there could be at least 100 septillion stars in space (1,000,000,000,000,000,000,000,000,000,00).

When God inspired Jeremiah to say, "the hosts of heaven *cannot* be numbered," He knew what He was talking about. To attempt to count all the stars in the heavens would be like trying to count all the grains of sand on the shores of the earth (Gen. 15:5).

It has been calculated that if all the people on earth were to count the stars, each person could count more than 50,000 of them without the same star's being counted twice! Science has proved that the Bible is correct. Or better yet, the Bible has proved science correct. And just think, the God who made the stars knows each one by name (Ps. 147:4)! Does all this sound unbelievable? Many people do find this hard to believe. If people can program a computer to store specific information into the millions, or make machines that can solve mathematical equations in just seconds, then why can't the God of this universe go far beyond our skills in numbering and naming stars?

Named. It is interesting to note that man has named some stars, and some of the names Job used over 4,200 years ago are used today. Notice the scientific truths attached to some of the named stars of his time. God asked Job: "Canst thou bind the sweet influences of *Pleiades,* or loose the bands of *Orion?"* (38:31). The Pleiades and Orion are *true* star groups.

Stars appear to remain unchanged. They are often spoken of as "fixed" because their patterns, or constellations, have not changed. Astronomers of our day, however, reveal a slight change in positions compared with the earliest observation records. The two stars at the opposite end of the Big Dipper are *moving* in one direction while the rest of the stars in the constellation are moving in the opposite direction. All the stars in this group are bound, that is, they are moving together, not in various directions like the stars of the Big Dipper. Science, centuries after God's question to Job, has confirmed the "binding" of these stars.

Singing. Another scientific statement

by Job speaks about how the "morning stars sang together" (38:7). "Singing stars?" you might ask. Yes! Through the discoveries of modern physics, many things have been learned about the *tonal* value of light. Experiments have proven that every light ray and every shade of color has a very definite phonetic value. The light of the sun or of the stars speeding through space carries sound. Our ears are just not tuned to hear the melodies.

Height. What about the height of the stars? Job gives us a scientific answer: "Is not God in the height of heaven? and behold the height of the stars, how high they are" (22:12). It is implied that there is a great distance from the earth to the stars. Astronomers have found this to be true by measurements using triangulation. *Triangulation* is the finding of a position or surveying by use of a compass.

Empty Space in the North. Job makes mention of an empty space: "He [God] stretcheth out the north over the empty place, and hangeth the earth upon nothing" (26:7).

Lord Rosse invented a telescope so powerful that newsprint could be read twenty miles away. With this microscope, it was discovered that in the northern part of the heavens there was a great empty space that did not contain a single star. In all other parts of the heavens there were billions, but none in the north. This area has been commonly called the "black hole." It is described as an invisible object because it has so much gravitational force that not even light can escape from it. It is located in the nebula of the constellation of Orion. Orion is estimated to be 1,500 light years above our solar system. (Recall that a "light

year" is the distance light travels—about 5.88 trillion miles—186,000 miles per second.)

What is the significance of this "black hole" in the north to the Bible believer? Since the Bible does mention it, some are of the opinion that it is the dwelling place of God Himself. There is no need for light there "for God *is* light" (1 John 1:5). We have already been reminded that God is in the "height" of heaven (Job 22:12). The psalmist tells us that His throne is in heaven (11:4), and Isaiah 66:1 informs us that "heaven is [His] throne."

When Lucifer sought to dethrone God, he said: "I will ascend into heaven, I will exalt my throne above the stars of God: I will sit also upon the mount of the congregation, in the sides of the north" (Isa. 14:13). What better place for God's throne and dwelling place to be than in this northern part of heaven? It is filled with God Himself and His glory. It is a place where we will be "absent from the body, and . . . present with the Lord" (2 Cor. 5:8). It is a place where there is no more curse and night. It is a place where God and the Lamb (Christ) shall reign on their thrones (Rev. 22:3, 5).

Constellations—the Zodiac. Job uses the Hebrew word *mazzaroth* in reference to "constellations," which implies he was quite familiar with them. This Hebrew name was originally used for a group of stars that seemed to form a configuration in the sky. The movement of the earth in its orbit causes the sun to appear to move in a circle through the heavens. The twelve constellations in this apparent path ("the ecliptic") are known as the Zodiacal constellations. While the astronomers know the meaning and purpose of these heavenly bodies, astrologers have sought to use them as signs to forecast the future of our mind and body. [See "Astronomy/Astrology" in Index.]

Different. Our most powerful telescopes can only reveal individual stars as a points of light. Astronomers can best classify stars by plotting them on a standard graph, along with the star's magnitude (its temperature versus its brightness). When this is done, every star will plot its own unique path on the diagram that is different from all other stars.

Stars differ in color, amount of light emitted, density, heat, and size. Our sun, which is a star, is over 1,000,000 times the size of the earth, yet there are some stars that are over a million times larger than our sun, and there are some that are smaller than the smallest planet, Mercury.

Science confirms the accuracy of Paul's statement in 1 Corinthians 15:41, "There is one glory of the sun, and another glory of the moon, and another glory of the stars: for one star differeth from another star in glory." Here is a clear scientific statement in the Bible that stars do differ greatly one from the other. The *glory* of the stars means "honor" or "praise." Each star is worthy of its own honor and must, therefore, have a specific structure for its own individual divinely ordained function.

Paul uses the analogy of the glory and individuality of each star to parallel believers and their individual functions within the body of Christ. Their faithfulness on earth will determine whether they will be as the glory of the sun, the glory of the moon, or the glory of the stars.

As Paul gives spiritual application to the sun, moon, and stars, Solomon does the same when he reminds young people to "Remember now thy Creator in the days of thy youth . . . while the sun, or the light, or the moon, or the stars, be not darkened . . ." (Eccl. 12:1–2). He desires for them a life that reveals the light of their Creator's countenance. It is so easy to forget God and the things of God, so remember Him while the sun is not darkened.

The sun is a type of the Lord Jesus Christ, who is the Light of the world. If not remembered in youth, He becomes darkened in their thinking as they grow older.

The moon, which gets its light from the sun, is a type of the church. If church has no meaning in youth, in later years it becomes darkness to the soul. The stars could well be a type of individual believers. If their Creator, who became Savior, is remembered in youth, their works will glorify their Father who is in heaven (Matt. 5:16).

Wandering. When Jude refers to wandering stars (v. 13), he is not necessarily making a scientific statement, but a scientific fact is included. He compares these wandering stars, or comets, to the false prophets and apostate teachers. Comets shine for only a short time. As one moves toward the sun, gasses vaporize to leave a trail behind it. As the comet begins to wander and move away from the sun, its gases freeze and the bright trail disappears as the comet moves into darkness. Just as the comet shines brightly for a short time as it faces the light (sun), so a false prophet appears as an "angel of light." As the comet wanders into darkness, so a false prophet goes out from true believers in Christ to show that he was not one of them (1 John 2:29).

The stars

a. rule the night (Ps. 136:9)
b. are infinite in number (Gen. 15:5; Jer. 33:22)
c. are named (Ps. 147:4; Job 9:9; 38:31–32)
d. are appointed to give light (Jer. 31:35)
e. revolve in fixed orbits or courses (Judg. 5:20)
f. appear in different magnitudes (1 Cor. 15:41)
g. appear after sunset (Neh. 4:21; Job 3:9)
h. are alluded to in navigation (Acts 27:20)

The stars are illustrative of

a. Christ (Num. 24:17; Rev. 22:16)
b. angels (Job 38:7)
c. God's power (Ps. 8:3)
d. praise (Ps. 148:3)
e. song (Job 38:7)
f. ministers (Rev. 1:16, 20; 2:1)
g. reward (Rev. 2:26–28)
h. glory (Dan. 12:3)
i. judgment and calamity (Jer. 8:2; Joel 2:10)
j. judgment, for pride (Obad. 4) apostate teachers (Jude 13)

4

The Earth

When one considers the earth upon which life exists, common sense should tell us that there is a Designer who created life. A child can see the logic in the days, or steps, of creation by God, as recorded in Genesis 1–2, which led to the creation of human beings and their physical needs.

Recent photographs by satellites show distant planets that are lifeless, void, and wasteless. The earth is unique among all other explored planets. For life to exist, certain elements must exist in proper proportions.

Temperature

The temperature on the earth's surface depends primarily on the distance of the sun from the earth and the rotation of the earth on its axis. Of secondary importance to the earth's temperature is (1) the surface area of the continents, (2) the amount of earth covered by light and heat reflecting masses of ice (glaciers), and (3) the amount of carbon dioxide and water vapor effecting the transparency of the atmosphere to both incoming and outgoing heat.

The earth's axis is tilted 23½ degrees, which causes the different seasons. During the spring months, the northern hemisphere is facing the sun, which brings the warm summer. During the fall months, it is facing away from the sun, which brings cold weather. If the earth was closer to the sun, the heat would parch the land and vegetation. We could not survive. If the earth was farther away from the sun, freezing temperatures would prevail. If the earth's axis were not tilted 23½ degrees, nothing but ice would exist on both the northern and southern hemispheres, and the temperature at the equator would suffocate life.

If there were no Creator to set laws in motion to control temperature, it would seem strange that the evolutionary process arrived at the exact temperature on the planet to perpetuate life. How did life exist until the earth evolved in a "natural progressive" state until it reached its proper position? Somebody is in control. These things did not happen by chance. God put the proper temperature on earth to keep glaciers from melting and causing larger ocean surfaces, which would flood too much land surface. He tilted the earth on a rotating axis to provide seasonal weather for life to exist.

Atmosphere

Scientists have calculated the proportions of gases in the earth's atmosphere that would be needed to sustain life. Their ratio should be 78 percent nitrogen, 21 percent oxygen, slightly less than 1 percent argon, and enough carbon dioxide to make up the difference of argon and the full 1 percent. Oxygen is the most vital. Too much oxygen would cause combustion to increase, rocks and metal would disintegrate more rapidly, and life would be in jeopardy.

Carbon dioxide, though only a small amount is in our atmosphere, is essential to plant life. Many experts have suggested that it is beneficial to talk to your plants. When we talk to them, we breathe carbon dioxide on plants and they give off oxygen. Have you talked to your plants lately?

How did evolving life exist before the gases developed into their proportions unless the Creator mixed them properly at the beginning of time?

Wind

We previously noted the relationship of the sun to the wind (Job 38:24). The Bible makes another scientific statement about the wind in Job 28:25—its *weight*. No scientist before Galileo was aware that air has weight, or pressure. Today it is common knowledge that this is true. Automobile tires carry "air weight," or "pounds" of air. Trucks and trains use air (weight, pressure) for brakes.

The types and functions of wind mentioned in the Bible are

a. north wind—drives away rain (Prov. 25:23)
b. south wind—warms and dries (Job 37:17)
c. east wind—makes for storms (Job 27:21)
d. west wind—drives away pests (Ex. 10:19)
e. Euroclydon wind—tempestuous (Acts 27:14)
f. whirlwind (Job 37:9)
g. drying wind (Gen. 8:1; Isa. 11:15)
h. wind restrains (Job 28:25)
i. wind raises (Ps. 107:25)
j. wind changes (Ps. 78:26)
k. wind assuages (Matt. 8:26; 14:32)
l. wind's origin (John 3:8)

Some of the decriptions of wind in the Bible are

a. storm (Job 21:18; Ezek. 13:11, 13)
b. tempest (Job 27:20)
c. great and strong (1 Kings 19:11)
d. mighty (Acts 2:2)
e. fierce (James 3:4)
f. rough (Isa. 27:8)

The wind is illustrative of

a. the operation of the Holy Spirit (John 3:8)
b. purity (Job 37:21)
c. the life of a man (Job 7:7)
d. the speeches of the desperate (Job 6:26)
e. terrors that pursue the soul (Job 30:15)
f. molten images (Isa. 41:29)
g. iniquity and destruction (Isa. 64:6)
h. false doctrines (Eph. (4:14)
i. the wicked (Job 21:18; Ps. 1:4)

j. judgments of God (Isa. 27:8; Jer. 4:11–12)

k. sowing a course of sin (Hos. 8:7)

l. vain hopes (Hos. 12:1)

Water

Genesis 1:9 implies that the earth is a water planet. Research on the formation of other planets reveals a lack of water on them. Our planet is singular among other planets because of the abundance of water and the temperature that allows it to remain liquid. This makes the earth unique for vegetation and habitable for human beings and animals (Gen. 1:9–10).

Someone has suggested that there are some 340,000,000 cubic miles of liquid water on earth. Since water expands when it freezes, our oceans and streams do not freeze from the bottom up. With an average temperature of 45 degrees F, the ocean helps control the earth's temperature, keeping it cooler at the equator and warmer in colder regions. Since water admits light through it without appreciable diffusion or distortion, it is possible for marine algae to perform photosynthesis below the ocean surface. Ocean currents caused by the earth's rotation serve to circulate seawater and prevent the equatorial seas from becoming too hot and the polar seas from becoming too cold.

Scientists weigh water by measure. Over 2,200 years before Christ, Job stated that God "weigheth the waters by measure" (28:25). The *density* of water is implied in this verse indicating that it has a weight or mass/volume.

The weight of water serves as a standard of comparison for gravity calculations in chemistry. Since ice has less density or weight than water, it is lighter and will float, resulting in preserving life in streams and lakes. And the evolutionist, by *faith*, says that chance brought all this about!

Clouds

Almost 3,000 years ago, King Solomon said, "If the clouds be full of rain, they empty themselves upon the earth" (Eccl. 11:3). Clouds play a large role in other natural phenomenon—lightning, rain, rivers, and water in general. Job spoke of some of the activities of the clouds.

1. Spreading of clouds. Weather reports today are a part of the news media. Science has so perfected this study that predictions can be given well in advance. Satellites can view one-half of the world at a glance and transmit pictures of cloud formations. Infrared photography enables meteorologists to see during the night, and around the clock watch is kept on the spreading of clouds to interpret high and low pressure areas.

When vapors of the earth ascend, they cool and condense to form clouds, tornadoes, and other weather systems. It was absolutely scientific of Job when he asked: "Can any [but God] understand the spreadings of the clouds?" (Job 36:29).

2. Balancing of the clouds. Clouds are balanced in the air by two forces—gravity, which pushes or pulls down, and rising warm air, which forces upward. This perfect balance keeps both moisture and dust-filled clouds aloft. Job's timely question about "cloud balancing" (37:16) is just one more scientific question he asked.

3. Numbering the clouds (38:37). Some have questioned that Job 38:37 is not scientific. The Hebrew text does not say that the numbering of each

cloud is an impossibility for us. Job means that only God, who has numbered the "hairs on your head" (Matt. 10:30; Luke 21:18), knows the number of clouds in the sky.

The thought here has to do with "cloud coverage," not counting each cloud, but a recording of cloud coverage—especially the number of storm clouds covering an area, or in our scientific age, covering the earth as a whole.

Clouds are
a. established (Prov. 8:28)
b. balanced in the air (Job 37:16)
c. spread out (Ps. 147:8; Job 26:9)
d. scattered (Job 37:11; Hos. 13:3)
e. disposed of (Job 37:15)
f. waters above the firmament (Gen. 1:7)
g. numberless (Job 38:37)

They supply
a. rain (Judg. 5:4; Ps. 104:13; Eccl. 11:3)
b. dew (Prov. 3:20; Isa. 18:4)
c. moderate heat (Isa. 25:5)

Clouds are illustrative of
a. Christ's finished work of redemption (Acts 1:9)
b. Christ's glory (Matt. 17:5; Rev. 10:1)
c. Christ's return—the rapture (1 Thess. 4:16–17)
d. protection (Isa. 4:5)
e. God's power (Isa. 19:1)
f. glory of God (Exod. 16:10; 40:34)
g. unsearchableness of God (Ps. 97:2–12)
h. promise of God (Gen. 9:13–17)
i. guidance (Exod. 13:21; Num. 9:17–23)
j. light (Pss. 78:14; 105:39)
k. defense (Exod. 14:19; Ps. 105:39)
l. forgiveness (Isa. 44:22)
m. victory (1 Kings 18:44–46)
n. witness of Christ (Heb. 12:1)
o. hostile armies (Jer. 4:13; Ezek. 38:9, 16)
p. the fraudulent (Prov. 25:24)
q. fleeting "goodness" of hypocrisy (Hos. 6:4; 13:3)
r. false teachers (2 Peter 2:17; Jude 12)
s. judgment of God (Lam. 2:1; Ezek. 30:3)

Rain and Rain Clouds

Job also mentions rain—water in the clouds (26:8). This verse mentions the fact that water is bound up in a thick cloud, yet the cloud does not fall or break beneath its weight (as a result of cloud balancing, Job 37:16). The weight of water vapor or minute drops of water can be tremendous. When these vapor droplets become too large to float with the cloud, they fall as rain (Job 36:27). As Solomon said: "If the clouds be full of rain, they empty themselves upon the earth" (Eccl. 11:3).

Rain
a. refreshes the earth (Ps. 68:9; 72:6)
b. makes the earth fruitful (Heb. 6:7)
c. replenishes springs and fountains (Ps. 104:8–11)
d. often accompanies lightning and thunder (Ps. 135:7)
e. often is destructive (Ezek. 13:13–15)
f. is occasioned by condensation of clouds (Job 36:27–28)

Rain clouds are illustrative of
a. greatness and goodness (Job 36:26–27; Acts 14:17)

b. mercy (Matt. 5:45)
c. encouragement to fear God (Jer. 5:24)
d. promptings to praise God (Ps. 147:7–8)
e. a promise to the obedient (Lev. 26:3–4)
f. the Word of God (Isa. 55:10–11)
g. doctrine (Deut. 32:2)
h. graces of Christ (Ps. 72:6; Hos. 6:3)
i. spiritual blessings (Ps. 68:9; 84:6)
j. righteousness (Hos. 10:12)
k. oppression (Prov. 28:3)
l. God's judgment (Job 20:23; Ps. 11:6)

e. eternal life (John 4:14; Rev. 21:6)
f. means of grace (Isa. 41:18)
g. a good wife (Prov. 5:18)
h. numerous prosperity (Deut. 33:28)
i. spiritual wisdom (Prov. 16:22; 18:4)
j. the law of the wise (Prov. 13:14)
k. Godly fear (Prov. 14:27)
l. guidance and satisfaction (Isa. 58:11)
m. backsliding (Prov. 25:26)
n. Israel's wickedness (Jer. 6:7)
o. corruption—the natural heart (James 3:11; Matt. 15:18–19)
p. punishment/judgment (Ps. 107:33–34)

Springs and Fountains

Isaiah states that rain "waters the earth" (55:10). For centuries it was believed that as rain descended, its waters only ran into streams, lakes, rivers, and the seas. We now know that rain seeps into the ground, thus making the surface moist for plant life. And, of course, as the rains fall upon the earth, plant life is not only nourished, but rain also supplies "ground water" for watersheds, springs, and fountains (Isa. 44:4).

Springs and fountains
a. are found in hills and valleys (Deut. 8:7; Ps. 104:10)
b. provide refreshment for beasts and fowls (Ps. 104:10–13)
c. bring fruitfulness to the earth (1 Kings 18:5; Joel 3:18)

Springs and fountains are illustrative of
a. God (Ps. 36:9; Jer. 1:13; 17:13)
b. Christ's blood (Zech. 13:1)
c. the Holy Spirit (John 7:38–39)
d. constant supply of grace (Ps. 87:7)

Ponds and Lakes

Ponds and lakes are also filled with rainwater (Ps. 84:6). They
a. supply gardens (Eccl. 2:6)
b. supply cities with water (Isa. 22:11; 2 Kings 20:20; John 9:7)
c. preserve fish (Isa. 19:10)

Ponds and lakes are illustrative of
a. gifts of the Spirit (Isa. 35:7; 41:18)
b. desolation (Isa. 14:23)

Rivers

Solomon, ca. 975 B.C., mentioned rivers in connection with clouds: "All the rivers run into the sea; yet the sea is not full; unto the place from whence the rivers come [precipitation from the clouds], thither they return again [by evaporation to form new clouds]" (Eccl. 1:7). Science agrees with this portion of Scripture.

Rivers
a. are enclosed with banks (Dan. 12:5)

b. flow through valleys (Ps. 104:8, 10)
c. part into many streams (Gen. 2:10; Isa. 11:15)
d. run into the seas (Eccl. 1:7; Ezek. 47:8)
e. supply drinking water (Jer. 2:18)
f. are used for commerce (Ps. 46:4; Isa. 23:3)
g. promote vegetation (Gen. 2:10)
h. are used for bathing (Exod. 2:5)
i. abound with fish (Lev. 11:9–10)

Rivers are illustrative of
a. grace in Christ (Isa. 32:2 with John 1:16)
b. indwelling Holy Spirit (John 7:37–38)
c. abundance (Job 20:17; 29:6)
d. peace (Isa. 66:12)
e. overflowing of divine love and grace (Ezek. 47)
f. fruitfulness (Ps. 1:3; Jer. 17:8)
g. eruption of invading army (Jer. 46:7–8)
h. heavy affliction (Ps. 69:2; Isa. 43:2)
i. God's judgment (Isa. 19:1–8; Jer. 47:2)

Seas

Seas (oceans) are mentioned in Genesis 1:9–10. The Bible contains a number of statements about these vast bodies of water, such as Genesis 1:9–10, and all of them are scientifically accurate.

Science today acknowledges that since over 70 percent of the earth's surface is covered with water, here is just one mass of water, which they call the "world ocean." This same thought is seen in our verses: "And God said, Let the waters under the heaven be gathered together unto one place, and let the dry land appear. . . . And God called the dry land Earth; and the gathering together of the waters called he Seas." We call them the Atlantic, Pacific, Indian, and Arctic oceans.

The Bible (Job 38:8–11) speaks of ocean boundaries. We mentioned previously that some 340,000,000 cubic miles of liquid water are on the earth, and if our earth were smooth, water could cover it to a depth of 12,000 feet. There are mountains in the ocean which, in valleys (recesses and trenches), store vast amounts of water. Some of our highest mountains could be swallowed up in the ocean valleys. This information was given by the psalmist centuries before Christ (33:7). This all has to do with keeping the oceans within their bounds, as mentioned by Job.

The channels of the sea are mentioned in 2 Samuel 22:16. A sea channel is a valley in the ocean floor. It has been revealed that life is found in these ocean depths, something that had been previously denied.

The psalmist mentioned "deep calleth unto deep at the noise of thy waterspouts" (42:7). This could well have been a reference to sea life *talking* due to this roaring. Sea life can communicate with each other. Dolphins and other fish and ocean mammals can "talk" to each other.

In recent years science has developed techniques to reach the great depths of the bottom of the seas. It is believed the deepest part of any ocean is about 7 miles (almost 37,000 feet deep).

Job mentioned these great depths (38:16). There are also great springs in the oceans—springs which empty into the oceans. Genesis 7:11 and

Job 38:16 mention "fountains [springs] of the great deep [oceans]." Not only did rain contribute to the flood of Noah's day, but fountains on the ocean floor contributed to it. Great pressure at the ocean's bottom prohibited explorers from examining its floor. Sophisticated equipment has enabled explorers to indeed discover "springs in the deep."

M. F. Murray concluded in 1860 that the ocean had a circulating system based on his reading of Psalm 107:23–30. Modern technology still holds to his conclusions. Currents are due to paths of the sea (Ps. 8:8). The cycles of rivers flowing into the oceans and vapor ascending into the clouds in turn send the water back to the earth in the form of rain. "If clouds be full of rain, they empty themselves upon the earth" (Eccl. 1:7; 11:3; Amos 9:6). This process, which was accepted by science around A.D. 1600, is known as the "water cycle" and has contributed to water movements (currents) that have created paths in the seas for ships to follow.

The seas
a. are of immense extent (Job 11:9; Ps. 104:25)
b. are of great depth (Ps. 68:22)
c. are replenished by rivers (Eccl. 1:7)
d. sand their barrier (Jer. 5:22)
e. are inhabited by numerous creatures (Ps. 104:25–26)
f. are raised by wind (Ps. 107:25–26; Jonah 1:4)
g. are sites of commerce (Gen. 49:13; Ezek. 27:3)
h. have waves that are raised (Ps. 93:3; 107:25), tossed to and fro (Jer. 5:22), multitudinous (Jer. 51:42), tumultuous (Luke 21:25; Jude 13)

The seas are illustrative of
a. righteousness (Isa. 48:18)
b. peace (Rev. 4:6; 15:2)
c. knowledge of God (Isa. 11:9; Hab. 2:14)
d. God's hiding place for sin (Mic. 7:19)
e. heavy affliction (Isa. 43:2; Lam. 2:13)
f. the troubled wicked (Isa. 57:20–21)
g. hostile armies (Isa. 5:30; Ezek. 26:3–4)
h. unsteadiness and devastation (James 1:5)

Water
In this chapter we have considered many forms of water, which contributes to life.

The uses and characteristics of water are
a. for man and beast (Exod. 17:3; 1 Kings 18:4–5)
b. for vegetation (Gen. 2:5–6; Job 14:9)
c. for culinary purposes (Exod. 12:9)
d. for washing (Gen. 18:4; 24:32)
e. described as fluid (Ps. 78:16; Prov. 30:4); unstable (Gen. 49:4); penetrating (Ps. 109:18); reflecting images (Prov. 27:19); cleansing (Ezek. 36:25; Eph. 5:26); congealed by cold (Job 38:29; Ps. 147:16–17); refreshing (Job 22:7; Prov. 25:25)
f. rises in vapor (Eccl. 1:7 with Ps. 104:8)
g. descends as rain (Deut. 11:11)
h. found in rocks (Exod. 17:5); springs (Josh. 15:19); pools (1 Kings 22:38; Neh. 2:14); ponds (Exod. 7:19; Isa. 19:10); fountains (1 Kings 18:5;

2 Chron. 32:3); wells (Gen. 21:19); brooks and streams (2 Sam. 17:20; Ps. 78:16); rivers (Isa. 8:7; Jer. 2:18); the seas (Gen. 1:9–10; Job 25:8–9); the clouds (Gen. 1:7; Job 26:8–9)

Water is illustrative of
a. the voice of Christ (Rev. 1:15)
b. salvation (Isa. 55:1; John 4:14)
c. gifts and graces of the Spirit (Isa. 41:17–18; John 7:28, 39)
d. the Word of God (Eph. 5:26 with John 15:3)
e. the support of God (Isa. 8:6)
f. contentment (Ps. 23:2)
g. exaltation (Num. 24:7)
h. wavering disposition (Gen. 49:4)
i. cowardice (Josh. 7:5; Ezek. 7:17)
j. strife and contention (Prov. 17:14)
k. wrath of God (Hos. 5:10)

The Earth and People

The watered earth provides the ingredients necessary for our very survival. The evolutionist believes such things evolved; the creationist believes a Designer was responsible—that this Designer is none other than God Himself, the Creator. Is the earth the only planet that has life? Are there essentials provided on other planets for the sustaining of life?

With the development of missiles during World War II, the construction of space capsules to orbit the earth, the landing of people on the moon, and the sending of other spaceships to remote planets, there are some scientists who believe that there is life on other planets.

These scientists think that life is flourishing on some distant planets, and the creatures are in some way des-perately trying to send messages to other life-forms across the vastness of space. There are those who claim they sight UFOs, which are supposed to contain beings from outer space. Imagination and fancy too often over-rule fact, and statements have appeared that there is life beyond our earth. A Roman Catholic priest was once quoted as saying that the church needed to prepare missionaries to send to other planets.

In 1969 when astronauts first visited the moon, part of their mission was to bring back information that would verify the existence of life on that satellite. No information has been found to verify that life existed on the moon. Many pictures have been taken via satellite of Mars, Venus, and Jupiter. No evidence of life appeared.

What should the Christian's attitude be in this matter of life on other planets? Is there life elsewhere? If so, what kind? These seem to be un-answerable questions. The Bible, however, gives an answer for those who might ask. "Ye are blessed of the LORD which made heaven and earth. The heaven, even the heavens, are the LORD's: *but the earth hath he given to the children of men*" (Ps. 115:15–16). Just as birds were made for the air and fish were made for the water, so humankind was made for this earth.

This can be proved by the fact that astronauts must have earth's elements—water, air, food, and clothing—to survive in outer space. Their spaceships and spacesuits are constructed so the body will be in the same atmosphere that is necessary for life on earth. Even when people walked on the moon, these require-ments were still essential for their survival.

We are told that a person's body is over 75 percent water. It is 400 degrees below freezing on Neptune. If humans ever reach this planet *as is*, they would be ice cubes in no time. If they took a trip to Mercury *as is*, they would be in for a hot time because it is 750 degrees Fahrenheit there.

We should praise God that He has given the earth to us. Evidence from all known sources show life only on earth. It was human beings that God created, made *on* this earth *for* this earth. The point is not to argue if life exists elsewhere, but rather to question whether or not those of us who know Christ as our Savior are faithful witnesses to those on planet earth who are yet unsaved? It was to *this* earth that God sent His Son to die for the lost. It is to *this* world that we are commissioned to "go and preach."

God is not the author of confusion. He would have made it perfectly clear to us in His Word if there were others in space who needed to be reached with the Gospel. He would have created our bodies in such a manner that if others needed to be reached elsewhere, we could go from planet to planet without needing the earth's elements to survive.

Before we close our chapter on the earth, we will consider more ancient biblical statements that are scientifically correct.

Lightning

Job 36:28 is scientifically correct in stating that the clouds drop and distill rain. Rain *distills*, not splashes, onto the earth. Science has confirmed that when water is sprayed into a charged area, drops are formed by vapor. In like manner, lightning provides the necessary charge to make vapor droplets unite, and "He maketh lightnings for

the rain" (Ps. 135:7; see also Jer. 10:13 and Eccl. 1:7).

Jesus spoke scientifically when He mentioned lightning in reference to His second coming (Luke 17:24). He spoke of this coming again "as the lightning, that lighteneth out of one part under heaven." He said "in that night there shall be two men in one bed; the one shall be taken, and the other shall be left. Two women shall be grinding [which is done in the morning]; . . . Two men shall be in the field [working in the daytime]; the one shall be taken, and the other left" (Luke 17:34–36). This sudden event is described as taking place while it is night in one part of the world, morning in another, and daytime in another. Because the earth is a sphere, part of it will be illuminated by the sun while and the other half will be dark.

In speaking of lightning, Job 38:25 correctly describes the way lightning travels as a *path*. It is a known fact that lightning travels on a charged path, sometimes only a few inches wide and as hot as 35,000 to 45,000 degrees Celsius.

Could sending messages by lightning be scientific? Job asked such a question: "Canst thou send lightnings, that they may go, and say unto you, Here we are?" (38:35). The apostle Paul prayed that the Word of God might have free course and be glorified (2 Thess. 3:1 with Ps. 147:15). Paul's thought, no doubt, was that prayer would cause God's message to take flight and reach multitudes of people within a short period of time. Today, thanks to radio, TV, and other forms of electronic media, it is possible for the message of His Word (as well as other messages) to be "sent by lightnings [electricity]."

Snow and Hail

"Hast thou entered into the treasures of the snow? or hast thou seen the treasures of the hail, which I have reserved against the time of trouble, against the day of battle and war?" (Job 38:22–23). Snow is known to be a scientific must for our survival. Some of its treasures include a topcoat to keep the earth from freezing; protection of winter seeds; a purifying, cleansing agent for the soil; a supply for streams and reservoirs.

Isaiah 55:10 mentions the snow's scientific value—that of coming down from heaven and watering the earth, making it fruitful (55:10).

Snow and hail have revealed their worth in times of battle. Napoleon and Hitler were both thwarted because of Russia's snow. The Israelites were assisted in battle by hailstones, which killed more of their enemies than were slain with the sword (Josh. 10:11). After several experiments to make the explosive TNT safe for shipment during World War I, it was discovered that snow water, which is absolutely pure, made it possible for the particles of impure water to be removed from the explosive. As a reward to the Jewish scientist who accomplished this feat, the British signed the Balfour Declaration in 1917 to give Jews a homeland in Palestine.

Snow
a. comes in the winter (2 Sam. 23:10)
b. is cold, instills fear (Prov. 31:21)
c. can be melted by heat (Job 24:19)
d. contains many treasures for the earth's good. It protects seed, purifies, covers the earth's soil, keeps the earth from freezing, and supplies streams and lakes with water

Snow is illustrative of
a. God's power (Job 37:5–6)
b. the Word of God (Isa. 55:10–11)
c. purity (Matt. 28:3; Rev. 1:14)
d. salvation (Isa. 1:18)
e. cleansing (Ps. 51:7)

Treasures in the Earth

As snow and hail are mentioned as treasures from the heavens, the Bible also speaks of the hidden treasures of the earth. Isaiah said, "I will give you the treasures of darkness and hidden riches in secret places" (45:3). We seem to take things in stride much better in the daylight than we do in darkness, yet most of earth's valued treasures are found only in dark, secret places. Gold, silver, diamonds, precious stones, coal, and oil are found in the deepest mines. Then, too, we need the darkness to enable us to appreciate the beauty of the moon, stars, and planets—the works of God's fingers (Ps. 8:3). Some treasures of darkness are metals, which
a. can be dug out of the earth (Job 28:1–2, 6)
b. are mixed with dross (Isa. 1:25) and dross is freed by fire (Ezek. 22:18, 20)
c. can be cast in molds (Judges 17:4; 1 Kings 7:46)

Gold (Job 28:1, 6; Ps. 68:13; Isa. 13:12) is illustrative of
a. saints after affliction (Job 23:10)
b. tried faith (1 Peter 1:7)
c. doctrines of grace (Rev. 3:18)
d. faithful servants (1 Cor. 3:12)

Silver (Job 28:1; Ps. 68:13–14) is illustrative of

a. the words of the Lord (Ps. 12:6)
b. the tongue of the just (Prov. 10:20)
c. wisdom (Job 28:15; Prov. 3:14; 16:16)
d. faithful servants (1 Cor. 3:12)
e. saints purified in affliction (Ps. 66:10)

Copper (Deut. 8:9) is illustrative of

a. decrees of God (Zech. 6:1–5)
b. strength and firmness of Christ (Dan. 10:6)
c. strength for saints (Jer. 15:20; Mic. 4:13)
d. drought (Deut. 28:23)
e. barren earth (Lev. 26:19)
f. obstinate sinners (Isa. 48:4; Jer. 6:28)
g. hypocrisy (2 Chron. 12:9–10)

Iron (Deut. 8:9; Job 28:2) is illustrative of

a. strength (Dan. 2:33, 40)
b. stubbornness (Isa. 48:4)
c. severe afflictions (Deut. 4:20; Ps. 107:10)
d. hard barren soil (Deut. 28:23)
e. severe exercise of power (Rev. 2:27)
f. insensibility of conscience (1 Tim. 4:2)

Precious stones are illustrative of

a. preciousness of Christ (Isa. 28:16)
b. beauty and stability of the church (Isa. 54:11)
c. saints (Mal. 3:17)
d. faithful service (1 Cor. 3:12)
e. glory and stability of the heavenly Jerusalem (Rev. 21:11, 19)

f. a virtuous woman (Prov. 31:10)
g. the superiority of wisdom (Job 28:18)

The Earth in Space

The Bible states in Job 26:7 that our planet earth "hangs upon nothing." In A.D. 1543 Copernicus made a bold statement that the earth hangs in space and revolves around the sun. Later, when Galileo came forth with his telescope, he proved Copernicus right. Galileo's proof brought down the wrath of the Roman Catholic Church and forced him to recant on his knees and deny his findings, but even though the church "won" then, it later had to recant.

It was thrilling when the American astronauts in 1968 circled the moon and took pictures of the "round earth hanging upon nothing in space" (see fig. 1). For the Christian, it is good to know that our God, who created the earth, "upholds all things by the Word of His power" (Heb. 1:3).

The Earth Is Round

Isaiah (750 B.C.) refers to the earth as being round: "The circle of the earth" (or more literally, "the roundness of the earth"; 40:22). Copernicus also had said that the earth was round. Ancient Egyptians had calculated the curvature of the earth as eight inches to the mile in erecting the Great Pyramid with perfect orientation (i.e., its sides face due east and west, north and south to a perfect degree). Columbus discovered the New World in 1492, and it was said then that the world was round. God's Word not only confirms this scientific fact stated by Isaiah but also by Solomon (ca. 970 B.C.) who said that it was God who "set a

Figure 1. The Earth as viewed from lunar orbit

compass [circle] upon the face of the depth [earth]" (Prov. 8:27).

The Four Corners of the Earth

Critics of the Bible point to a verse they think is unscientific. Isaiah (ca. 750 B.C.) spoke of the "four corners of the earth" (11:12). The apostle John (ca. A.D. 95) also used this same expression. Is such a statement scientifically correct? Is it just a figure of speech?

It actually refers to the four directions or extreme limits of land. The Hebrew word for *corners* is "borders" (Num. 15:38); "four corners" (Ezek. 7:2: Isa. 11:2); "ends" (Job 37:3; 38:13); and in the Greek, used by the apostle John in Revelation (7:10), it is "divisions" and "angles," such as a map is divided into quadrants, shown by the four directions—North, South, East, and West. Isaiah and John did not mean that the earth was flat with four corners. But is there any scientific proof of the earth having "four corners"?

Scientists at Johns Hopkins University have said that the four corners of the earth are a reality. Military satellites have detected "corners" in the form of four plateau-like areas, so vast and subtle that ordinary means of measuring have left them unnoticed until now.

They were found to be equidistant from each other, each covering several thousand miles. The first corner was centered in Ireland. The second extends from New Guinea across the equator toward Japan. The third lies south of the tip of Africa and extends halfway to Australia, and the fourth is west of Peru.

Dr. Robert R. Newton, supervisor of space research analysis at the Johns

Hopkins physics laboratory, said the findings resulted from radio soundings taken from six satellites launched between 1961 and 1963. These plateaus exerted greater gravitational force on the satellites and pulled them closer to the ground, thus revealing the actual presence of the four corners of the earth.

Summary

The questions of this age demand answers. The old adage "I'll believe it when I see it" seems uppermost in many minds. Yet, one of the greatest tricks of Satan is to get people to believe something that is said over and over, whether it is right or wrong, whether there is proof or not.

Scientists in the field of evolution have presented theory as fact. Proof is lacking, but people believe what they say—proof or no proof. When we consider what evolution teaches, people who believe it are to be prayed for. We know that God loves them and Christ died for them, but there will come a time when His grace can no longer be extended. Psalm 2 gives a picture of God's reaction to those who have ignored or refused His claims on them. He looks upon them in love, in pity, as being educated beyond their intelligence, as knowing more and more about less and less until they know everything about nothing. Then God laughs (Ps. 2:4).

"He [God] hath made his wonderful works to be remembered" (Ps. 111:4).

From the dawn of time, people have looked at the intricate, mathematical perfection of the amazing universe in which they find themselves and cry out two inevitable queries: "Where did we come from?" and "Why?"

The first question has only one answer—Creation. The works of God are the unanswerable proof of the existence of God. So the first question is answered by a *fact* of God: He created.

It is the second question that constitutes the real enigma. *Why* should God create a complex and extensive universe? As far as science can answer, there is no other orb in space which is populated or inhabited by people. Light years apart from each other, the globes sail serenely through space, apparently indifferent to each other and unknown to all except the occupants of earth. Reason falters as it seeks to make an estimate of the size and mass of these other worlds, in spite of what science has learned from its telescopes. What was the purpose, or what is the use of such colossal expenditure of material? We are certain that God is never profligate nor wasteful, hence we have constantly sought for a reason for the stupendous extent of creation. Angels do not need these worlds; heaven is their habitation. People may reach a few planets in space, but to them, they are just awe-inspiring mysteries to be studied the best they can.

God made *all* these things in creation to encourage us to remember Him through His wonderful works. Each day these works tell us of the glory of God, and the firmament shows us the handiwork of His fingers (Ps. 8:3; 19:1). The God who is not willing that any should perish is also not willing that He should be forgotten, since to forget Him results in sin, rebellion, estrangement, and hence eternal loss of soul. He has done all this so that the creature called human should never be without a witness of

Himself. He set in motion His creative acts so that someday we would glorify Him and enjoy Him forever through His Son Jesus Christ, who died for our sins (Rom. 5:6–11).

The reader can believe the theories of evolution (1 Tim. 6:20) or accept what God said He did—"In the begin- ning God created the heaven and the earth" (Gen. 1:1). If we believe in evolution, we might as well eat, drink, be merry, then die. We lose nothing and gain nothing. But if the Bible is right, we gain everything. For to live is Christ, and to die with Christ is gain (Phil. 1:21).

5

The Earth's Age and Length of Days

There is a heated debate among theistic evolutionists and creationists as to the age of the earth and the actual length of time of the seven days recorded in the first two chapters of Genesis. Evolutionists claim that the earth has been in existence for billions of years, and others say that each day of creation could actually be millions of years.

Some people compromise their beliefs and hold to "theistic evolution" or "progressive creationism." This equates the geological ages with the six days of creation of Genesis, thus the so-called day-age theory. It adopts the standard evolutionary framework of history but allows for God to "create" various entities along the way, particularly at points where there are gaps in the fossil record. Such progressive creationists generally believe in the Big Bang theory of the universe, the naturalistic evolution of the stars and galaxies, the development of the solar system some 5 billion years ago, and the evolving development of the different forms of life on earth.

Creationists believe that their opponents are wrong because their timetable does not coincide with sufficient scientific evidence and statements in the Bible. Creationists believe in a young earth and that the six days of creation were twenty-four-hour periods per day. When verses other than those in Genesis 1 and 2 are considered, a young earth seems to be the logical conclusion.

The Earth's Age

For a number of years Bible believers were taught, according to Ussher's chronology (popularized by the old *Scofield Reference Bible*), that Adam was created in 4004 B.C., which would make humankind almost 6,000 years old, and the earth just a few days older, that is if each day were twenty-four hours long. There are some archaeological discoveries, however, that date the beginning of humankind back to 8,000 years B.C., making the human race at least 10,000 years old. No one can pinpoint our exact age, giving the day and date of creation.

We are assured from the Scriptures that death did not enter the world until Adam and Eve disobeyed God and brought a curse upon the earth

(Rom. 5:12; 8:20–22). Such verses contradict the evolutionist's theory that fossil finds are millions of years old. But when we consider the flood of Noah's day—a worldwide flood— evidence of it and its effects upon the earth support the theory of a young earth. Historical evidence shows that in every part of the world there are traditions and records that speak of a great flood [see "Flood, Worldwide" in Index].

The science of geology (rocks and fossils) points to a great worldwide catastrophe. With the vast amount of water that covered the earth weighing billions upon billions of tons (Gen. 7:11–12), there must have been terrifying volcanic eruptions and shifting faults causing earthquakes to open up huge spaces for water to pour in, swallowing vast amounts of rock and sediment—plant life, trees, animals, and humans. Two-thirds to three-fourths of the earth's crust is covered with sedimentary rock. Evidence shows that thick layers of sediment were deposited in a short period of time—not gradually over millions of years. For anything to become fossilized, it must be quickly buried in sediment, otherwise it would decay or be devoured by scavengers. The sudden death of the frozen mammoths, the wiping out of dinosaurs, and the many fossilized shoals of fish all point to a terrible catastrophe like a flood.

Coal, for example, which took millions of years to form according to the evolutionist, shows evidence that seams were formed when vegetation was uprooted and redeposited by flood waters. Trees, marine life, vegetation fossils, a gold chain, an iron pot, and a human skull have all been found in coal deposits. An amazing coal mine at McDade Park in Scranton, Pennsylvania, has stalactites that grow on the coal at an alarming rate. The mine was first dug in 1921, and all the stalactite growth has occurred in the past seventy years or less. One vein dug between 1958 and 1960 has a stalactite 12 ¼ inches long and still growing. In another area of the mine an entire wall is covered with calcite deposits and stalactites that measures several inches. The longest stalactite is 20 inches. Evolutionists would claim that this stalactite formation took millions of years to form, yet all this has happened in the past seventy years. The tour guides in these mines point out a geological enigma—a huge rock with unusual water marks, possibly relating to some great flood. Arrowheads, human bones, and animal bones have been found in the coal mine, while evolutionists claim coal was formed millions of years before humans.

The arrangement in which fossils are usually found in rocks is fish, amphibians, reptiles, mammals, plant life, trees, fowls, and people. If people are included in fossils—and such discoveries have been made—the earth could not be as old as evolutionists make it out to be before people came into existence. Such fossils, as mentioned, fit in with Genesis 7:21: "And all flesh died that moved upon the earth, both of fowl, and of cattle, and of beast, and of every creeping thing that creepeth upon the earth, and every man." Everyone died, that is, except for Noah, his family, and the animals taken aboard the ark (Gen. 7).

For the evolutionist to ignore a flood of the magnitude recorded in the Bible and substantiated by other historical records, is to ignore bona fide evidence that caused fossil-producing sediment. The Genesis flood has been the best promising evidence for the formation of fossil-bearing sedimentary rocks on a worldwide scale the earth has ever experienced and goes a long way to give credence to a young earth instead of an old one.

When Noah and his family disembarked from the ark, God promised He would never again destroy the earth with a great flood (Gen. 9:11, 15). If Noah's flood were only local, then the biblical flood is false. And if it were local, there would have been no need for Noah to have built an ark for his and some animals' survival since he had one hundred years warning. He could have climbed to higher ground.

There is a warning for us attached to this worldwide flood. Christ based His second coming and judgment on the fact that Noah's flood judged all humankind (Matt. 24:36–39; Luke 17:26–27). A local flood implies only a partial judgment. Likewise, Peter based his argument of future events on the historical fact of the global flood of Noah's day (2 Peter 3). All things considered, few doctrines are taught as clearly in Scripture as that of the worldwide flood of Noah's time.

The Days of Creation

If we can determine the length of each day in Genesis 1, we can better understand the age of the earth. When the Bible speaks of a day as a thousand years, critics say that this favors their view of an old earth (Ps. 90:4; 2 Peter 3:8). These verses show this expression to be a figure of speech—saying that God is not restricted to time as we are.

The word *day* can mean
1. from sunrise to sunset (Gen. 1:5; Ps. 74:16)
2. a period of twelve hours (John 11:9)
3. time in general (Judg. 18:30; Job 18:20)
4. length of life (Gen. 5:4)
5. a time of opportunity (John 9:4)
6. the day of judgment (Joel 1:15; Amos 5:18)

When making a study of any subject in the Bible, the context must be considered—not just one verse or word. A number of verses speak of a day as a twenty-four-hour period. Here are some examples:

"And [Laban] set three days journey between himself and Jacob" (Gen. 30:36).

"And the glory of the Lord abode on mount Sinai, and the cloud covered it six days, and on the seventh day He called unto Moses" (Exod. 24:16).

"Remember the Sabbath day to keep it holy. Six days shalt thou labor and do all thy work: but the seventh day is the Sabbath of the Lord. . . . For in six days the Lord made heaven and earth, the sea, and all that is in them, and rested the seventh day" (Exod. 20:8–11).

The meaning of the word *day* in the above verses must be seen in relation to the word *day* in Genesis 1:5 with the use of the expression "evening and morning were the first day."

Day in Genesis 1 means the same twenty-four-hour period we have in other verses that speak of this period of time. People do not work six days of an indefinite period of time, especially when it comes to the time of which an evolutionist speaks! People used to work from sunup until sundown (*day*) with night (*evening*) to rest, making it a twenty-four-hour day. They couldn't survive otherwise. So look at the six days of creation as twenty-four-hour periods of time.

As we take into account the possibility of the flood of Noah's day bringing to pass concrete evidence to support rapid fossil deposits happening as a result of such a catastrophe and sufficient evidence to show that a day is a twenty-four-hour period, both the flood and the twenty-four-hour day are contributing factors to a young earth.

6

Scientific Illustrations in the Bible

Throughout the Bible there are a number of verses which list scientific facts and subjects that have a scientific application. Let's examine some of those subjects and the Scripture that enlightens them.

Medicine and Sanitation

The book of Leviticus, written by Moses ca. 1500 B.C., lists several subjects that modern science accepts as fact.

As previously stated, Moses was schooled in the wisdom or sciences of Egypt (Acts 7:22). These ancient Egyptians excelled in medicine and practiced it scientifically. They left two documents which tell of their medical practice. One is called the Ebers Papyrus, which deals with internal medicine and diseases, and the other is called the Edwin Smith Papyrus, the oldest surgical document known. This treatise analyzes many disorders common to man, including wounds, fractures, dislocations, tumors, ulcers, and abscesses. In surgery, lint was used for absorbents. Stitching or adhesive plaster was used to close incisions. Salves were used

extensively on wounds. Artificial teeth were also common to them, and they knew of a "magic" fluid in the body that with the pulsing of the heart was in every vessel and that loss of this fluid could be fatal. Minerals and herbs were prescribed that are comparable to ours in therapeutic value. Belladonna was used to check bladder spasms, and poppy was administered for pain and to induce sleep—it is used today with other drugs in connection with spasms and seizures. We profit today by their graphic accounts of eye diseases, jaundice, fevers, and ideas to control the spread of disease.

If Moses applied any of the medical science of his day, we have no record of it. But in the book of Leviticus, we note that he went much further than what has been found in Egyptian records. What he did prescribe is a part of medical science of our day, and it was in keeping with God's promise: "And the LORD will take away from thee all sickness, and will put none of the evil diseases of Egypt, which thou knowest, upon thee" (Deut. 7:15). This implies *precaution*, something the Egyptians failed to mention in their documents. Fatalities often occur when precautionary measures are not taken.

Lip Covering (Mask)

Lip covering is mentioned in Leviticus 13:45. Surgeons today would not dare operate without such a mask. Many times before entering a patient's room in a hospital, visitors must don a gown and a mask to keep from spreading germs. Moses gave such precautionary advice about 3,500 years ago, long before Pasteur discovered germs.

Quarantine

The Bible is the only ancient book in the world that insists on quarantining contagious diseases, so said Moses (Lev. 13:45–46). Today's medical science knows of this need. With the discovery of germs, soap commercials have a field day stressing cleanness. Moses told Israel to do this centuries ago (Lev. 14:8–9).

Why do we have sewage plants today? Science tells us that without proper disposal, typhoid fever would be common among us. Moses recognized this fact when he instructed people to bury body waste with a shovel (Deut. 23:13).

Disinfection

Surgeons preparing for an operation will scrub their hands for about seven minutes under running water. Unless this continuous washing is performed, germs will be carried under the scales of their skin and transmitted to the patient. If hands were washed in a basin of water, no matter for how long, germs would contaminate it. Running water carries away the germs until the hands are surgically clean.

Such instructions are given in the Bible (Lev. 15:13). Moses also instructed the Israelites to wash any contaminated clothes for fear of spreading germs (Lev. 15:25–27). All of these instructions were given long before modern science knew what a germ was!

Artificial Respiration

This is a measure that replaces natural breathing in such cases as respiratory paralysis, drowning, electrical shock, choking, gas or smoke inhalation, or poisoning. In the absence of mechanical respirators, mouth to mouth resuscitation is practiced. Such a case is recorded in the Bible, when it is indicated that Elisha "stretched himself upon the child face to face." He employed mouth-to-mouth resuscitation to stimulate the lungs (2 Kings 4:34–35). This scientific procedure took place about 2,740 years ago.

Pharmacy and Pharmacology

There are no prescriptions as such in the Bible. However, from various Old Testament passages, we can deduce that the ancient Hebrews were well aware of the apothecary's art and that there was a sufficient amount of scientific medical knowledge to bring about desired results.

1. Mandrake. Among the powers attributed to this plant are increasing wealth, arousing passion, and overcoming barrenness.

2. Balm of Gilead. This medicinal herb is mentioned many times in Scripture (Jer. 8:2, 22; 46:11). Gilead is Central Transjordan, whose hills were famous for such herbs. According to Jeremiah, it was used as a palliative—to ease pain (51:8–9).

3. Nitre (niter) or soap. Nitre was

used as a cleansing agent and surface antiseptic (Jer. 2:22).

4. Oil. Oil was employed to dress wounds, bruises, and festering sores (Isa. 1:5–6). This reference also shows that drainage was accomplished by pressure around the infected area.

5. Fig. A New England physician has written a book titled *None of These Diseases*, in which he lists any number of "old-time" remedies for various ailments. His contention is that they worked in days gone by, and why not try today. King Hezekiah did not have modern scientific techniques to cure his boil, so Isaiah applied a fig to draw it out, and Hezekiah was healed (Isa. 38:21).

Pure Food and Water

It is a scientific fact known by Moses that healthy food and pure water are necessary to sustain life (Lev. 11). His meat diet roughly corresponds with that of ours today. Moses' diet forbade such animals as swine and rabbits, both of which are susceptible to infectious parasites. Even though today they are cleanly fed and well cooked, they can still be a source of disease, especially fresh pork. Israel was told not to touch the bodies of dead swine because these parasites can be communicated simply by handling such pork. If an animal was not killed by the hand of people, the eating of it was forbidden by God (Deut. 14:21). Animals slain for food are fine, but those which die by themselves crawl with insects, all of which are carriers of disease.

The need for pure, fresh water was stressed by Moses in his day (Lev. 11:36). It has been less than one hundred years since it was learned that

typhoid fever, cholera, and other contagious diseases were spread by contaminated water. How scientifically up-to-date is the Bible!

Surgery—Circumcision

The only surgical operations mentioned in the Bible are *castration* (Deut. 23:1), of which we have no record in the Scriptures, and *circumcision*, which was commanded of all Jewish male infants (Gen. 17:10–11). There are some physicians in our day who contend that there is no justification for this procedure, but it has been standard practice in the United States since about 1940 to circumcise all males. It is done soon after the birth as a matter of convenience before mother and baby are discharged from the hospital. But the Bible says: "And in the eighth day the flesh . . . shall be circumcised" (Lev. 12:2–3). The instrument used was a flint (Exod. 4:25).

It is a matter of medical knowledge that circumcision should be done on the eighth day. A baby's blood is saturated with antitoxins, or disease-fighting elements, that it received from its mother before birth. For the first week of life it is protected against infection. There is also a blood-clotting agent that increases healing during the first week, and its normal concentration increases about the beginning of the second week of the baby's life.

Since the disease-fighting antibodies begin to decrease after the first week, operations *after* that time have a greater risk for infection. Operations *before* that time can be in danger of hemorrhage. Hence the safest time [according to the late M. R. De Haan, M.D.] for surgery is at that point where both the disease-fighting qualities and the blood-clotting ability are at their highest point—the eighth day.

God certainly knew what He was talking about when He instructed Moses centuries before Christ in the matter of the time for circumcision.

Circulation of the Blood

William Harvey, an English physician who lived in the mid-1600s, proved that blood circulated from the heart through the arteries and then back to the heart through veins. He also believed there were small vessels that unite the arteries and veins but was unable to prove it. Soon afterward, a physician in Italy discovered these small vessels, calling them *capillaries*. These discoveries confirm Moses' statement in Leviticus 17:11, "The life of the flesh is in the blood."

The heart is the organ that keeps up blood circulation. This interesting machine is about the size of a fist and weighs a little over a one-half pound. Divided into four chambers, it is enclosed in a sac, the pericardium.

The heart beats an average of 70 times a minute, 4,200 times an hour, 100,800 times a day, and 36,792,000 times a year. If one reaches 70 years, it will have beaten 2,575,440,000 times. Six hundred fifty thousand gallons of blood is the volume pumped in one year's time—enough to fill more than 81 tank cars of 8,000 gallons each. The heart generates enough energy in 12 hours to lift a 65-ton tank car one foot off the ground. An average person's blood circulates through about 12,000 miles of "highways," or the approximate distance of a round trip to the Holy Land from New York City. Only a Creator is capable of making such a circulatory instrument.

Agriculture

Pest Control

A surefire remedy for pest control was given centuries ago, yet in spite of advanced chemicals in our day to control them, we are still plagued with some insects, often with no remedy. Moses commanded Israel to set aside one year in seven when no crops were to be raised (Lev. 25:1–24). God promised sufficient harvest in the sixth year to provide for this period.

Following this plan, the insects would spend their winter in the stalks of last year's harvest and hatch eggs in the spring in the new crop. If one year no crops were planted, there would be nothing for the insects to subsist upon and they would be controlled by this method. Farmers today use crop rotation as a means of pest control, but insects often survive.

Purebred Stock

"Thou shalt not let thy cattle gender with a diverse kind" (Lev. 19:19). This was God's instruction some 3,500 years ago for the improvement of stock by scientifically selective breeding.

Science has found out that by breeding the strong with the strong, a pure strain of superior stock is produced (note also Deut. 22:10).

Cross-pollination

"Thou shalt not sow thy field with mingled seed" (Lev. 19:19). Over thirty centuries after this statement was made, science found out that the secret of producing better grain is to avoid cross-pollination. Should citron, for example, be planted with or near watermelon, the melons would taste like citron (see Deut. 22:9).

Substances Weighed and Measured

Isaiah (ca. 715 B.C.) brings out the scientific fact that substances are *weighed* and *balanced* (40:12). Chemists discovered that all substances *must* be weighed and measured. This has been labeled *isostatic balance*, or equilibrium. For example, table salt is labeled "NaCl" (Na for sodium and Cl for chlorine). The atomic weight for chlorine is 35.5 pounds. In 58.5 pounds of salt we have 23 pounds of sodium and 35.5 pounds of chlorine. Only in these proportions will these two combine.

We term water as H_2O, and that means two parts hydrogen and one part oxygen. The combining weight of hydrogen is 2 and the combining weight of oxygen is 16. To form 18 pounds of water, God carefully measured out these proportions. Water can be formed *only* by mixing these two gases in this exact amount. Ingredients of each substance can be combined only as they are measured or weighed out in exact proportions.

Isaiah, in expressing this great scientific fact, shows that God knew exactly what He was doing when He weighed and measured the components in all the substances He created. Evolution, no matter how many millions of years it would have taken, wouldn't have been able to come up with the right balance.

Fowls

There are many statements about birds in the Bible, the first being that God created them (Gen. 1:20). The evolutionist would have us believe that birds evolved from reptiles, which in turn evolved from fish. But when all the facts are considered in the matter of the design and construction of birds, there are too many obstacles to hurdle to accept the evolutionary theory.

The bone structure—usually thin, hollow, light, and strong, many having air pockets connected with its lungs—helps make a bird lighter in flight. They have no teeth or jaws, and the food they consume is rapidly converted to energy instead of fat. Flapping its wings gets the bird aloft. The combination of air pressure from below and suction from above causes lift. By flapping the outer parts of its wings, the bird pushes the air backward, driving itself forward. The robin can fly up to 30 miles per hour. The spine-tailed swift has been clocked at 218 miles per hour.

Their legs have knee joints which work in the opposite direction from those of most animals. This is for the purpose of "shock absorbers" when landing and for an upward swing when taking off.

To enable a bird to maintain a higher temperature in colder altitudes in which it flies, the heart has four separate compartments that separate vein and arterial blood for upper flights. Its blood has more red corpuscles per ounce than that of animals. Its food supply is so rapidly burned as fuel in flight that it is required to eat several times hourly. The tiny chickadee can maintain a body temperature of 105 degrees Fahrenheit even though the temperature outside is 40 degrees below zero. No wonder Solomon, who was a lover of birds, said that one of the things too wonderful for him to understand was the way of an eagle in the air (1 Kings 4:30–34; Prov. 30:18–19).

Did birds practice leaps for millions of years after evolving from reptiles until they learned to fly, or did the Creator of living things equip them with the design and balance for their existence? I know that God did. It is no wonder, then, that God said "It is good" when He finished creating birds on the fifth day (Gen. 1:21–23).

Let us keep in mind that God's Son, Jesus Christ, gave specific attention to fowls (Matt. 6:26). Observe the following two illustrations and decide for yourself if these birds evolved or were created with a specific design.

The ouzel bird is found among the mountain streams where water is the fastest, among falls and rapids. They build their nests near the brink of a fall and precede those who fish downstream, darting from rock to rock. According to ornithologists, this is the most buoyant of all the birds on record. It can float on the surface of water like grease, seemingly riding above the water, instead of being partly in it like ducks or geese. It would seem impossible for one of the ouzels to sink, but an observing watcher is startled to see one suddenly descend into the water. There this strange creature of *three* worlds—the land, the water, and the air—calmly *walks* on the bottom of the stream just as if it were made of iron instead of flesh and feathers and bones. When the feeding bird has filled its beak with all it can hold, it wades out to the bank, shakes itself, swallows its mouthful of food, and a few seconds later it takes off to float on the stream again.

The ouzel has a muscular apparatus that can instantly exhaust the air from its body and give it the weight needed to sink in water. It comes back to the surface to fill its body once again with air and instantly regains its lost buoyancy to float away on the rushing stream. To float like a cork or sink like a stone at will would require designing that is at present past the ability human reasoning and evolutionary theories.

If the ouzel evolved, it must have stayed down for a couple hundred or so millions of years the first time it submerged. With a big mouthful of food it would have choked to death in this time, or it would have been covered with the silt of a swift-moving stream or suffocated for lack of air.

It was once thought that scavenger fowls such as the vulture (Job 28:7) found their food by the means of a keen sense of smell. Ornithologists have done a number of experiments and found that vultures have little, if any, sense of smell. Rather, they discovered that vultures have remarkable vision—that the shape of the cornea will vary while the bird is descending, thus enabling it to keep perfect focus. Did this focusing cornea develop, or was there a Designer? If it developed, how many crash landings did it have to make for several millions of years before it learned to hit a target? You are aware, I am sure, that this first crash landing would have killed the vulture, and then it would have taken about another two hundred million years to produce a second vulture.

Fish

The coelacanth is a fish whose origin is said to date back 400 million years. *National Geographic* (June 1989) reported the catch of a coelacanth off the Comoro Islands in the Indian Ocean. According to the evolutionist, the ancestors of this fish were probably land animals. It is a *ganiod* fish, so called because of its shallow spine. It is beautiful, with hard, glossy, enameled scales.

Even though scientists thought this fish to have been extinct for 60 million years, one was caught off South Africa in 1938, and several have been caught since. The article in *National Geographic* said the recently caught fish was brought to the United States. It has undergone seven hours of 3-D computerized X-ray scanning and thirteen hours of MRI (magnetic resonance imaging). The lengthy tests were designed to provide detailed data on the fish's tissue. Scientists also studied the genetic and biochemical makeup of the dissected fish.

This story is like a lot of others I have heard. Starting out 400 million years ago, for the next 340,000,000 years things were going along nicely until 60 million years ago we were confronted with the coelacanth's demise. However, a resurrection took place in 1938, and evolution is alive again! Or is it? Possibly the Lord played a trick on the scientists of evolution just to show them Who's Who!

"God created great whales, and every living creature that moveth, which the waters brought forth abundantly, after their kind" (Gen. 1:21). Not so, says the evolutionist. There was an article in the *Reader's Digest* (May 1989) called "Whales: Gentle Giants of the Deep." Many people think that 60 million years ago that the ancestors of modern whales were four-legged, wolf-size animals living on the shores of lagoons where an abundance of fish and shrimp enticed them to try wading.

As nature favored those best equipped for swimming, evolution began reshaping them. Forelegs shrank into flippers, hind legs disappeared, tapered tails grew, the nose moved to the top of the head, and the insides were reconstructed. As a result of these amazing transformations, they are now helpless on land. The only thing I found to be true in this article was its title.

Animals

During God's timetable of His creative acts as recorded in the Bible, animals followed sea life (Gen. 1:20–23). Here again, one must decide if animals were created or if they evolved. We can give only a few illustrations about some to see if they could have developed into what they are now, or if the way they are now is the way they started in life.

Dinosaurs

The dinosaurs have become a popular topic of conversation today, especially among children. The information propagated about them says that, generally speaking, the dinosaur's age could be at least 230 million years.

That they existed, none will deny. The Christian holds the position that they were a part of original creation. They believe that Noah took two, a male and a female, into the ark. Size does not enter the picture, whether young or adult, since the size of the ark could easily accommodate either [see "Ark, Noah" in Index]. We can keep in mind our discussion about the "how" of fossils, which would account for dinosaur bones and the possibility of a much younger age than 230 million years.

There is also the possibility that due to a climate change after the great flood, extinction brought their existence to an end. Varied animal life is becoming extinct even in our day, as concerned environmentalists tell us.

It is amazing how evolutionists can

take a bone, tooth, jaw, vertebra, skull, hip, or shoulder blade and make a full skeleton. They can design it to suit their fancy. If enough bones are found, they can, to their satisfaction, construct an animal the way they think it looked. However, it is true that some complete skeletons of dinosaurs and some large deposits of dinosaur bones have been found, so there is no question how these beasts looked.

One interesting item that came to light was the discovery in 1908 of a skull in England which was labeled the Piltdown Man. He was supposed to be part of a chain of developing humans during the Pleistocene period, 200,000 to 1,000,000 years ago. A body was made to order, and such museums as the Smithsonian Institution had a statue of him placed with other homosapiens to show the "true" development of humans. It was shown in 1950, however, that Piltdown Man's jaw and canine tooth had been altered to "look human." The *Encyclopedia Britannica*, Smithsonian Institution, *National Geographic* and others had to eliminate his figure from their drawings of man's evolutionary stages. Yet these organizations are still bold to set forth their erroneous views.

Evolutionists, in their claim that fossil beds were deposited millions of years ago, say that simple forms were found below more complex forms. But fossil footprints of human beings have been found with tracks of huge dinosaurs in the bed of the Paluxy River of Texas. This fits the biblical picture that humans were contemporary with all kinds of animals in order to have dominion over them (Gen. 1:28 with James 3:7).

Recently, near the Glen Rose dig, while witnesses watched TV cameras record the event, thirty-six new dinosaur tracks, twelve new human footprints, a human hand print, and a saber-tooth tiger print were revealed by removing a one-foot-thick limestone ledge.

The Lancaster, Pennsylvania, *News Era* (June 26, 1989) reported a dinosaur found at a construction site in the Washington, D.C., area. Peter Kranz, an amateur paleontologist, was leading children on a dinosaur hunt. As he was explaining to them what a dinosaur bone looked like, he reached down to pick up a bone, and to his amazement, it was a dinosaur bone! Both children and parents found more bones—the skeleton of a 20-foot mesosaur (reptile). The Smithsonian Museum of Natural History researchers say this could be the best find this century. What a statement, coming from those who believe that fossils of this kind were buried deep in sediment. We do wonder why, if these bones make up what they say they do, they were found so close to the surface. Perhaps, as with most dinosaur bones, they died out fairly recently on a *young* earth, instead of so many millions of years ago.

Cows

When one considers the digestive mechanism of a cow, evolution seemingly crumbles. One cannot help but see the intricate design of the cow's digestion. Because the cow's food must be so finely broken down before it can be absorbed into the blood stream, it goes through the following process.

A cow eats, hastily chews, and swallows fodder into its first stomach. Any fluids the cow drinks will go directly into the second stomach. The fodder in stomach number one is partially digested and passed into stomach number two. There it is saturated with the fluid and left until the cow has time to chew. By a simple muscle contraction the cow re-chews the food from stomach number two. When it is swallowed this time, it goes into the third stomach. There it is refined and passed on to stomach number four, where the process of digestion continues until it is converted into fluid. In this state the food passes out of stomach number four into the blood stream of the cow as is the custom of all mammalian digestion.

The purpose of this ordered process is to reduce the solid food to a fluid in order to pass the nutrients on to the bloodstream.

In all the world of nature, it is easy to believe that a Creator did something for the cow that no process of evolution could ever do. Without this digestive process the cow would not be able to benefit from the nutrients it eats. It would not be able to survive.

Camels

The camel is a most amazing animal. Someone once said that when God finished creating all the animals, He took the parts left over and made the camel. Someone else has said that a camel is a race horse put together by a committee. It is an amazing piece of handiwork.

When a camel is hungry, it will eat almost anything—a leather bridle, a piece of rope, its master's tent, or a pair of shoes. Its mouth is so tough that even a thorny cactus doesn't bother it.

The dromedary camel has one big hump of fat, not water, weighing about eighty pounds. The body automatically takes this fat and feeds on it when no food is to be found. This causes the hump to shrink, and it soon tips to one side. But when it finds an oasis and begins to eat again, it builds the fat back up. In the water-scarce desert, it might be eight days before a camel can get a drink. Much weight is lost, sometimes as much as 225 pounds. When water is found, it can drink up to twenty-seven gallons in just ten minutes and gain back its lost weight immediately. It was made for survival in the desert.

People use the camel for transportation because it can travel through sand dunes so well. It has specially engineered "sand shoes" caused by a super-tough piece of skin stretched between its two long bony toes. Its hooves are wide, and they will stretch wider when the camel steps down on them so the feet do not sink into the soft, drifting sand.

Sometimes a big sandstorm blows across the desert, but that doesn't bother the camel. It has special muscles in its nostrils that partially close, keeping the sand out but letting in just enough air to breathe. It has very long eyelashes that hang over the eyes and keep out the blowing sand. If a grain of sand should slip through and get in the eye, there is an inner eyelid that automatically wipes the sand off the eyeball like a windshield wiper.

One would have to admit that the camel is a very highly engineered animal. Things like this just don't happen via evolution. They have to be planned by Someone who is intelligent and logical, who knows what is needed in a particular area. The Bible, the Creator's Book, tells us just who this Great Designer is—none other than Jesus Christ Himself (John 1:3).

It must be conceded, since no one was present to observe what happened in the beginning of time, that we can only believe one of two things—speculation, which leads to the evolutionary theory, or faith, which simply tells us that the Creator brought all things to pass.

Whether we study plants, trees, fowls, fish, animals, or people, there is always one scientific fact the evolutionists cannot answer when it comes to that which is observable, and it is this: *like produces like.*

One does not have to accept the statement of the Bible to recognize this as fact—"after its kind," or to paraphrase, "like produces like" (Gen. 1:21, 24). Even when the first man reproduced a seed, it was "in his own likeness and image" (Gen. 5:3).

Look at it this way. One would shudder to think what would happen if a poisonous snake were crossed with a chicken, a crocodile with an elephant, a porcupine with a skunk. Ridiculous statements, yes, but seemingly logical to evolutionists, in view of their claiming that wolves became whales, fish became fowls, apes became humans.

Without the rigid enforcement of the "like produces like" law, the earth would be peopled in one generation with such abominable monstrosities as to render life unsupportable for intelligent beings. As for me and my house, we are so thankful that a wonderful Creator designed things after their kind, not only for our physical benefit, but also for our spiritual well-being.

Our Identity

There are so many things in the Bible which set people apart from all other creatures. Things such as articulate speech, the capacity for invention, our bodies, our morality, conscience, and influence mark people as special creatures. Christians believe that people are God's crowning act of creation (Gen. 1:26–27). In reference to humans being made lower than the angels in Psalm 8:5, the Hebrew word for "angels" is *Elohim*, the same word used for God in Genesis 1:1.

One mark of our identification which sets us apart from each other is our fingerprints. In 1893 a book was published titled *Finger Prints*, by Sir Francis Galton. His theory was that every person in the world has different fingerprints. Scotland Yard of England experimented with this theory and caught over 300,000 criminals in three decades with the method of finger-printing. Job said, "He [God] sealeth up the hand of every man; that all men may know His work" (37:7). Some have suggested that the word *sealeth* means that God "marks" us with a seal or that He makes a little different mark in the hand of everyone, that all may know or recognize His handiwork. There is no such mark on other creatures. Why humans?

The word "sealeth" also means "to shut up, or stop," implying God's last act of creation before He rested on the seventh day. God said of His last day of creation that it was very good. "Sealeth" also carries with it the thought of keeping people secure—certainly with no possibility of evolving into something else. It is a known scientific fact that we alone have the unique identification of fingerprints.

7

More Scientific Illustrations in the Bible

There are some accounts in the Bible that scientists have labeled as myth and legend. This raises the question: Why have critics of Scripture attacked the validity of the accounts in the Bible that relate to science?

The simple answer is that they have not taken the time to read, study, and examine these stories. They deride their accuracy and question their probability, solely on the basis of what they have *heard* about the so-called inaccuracies of these accounts. Keep in mind that their position is one of *faith*. What they believe is by faith, taking what another has said without making a thorough study for themselves.

The honest researcher, undaunted by the laughter of empty objections, proceeds to investigate and find truth. They will study the whole account before making judgment. It is amazing what one will learn when consideration is given to *all* known facts. He might even learn something his scholarly associates refuse to believe. What are some of these interesting biblical accounts?

The Size of Noah's Ark

When we consider the magnitude of the worldwide flood and the deliverance of Noah and his family, some method of escape had to be provided—an ark. The account of its building is found in Genesis 6:14–16. In examining these verses, we find something significant.

Its dimensions are nautically sound—300 cubits long, 50 cubits wide, and 30 cubits high. The ancients did not build ships to such exacting specifications, but Noah, taking God's blueprint, did. End to end it was exactly six times as long as it was wide, the same as some naval vessels of our day. Whether the ancient cubit was 18 or 22½ inches long, the ratio is the same—six to one. If 22½ inches, the ark was 562½ feet long, 93½ feet wide, and 56¼ feet high. This is small compared to some ocean liners and aircraft carriers of our day, but Noah's ark, if built with a flat bottom, square on both ends, and straight up the sides, had no wasted space in bow or stern. This means it had the tremendous capacity of a little over 2,958,000 cubit feet—a colossal cargo space. To put it in modern terms, it would take a railroad train of almost 1,000 freight cars to carry this enormous load or to provide this amount of space.

As we will note in the archaeological section, there are some legendary stories that make the ark even larger than Noah's. A Grecian account makes it 3,000 feet long and 12,000 feet wide.

Critics still say that they don't know and cannot know the exact size of Noah's ark, but they do know that it could *not* hold two of every kind of animal. How ridiculous! If one does not know the size of something, how can they know what would fit into it? How foolish to argue the scientific impossibility to get the number of animals into the ark as the Bible states (Gen. 6:19–20). Out of all the living creatures known to the science of biology, approximately 60 percent live in water. Over 95 percent of all fossils are marine creatures. Does this mean that all marine life died in such a catastrophe as a universal flood? Not necessarily since air pockets and various temperatures, chemistries, and sediment loads tend to remain segregated, which would have allowed some fish to escape. Fish did not need to be taken from their habitat—only living creatures on earth, as Genesis states.

Noah did not have to find room in the ark for every variety and specimen of animal, bird, and creeping thing alive in the world today. The problem of the ark's size is now simplified. The specified command is to take two animals of each kind. A *kind* is a species and may be described as those which crossbreed with fertility. Crossbreeding will produce variety of the same species but is different from *kind*. Noah was to take pure strain of every available creature. Any variety has

arisen by the process of mutation. It is not too much to say that the present varieties of living things could have arisen from an original pair of each kind. In the case of Noah, he did not need to take a pair of every known variety on board the ark—just take two of each pure strain.

How many true species are there? In considering the size of every species—*each kind*—as Scripture mentions, there certainly are not as many kinds as there are varieties of animals and birds between the size of mice and sheep. There are fewer between the size of a sheep and the size of a camel or a giraffe or an elephant. Out of the 40 percent of creatures that live on land, 70 out of 100 are insects, which do not take up much room. Think how many could get by with free room and board on just one elephant!

Let us not forget that 2,958,000 cubit feet or about 1,000 railroad cars is a lot of space. Such space means it was sufficient to carry eight people and some of the true species—seven male and seven female of each of the clean animals and the fowls, and a male and female of each of the unclean animals (Gen. 7:2–3). There would also been plenty of room for food storage. [For archaeological evidence of a universal flood, see "Flood, Worldwide" in Index.]

Lot's Wife—A Pillar of Salt

According to Bible critics, another scientific inaccuracy in the Bible is the account of Lot's wife having been turned into a pillar of salt (Gen. 19:1–26). In the context of Genesis 19 we notice that God pronounced judgment upon the cities of Sodom and Gomorrah for their wickedness. He warned Lot and his family to escape for their lives and not look back. But as God was pouring down fire and brimstone from heaven, Lot's wife looked back and became a pillar of salt.

Archaeological discoveries in Pompeii, Italy, shed some light on this subject. Pompeii, like Sodom, shows mute evidence of vast volcanic deposits. In A.D. 79 Mount Vesuvius erupted. Its poisonous gas asphyxiated many Pompeiians in their sleep and then covered the city with a layer of volcanic ash to a depth of about twenty feet. There they remained until archaeologists went to work in the late 1800s.

On one dig, workers noticed that their picks would strike some hollow places in the ash, and the director instructed them to open another hole near the first one to act as a vent. He then pumped plaster of Paris into the hollow space and allowed it to dry. After breaking away the brittle ashes from around the hardened cast, they were amazed as they gazed upon perfectly preserved forms of sleeping men, women, children, and even dogs. As a result of being covered by ash, not lava, buildings were also preserved, paintings and all. One can see Pompeii today exactly as it looked almost 1,900 years ago.

What happened to cause these humans and animals to retain their physical forms? The late Dr. Harry Rimmer said that volcanic ash contains many chemicals that are water soluble. With time the ash metamorphosed into a soft stone, similar to pumice stone, that water could flow through. The chemical content of the ash worked quickly on the forms of the deceased and wrought a chemical change which turned their bodies into some chemical, crystalline substance of sufficient hardness to permit the surrounding ash to retain a perfect cast of the buried bodies as it slowly formed into soft stone. Under the action of water, leaking through the porous rock, the concentration of chemicals which had been a physical form melted and disappeared. But the ash retained the shape and features, even the hairlines and expressions!

After a score of centuries, we are able to look upon these citizens of Pompeii once again. Many forms are on display in the Pompeii museum.

The recovered forms of a once thriving city must have changed into a pillar of salt of some variety. This word *salt* is used in its true chemical sense. The term *pillar of salt* cannot be limited to sodium chloride—common table salt—but must be used as a chemical substance.

The term *salt* can be applied to any mineral salt, saltpeter, an iron salt, etc. We can't say how long it would take for someone's body to turn into a form of salt. It would depend upon the nature of the chemicals, the amount of heat, the degree of pressure, and the strength of the solution involved. We can only say that at Pompeii, the exact conditions that prevailed at Sodom were present.

Excavations in and around the region of Sodom at the southern end of the Dead Sea reveal a large, thick stratum of salt. Over this were large quantities of sulfur, or brimstone. The place was a burned-out region of oil and asphalt where a great rupture took place in the strata centuries ago. Formerly, there had been a subterranean lake of oil and gas beneath Sodom, and in some mysterious way it had been ignited. A tremendous explosion took place, which carried the asphalt and sulfur oil into the air far above the city. This burning brimstone, mingled with the salt and fire, rained down from heaven (Gen. 19:24–25).

This is not to say that God did not perform a miracle in the destruction of this city. He could have rained down fire and brimstone without a volcanic eruption. However, in performing other miracles, He often used acts of nature to accomplish His purposes (e.g., a storm of hail stones to rout the enemies of Israel in Josh. 10:11).

The reference concerning Lot's wife becoming a pillar of salt is very interesting in light of what we have just discussed. It is stated that she "looked back from behind." She did more than merely stop to see all that was taking place. Having left the city with her husband and daughters, she literally lingered behind—she straggled behind the others. It is quite clear that "back from behind" means she had deserted the group. Lot had moved so swiftly that he was already in the city of Zoar when fire and brimstone began to fall. Because Lot's wife lingered behind, she evidently was engulfed in clouds of volcanic gas and buried beneath volcanic ashes, just like those at Pompeii.

When we consider the word *became*, it allows this thought: In due process of time she became a pillar of salt, like those at Pompeii. Regardless of the "how," Christ warned us against disobedience by simply saying, "Remember Lot's wife" (Luke 17:28–31). Why remember her? Remember her privileges—instructed in the faith, related to Abraham, forewarned of impending danger. Remember her fate—merited, sudden,

final. Let us be aware of earthly entanglements and never question God's commands.

Joshua's Long Day

This long day of Joshua (Josh.10:12–14) has come under the criticism of unbelieving scientists for some time. It is interesting to note that parallel accounts of the records of other nations show that the incident of this long day of Joshua is not an isolated one.

There is indisputable evidence from the modern science of ethnology that such an event occurred as Joshua records. In ancient Chinese writings there is a legend of a long day. The Incas of Peru and the Aztecs of Mexico have a similar record. There is a Babylonian and a Persian legend of a day that was miraculously extended. Herodotus, an ancient historian, recounts that while in Egypt, priests showed him temple records where he read of a day that was twice the natural length of any day ever recorded.

Yet Joshua's long day has been pointed out by many critics as a myth. Joshua said, "Sun, stand thou still upon Gibeon . . . and the sun stood still." Since it is a scientific fact that the sun does not revolve around the earth, critics point this out in glee as but another mistake in the Bible.

Scientists know that the spinning of the earth on its axis is the result of the gravitational pull of the sun. A reduction in the gravitational pull of the sun would result in the slowing down of the rotation of the earth, thus prolonging the day, or time.

Did Joshua have this scientific data in his day? Did he think that the sun moved from East to West and that for time to be prolonged the sun must stand still? By modern standards, he was a primitive man, in a primitive culture, with primitive misconceptions. He probably knew very little about the planet upon which he lived, its chemical compounds or shape. He knew even less about the solar system. As far as Joshua was concerned, practically everyone believed the earth was flat, the sun rose in the East, and hours later, it sank into the West. Did Joshua know that the earth upon which he stood really was a sphere about 8,000 miles in diameter? He had no idea that there were close to 200 million square miles of earth's surface, 71 percent of which was water. He was unaware the earth was spinning on its axis in a cycle every twenty-four hours (23 hrs., 56 min., and 4.09 sec. to be exact). And he didn't even know that the earth was traveling through space about 18½ miles per second. Did he know that the sun he was commanding to stand still was 93,000,000 miles away, that at its core it was over 30,000,000 degrees Fahrenheit, or that it was over 100 times bigger than the earth? Did he know that the earth made a complete orbit around the sun yearly?

No, he didn't, but He knew his God! He knew that God had promised to go before His people and fight their battles to give them victory (Josh. 10:8). And in this battle he saw victory in his grasp, but time was running out. If he didn't conquer the enemy before dark, they would regroup and attack Israel the next day. Knowing his God, his God's power, and his God's promise, he called out to Him for help, and in the presence of all the Israelites, he commanded the sun to stand still.

Joshua had no idea that his command slowed down 6.6 sextillion tons of spinning gravel and water to give Israel victory over her enemies. But did Joshua know something that would have met with the approval of today's scientific establishment? His command in the Hebrew tongue was *not* "Sun, stand still," but "Sun, stop working." It was then that the gravitational pull of the sun lessened and had its effect on the earth. It was then that the earth began to slow down and the day was lengthened.

Sir Edwin Ball, the great British astronomer, found that twenty-four hours had been lost out of solar time. Where did it go and what was the cause of this strange lapse, and how did it happen? Such would puzzle any scientist.

Professor C. A. Totten of Yale challenged the famous astronomer to read the Bible to see if it would account for the missing day. When the astronomer came to the portion of the long day in Joshua, he rechecked the figures and found that at the time of Joshua there were only twenty-three hours and twenty minutes lost. His skepticism justified, he told Dr. Totten that the Bible was in error because it had made a mistake of forty minutes.

Totten showed him that the biblical record does not say twenty-four hours, but rather "about the space of a whole day." He suggested the astronomer continue to read through the Bible. He then found that God, through the prophet Isaiah and in answer to king Hezekiah's prayer, promised to add fifteen years to the king's life. To confirm this promise of extended life, the shadow of the sundial was turned back ten degrees (2 Kings 20:1–11; Isa. 38:1–21). Ten degrees on a sundial is forty minutes on a clock's face. The missing time had been accounted for, and with bowed head the astronomer acknowledged and worshiped its Author saying, "Lord, I believe."

Jonah—The World's Biggest Fish Story

Of course the world's greatest fish story comes from the Bible. And who believes this fish tale about the prophet Jonah being swallowed by a whale and surviving after three days and three nights in its belly? Christians do. One Christian said it was easy for him to believe the story, but it was hard for him to understand how the whale could keep a backslidden preacher in its stomach for three days and three nights.

A little country girl on her way to Sunday school was chided by the town loafers because she was carrying her Bible. Asked what her lesson was about, she said "Jonah and the big fish." Asked to explain how a fish could swallow a man and then spit him up, she said she couldn't explain it, but when she got to heaven she would ask Jonah and he would explain it. One of the loafers asked her, "What if Jonah isn't in heaven?" She replied, "Then you ask him!"

Like the little girl, maybe we, too, don't understand all of the details of this situation, but there is sufficient scientific evidence to lend support to its credibility.

Some who have studied the book of Jonah say that it is a ridiculous fairy tale. They brand Jonah as a fictitious character, a legendary hero of Jewish folklore and fable.

But Jonah is as historical as Alexander the Great. Second Kings 14:23–25 authenticates his character, mentioning his father, listing his residence and the current king of his day.

None other than Christ Himself gave testimony about the historicity of Jonah and his ministry. It was in reference to His resurrection, using Jonah's experience in the belly of the fish for three days and three nights (Matt. 12:38–41). If we can't believe Jesus, whom can we believe?

There seem to be two arguments concerning Jonah's story. One says that God had prepared this monster to swallow Jonah. The evolutionist, of course, ridicules this statement. But if God cannot prepare a fish to swallow a man, then He indeed is inferior to man, and we know this is not true.

The second argument against this story of Jonah is that a whale's throat is too small to swallow a man. Jonah does not call it a whale but a "great fish" prepared by the Lord (1:17). The New Testament translators do refer to this account as a whale, but the Greek word used is *ketos* and means "huge fish" or "a sea monster," identically the same as the great fish in Jonah. A whale is a mammal. It would be scientifically incorrect to speak of a whale as a fish. Time and space will not permit a discussion of all the differences between the two, but suffice it to say it would still be reasonable and scientifically demonstrable that a whale could have swallowed Jonah.

Some whales, known as the denticete, have teeth. The mysticete whale has none. This second group of whales has a curious habit of feeding. They open their mouths, submerge their lower jaws, and rush through the water at a terrific speed. When its gigantic mouth is filled, it closes its jaws and curls its lips. Muscular pressure on the tongue forces the water out of his mouth. When the water is all expelled, whatever is left in the mouth is swallowed—an enormous amount. Some whales have measured almost 100 feet long, which means their stomachs are also large. Their stomachs are complex, having from four to six chambers in which any one could accommodate a small number of men. All whales have an air storage chamber in their heads—an enlargement of the nasal sinus—and in a very large whale this storage tank/compartment would measure 14 feet long, 7 feet high, and 7 feet wide. As mammals they must have oxygen. Having no gills, they can stay under just so long and then must emerge for air.

An article in the *Cleveland* (Ohio) *Plain Dealer* (1930) told of a dog that was lost overboard from a whaling ship. It was found in the head of a whale two days later *alive*, and none the worse for its unnatural journey. While it says that Jonah was in the fish's belly a day and a night longer than this dog, no man would have had difficulty being in a whale's air chamber a day more.

There is a whale shark known as the *rhinodon typicus,* which sometimes reaches a length of 50 feet. One has been caught that was 70 feet in length. Like the mysticete whale, it has no teeth. There is a record from the Hawaiian Island of Maui of a rhinodon (whale shark) which was caught. Cutting open its stomach, inside was the skeleton of a sailor who had been reported missing for thirty days. This whale shark had swallowed a man whole!

Another incident, reported by the Museum of London, is of a fisherman who fell overboard in the English Channel and was engulfed by a rhinodon. Forty-eight hours later the whale was caught, and when the fishermen cut it open, the man was unconscious but alive, and he survived. Certainly if a man in the ordinary course of nature can exist this long inside a great fish, a prophet of God could stay a day longer, couldn't he?

The summary of this incident in Jonah's life is that there are some creatures in the seas that are capable, in the course of their nature, of being hosts to people like Jonah. It is impossible to state whether God prepared this fish in the natural order of generation and birth or whether it was a special creature made just for the occasion. Either way, it was possible to have happened. The Bible said it did, and upon the authority of Jesus Christ and the weight of attested reason, let us acknowledge the truth of this account.

The Wounds of Christ

"He was wounded for our transgressions, he was bruised for our iniquities: the chastisement of our peace was upon him; and with his stripes we are healed" Isaiah 53:5.

There are five classifications of wounds known to surgeons.

1. The contused wound is one that is caused by a blunt instrument. Such would result from a blow by a rod, as it was foretold by Micah (5:1). This was fulfilled when they smote Christ with a reed (rod—Matt. 27:30 with John 18:22 RSV margin).

2. The lacerated wound is one that is produced by an instrument which tears. Christ was lacerated as a result of scourging (Ps. 129:3; Isa. 50:6; Matt. 27:26; John 19:1). It was on His lacerated back that the cross was laid.

3. The penetrating wound is one that is deep, caused by a pointed instrument. This happened to Jesus when they placed upon His head a

"crown of thorns" (Matt. 27:29; John 19:2). These wounds were deepened by the blow of the rod as they smote Him on the head (Matt. 27:30).

4. The perforating wound is one that receives its name from the Latin word meaning to "pierce through." The iron spikes were driven between the bones, separating but not breaking them—"They pierced my hands and my feet" (Ps. 22:16). The New Testament writers do not make mention of the actual driving of spikes into His hands and feet, but evidence presented to Thomas is sufficient that it happened in His crucifixion (John 20:24, 25, 27–29).

5. The incised wound is a cut, one that is produced by a sharp-edged instrument. As a spear was thrust into His side, "forthwith there came out blood and water" (John 19:34). This wound was inflicted by the practiced hand of the Roman soldier to make certain that whatever vestige of life was present would be extinguished, but while it was not the cause of death in the case of Christ, it was an assurance to all that death had actually occurred. It was also in fulfillment of the Scripture which says, "They shall look upon me whom they have pierced" (John 19:37).

The very sight of seeing both blood and water coming from the wound was a startling surprise and of deep interest to John. Piercing started a flow of water from the pericardium (the sac around the heart), and the blood started flowing from the heart. The fluid (water) which encases the heart lubricates it to help facilitate the heart's motion. The amount of this fluid is about a teaspoonful. It may be asked how John saw such a small quantity of water.

A standard medical work by Mallory and Wright, *Pathological Technique,* explains that the normal amount of the pericardium fluid is about a teaspoonful, but it may increase to 100 c.c. (24 tablespoonsful) where the death agony is prolonged. Here, then, is confirmation by those in the medical field of the mute testimony borne by the water to the intense suffering of our Lord. The last wound inflicted on His body proclaimed both purification and redemption, for the very spear that pierced His side drew forth His blood for our salvation from sin.

The Resurrection of Christ

The resurrection of Christ is the very cornerstone of our Christian faith. The Bible states "[Jesus] was delivered for our offenses, and was *raised* again for our justification" (Rom. 4:25), and "If Christ be not *risen* . . . your faith is vain" (1 Cor. 15:14).

From a scientific viewpoint, the resurrection is plausible. Many years ago a certain scientist said dogmatically: "At death the life of a man is snuffed out like a candle flame."

At the end of World War II the eminent director of the Army Ballistic Missile Agency, Dr. W. Von Braun, explained that it is a *known* scientific fact that nothing in nature disappears without a trace. Nature does not know extinction. All it knows is transformation!

This scientist says that everything science has taught him through the years strengthens his belief in the continuity of our spiritual existence after death.

The Bible has been saying for centuries that there is a spiritual life after death! Jesus Christ came to bring immortality to light, to show the way beyond the grave. He *is* risen, and those who experience His saving grace shall one day be raised incorruptible.

Summary

In this first section we have dealt with science—theories propounded by the evolutionist regarding origins, matter, and life, and what the Bible has to say in regard to these theories. Critics of the Bible have used all the artillery they can muster to blast the Bible into dust, but like the anvil that is beaten continually and still stands, so does the Word of God!

Science itself is evolutionary, constantly changing opinions and theories. We must not forget there are errors in scientific thought (as mentioned about the Piltdown Man). The opinions of scientists change so rapidly it is reported that the Louvre Library in Paris contains more than three and one-half miles of bookshelves holding volumes of science that have become obsolete in fifty years. And to think that those measurements were taken over fifty years ago!

Creation and Evolution

In our summary of creation versus evolution, we note that the apostle Paul relied heavily on creation by God as he presented the Gospel. To accept God as Creator, one must accept law and order—laws that are made and given by a Master Designer. The people of Paul's day were not acquainted with laws that governed the universe, but people have always lived in a law-abiding universe, and there are certain laws that cannot be attributed to people or chance.

If the God of creation is the Lawgiver, He has the right to make laws suitable to order; He has the right to impose them, and they are always good for His creatures. If such laws are ignored and the Lawmaker, or Creator, is denied, then one's philosophy will be that people are their own god, they control their own destiny and will live according to the "lust of the flesh, the lust of the eyes, and the pride of life." They will live according to the world, the flesh, and the devil (1 John 2:16). This is modern humanism.

As any believer of the Bible knows, there are two systems in the world—those who believe in the God as Creator and the evolutionists. The latter will sneer at the creationists, not only for their belief in *direct* creation, but in their proclamation of the Gospel and other biblical truths. When creation by God was taught in our churches, there was a sense of the presence of God our Maker. Creation was not denied in our public schools when the Bible was read, the printed Ten Commandments were posted, prayer was offered, and there was a measure of respect for moral laws. But as Darwin's theory of evolution, the philosophy of socialism (communism) by Karl Marx, and the psychoanalysis of Sigmund Freud got a foothold in our educational system, the Bible took a back seat. Its laws and morals were questioned, and society went askew.

Human nature, being what it is (Jer. 17:9), has thrown law and order overboard and replaced it with the evolutionist's doctrine of humanism, with self taking complete control of the mind. The Bible says: "As a man thinketh in his heart [mind], so is he" (Prov. 23:7).

When Paul appeared before Jews and Greeks, he was determined to know no one save Jesus Christ and

Him crucified, using the Old Testament Scriptures of the Jews to show that Jesus was the Messiah, the Son of God (1 Cor. 2:2; Acts 9:20). When the Jews refused to believe, Christ then became a "stumblingblock" to them (1 Cor. 1:23). Paul would then turn to the Greeks or Gentiles. Before he could preach the Cross, which was foolishness to them, he often had to show that their belief in a form of evolution had ignored a need for a true God in their thinking; a God who created them; a God who had authority over them. This was a truth they sorely needed to know and believe. Therefore, his approach to them first was on the basis of creation by the God who made the world and all things in it, the Lord (authority) of heaven and earth (Acts 17:24).

These Greeks did not believe in such a God. They were just as ignorant of this as multitudes are in our day. They, like the fool, say in their hearts, "There is no God" (Ps. 14:1a). The Cross is as foolish to them as it was to the pagan Greeks of Paul's day.

In Acts 14, where those at Lystra thought Paul and Barnabas were gods, we note that Paul's first approach to them was to affirm the true God of creation saying, "We also are men of like passion with you, and preach unto you that ye should turn from these vanities unto the living God, which made [created] heaven, and earth, and the sea, and all things that are therein" (Acts 14:15).

He then talked about people "walking in their own ways" as all humanists do. Although Luke does not tell us more of Paul's message, we can be sure that he did not leave them without presenting the Gospel.

Paul's approach in his famous ser-

mon on Mars' Hill was to first familiarize his hearers concerning the true God of creation (Acts 17:24–30). He also pressed home the point, according to one of their poets, that they were not in the world by any chance but were the offspring of a Creator, having been created by Him, and that we *all* have the responsibility to Him to repent, because He has appointed a day of judgment for those who are His offspring (vv. 21–31). Since some believed, notably a chief philosopher, we can be assured Paul concluded his message with a Gospel presentation and appeal.

In our day when we face the same problem as Paul with pagans, we, too, can use this method to reach those steeped in the unbelief of evolution and humanism. As long as the philosophy in America is such that people regard the preaching of the Cross as foolishness, it is high time we wake up to some biblical methods like creation and evangelism and try to stem the tide of humanism. It will work if we try, as it did with Paul.

No Christian in their right mind would expect everyone to believe as they do. It would be wonderful if everyone believed the Bible. Even though God has commanded all to repent, not all will repent (Acts 17:30). Not many mighty (capable), not many wise (intelligent—wise in their own conceits), not many noble (wellborn), are called. God has chosen the foolish things of this world to confound the wise, and He has chosen the weak things to confound things which are mighty (1 Cor. 1:26–27).

Intellectual, conceited scholars of learning are too proud to consider a view other than theirs. Peer pressure keeps most of them from even thinking there is another side of a coin. They would have to unlearn too much of what they know, so as a result they blindly accept only what they want to believe. The facts do not matter. They do not have a capacity for objective thinking. Too many textbooks would have to be rewritten. They are content with the status quo. So, they remain unbelieving, humanistic, and evolutionistic. This is their religion—their faith, their belief. As someone said: "It is a sad cliché in science to say that old theories never die—only their proponents do."

As we have mentioned before, if evolutionists are right, we have nothing to lose. We will all die like animals. In death, no life hereafter; in the grave, no recognition. However, if the Christian is right in their beliefs in what the Bible teaches concerning creation, sin, and life hereafter, then the unbeliever loses everything!

What the Unbeliever Loses

1. Salvation for their souls from a Devil's hell. Eternal life is attained only through faith in Jesus Christ (Mark 8:36; John 3:16; Eph. 2:8–9; Rom. 10:9–10).
2. Deliverance from the guilt and penalty of sin, forgiveness, and their past blotted out (2 Cor. 1:9–10a; 1 John 1:9; Ps. 103:12; Isa. 38:17; 44:22).
3. Becoming a "new creation" in Christ—having a brand new start in life with God (2 Cor. 5:17).
4. Peace, joy, and satisfaction in Christ (Isa. 57:20–21; Rom. 5:1; 14:17; 15:13; 1 John 1:4; Ps. 107:9; Eph. 2:13–14).
5. One they can go to (Christ) in time of need, whether physical, mental, under stress, financial difficulty, or spiritual strain (Heb. 4:16;

1 Peter 5:10). He will give extended grace to help in our infirmities (2 Cor. 12:9–10; Ps. 55:1–18).
6. Encouragement to overcome the world, the flesh, and the Devil (1 Cor. 10:13; 2 Cor. 1:10b; Eph. 6:10–18; James 4:7; Rom. 8:37).
7. The Word of God to help become all that God intends them to be (2 Tim. 2:15; 3:16–17; John 15:3; Rom. 8:28; Josh. 1:7–8; Ps. 119:9, 11, 105).
8. Fellowship with those of like faith (1 Cor. 12:25; Gal. 6:2; Eph. 4:2, 32; 1 Peter 3:8; 4:9; Heb. 10:25).
9. The blessings of the Lord to share with others—show and tell (Ps. 107:2; Matt. 10:32–33; Mark 5:19; Luke 8:39).
10. A hope beyond the grave—something to live for and to die by—something to look forward to (Titus 2:13; 1 Peter 1:3–9).
11. The privilege of being with the Lord forever, and a reunion with your saved loved ones (1 Thess. 4:13–18).
12. A new body, free from pain and sickness (Phil. 3:20–21; 1 Cor. 15:50–57; 1 John 3:2).
13. Deliverance from the very presence of sin itself (Heb. 9:28; 2 Cor. 1:10).
14. A new home in heaven forever (1 Peter 1:14; John 14:1–3). Like Abraham who looked for a city whose builder and maker is God, the believer is home at last with Christ. [See "Heaven" in Index.]

Talk about a hope—a salvation—a life! Who else but the God of creation, the God who became our Savior (John 1:1–14). He alone could give such to those who accept His Word for its true intent [see "Bible: Subject and Design, Purpose" in Index], and who are personally acquainted with His Son as Savior. What a gift for a simple faith in God, the God of creation. What a complicated and *greater* faith it takes to believe in something that offers absolutely *nothing* like the evolutionist, the humanist, and the atheist.

A philosopher once said: "I believe in God because, like all people before they invent reasons for disbelieving, I find it much more intelligent to believe than not to believe."

Search the heavens, for truth is there. As long as the stars shall shine, as long as the earth shall spin on its axis, as long as life on earth as we know it shall exist, they all attest to the truthfulness of the scientific facts in the Bible (Ps. 19:1). But though we search for truth in scientific statements in the Bible, and, thankfully, finding that the Words and works of God agree, better to search this old Book for in it we find that they testify of Jesus Christ, and in Him and Him alone do we find eternal life (John 5:29). His name and works are high above, but His Word is above all, and when heaven and earth shall pass away, the Word of God shall endure forever (Matt. 24:35; Ps. 138:2).

SECTION TWO

Prophecy in the Bible

1

Fulfilled Prophecy in the Bible

This chapter will serve two purposes: one, to see what God has to say about false prophets and what believers should do to steer clear of error, and two, to illustrate how fulfilled prophecies confirm the Scriptures.

God Himself points to prophecy as an absolute proof that it is He who speaks. We find these words spoken by God to the prophet Isaiah: "I am the Lord: that is my name: and my glory will I not give to another, neither my praise to graven images. Behold, the former things are come to pass, and new things do I declare: before they spring forth I tell you of them" (42:8–9). "I am God, and there is none else; I am God, and there is none like me, declaring the end from the beginning, and from ancient times the things that are not yet done, saying, my counsel shall stand, and I will do all my pleasure" (46:9–10).

In other words, only God knows the future. And when God spoke, be sure His prophet was accurate 100 percent of the time. There have been some, even in our day, who have made some correct predictions, such as Vice President Agnew and President Nixon leaving office before their term expired. Jeane Dixon, by her own admission, is correct only half the time. This certainly does not qualify her as a prophetess of God. God's prophet could not afford to be wrong even *once!* As a mouthpiece of God, the prophet had to be accurate, for God cannot lie. As you read such prophets as Isaiah, Jeremiah, and Ezekiel, you will find little phrases at the end of a prophecy which say: "That ye may know that I am the Lord" (Isa. 45:3; 49:23; Jer. 44:28–29; Ezek. 5:13; 6:14). In these verses we note the one true test of prophecy, and such encourages the believer because they know they have a "more sure word of prophecy" (2 Peter 1:10–21).

False and True Prophets

It is interesting to note that no other religion has ever attempted to prophesy in the sense that the Scripture uses prophecy. There are several basic rules to the nature of prophecy which show the credibility of biblical prophecy.

1. A prophecy must contain specific

details that no human foresight could imagine. It must be a prophecy in which there is no double meaning or misleading statements that exclude accident and/or guesswork.

2. A prophecy must have proper timing. It must be spoken long before the event takes place so that the lapse of time makes it impossible for the prophet himself to bring its fulfillment to pass.

3. A prophecy is fully accredited only by its historical fulfillment.

It is an acknowledged fact that human wisdom cannot gaze ahead into time and predict the future with accuracy. How true is Proverbs 27:1— "Boast not thyself of tomorrow, for thou knowest not what a day may bring forth." But if events are set forth in writing long before they come to pass, then God must have inspired that writer.

Satan, however, is most desirous to lead people into error and often uses false prophets to do his damning work. God warned the children of Israel through Moses about these so-called prophets (Deut. 13:1–5; 18:20–22). In the first section on science, mention was made about astronomy being a true science—a study of heavenly bodies, the "ordinances of heaven," being signs (Gen. 1:14–15).

There is a *false* science that springs from astronomy called astrology. Astrology is a form of prophecy called *divination*. In this erroneous prophetical set-up, astrologers say that heavenly bodies have influence upon our destinies. They take the twelve signs of the zodiac, set certain dates around these signs, and make predictions based on these signs. Astrologers then profess to tell you your horoscope (or future), which is based on one's character and personality traits and the relative positions of planets and signs of the zodiac at specific times (near or soon after one's birth).

There is nothing in the Bible that condemns the astronomer for studying the heavenly bodies to gain more knowledge of their true purposes. However, the Bible does have much to say about astrology. Astrology, and many forms of divination, were practiced by heathen nations centuries before Christ. This is seen in the commandments given by God to Israel forbidding them to practice such "abominations" (note Jer. 27:9–10).

Since the custom of divination was common among the heathen, God restricted Israel from such, thus implying that these forms of prophetic worship were of the Devil. Yes, astrology *is* a religion, a religion promoted by Satan and opposed by God.

Not only did God oppose astrology, He condemned astrologers to death (Deut. 18:9–15; Isa. 47:13, 14 with Deut. 13:1–5). Astrology, or "star worship," was a part of idol worship (2 Kings 17:16–17; 23:4). Star worship is further seen in idolatry when Amos linked the offering of humans as sacrifices to the god Molech with Chiun, which is the planet Saturn (Amos 5:25–26). When Stephen was berating the religious leaders of his day, he referred to the same sin of Israel that Amos did in Israel's wilderness journey by mentioning *Remphan*, which is Saturn or Chiun (Acts 7:41–43). [See "Chiun (Raphan)" in Appendix.]

There are many things involved in the art of astrology and fortune-telling, which in essence embraces mediums, familiar spirits, wizardry (spells), witchcraft, enchantment, necromancy, and belief in the signs of zodiac. King

Saul's consulting with a witch at Endor is a good example of this practice in ancient times (2 Sam. 28:7).

When King Nebuchadnezzar of Babylon came up to besiege Jerusalem, he used three forms of divination to determine what he thought would be the best approach to attack this city (Ezek. 21:18–24).

The stars and other heavenly bodies were given to us by God to provide light and guidance, not to predict the future. Our custom through the ages has been to take that which is good and turn it into evil. Continual warning was given by God against astrology, which embraces the following:

1. False prophets, which have already been discussed.
2. Necromancers, or mediums (Deut. 18:11). Necromancers attempt to communicate with the spirits of the dead. The necromancer seeks to discover the future from them, believing that the dead are no longer bound by mortal limitations and can foresee future events. Another term used in connection with necromancer is *familiar spirit*, which is a demon or evil spirit believed to act as an intimate servant to contact the dead. Many warnings were given to Israel concerning familiar spirits (Lev. 19:31; 20:6, 27; 1 Sam. 28:7–9; 2 Kings 21:6; 23:24; 1 Chron. 10:13; 2 Chron. 33:6).
3. Witchcraft (Exod. 22:18; Deut. 18:1–12; Nah. 3:4–7). Witchcraft has to do with having a conference with the Devil to consult him to do some diabolic act.
4. Soothsayers (Mic. 5:12; Josh. 13:22; Isa. 2:6). A soothsayer is one who claims to have super-

natural power to foretell events. See also Acts 16:16–18.
5. Wizards (Lev. 19:31; 20:6–7; Isa. 9:19–20). A wizard is a conjurer who uses sleight-of-hand with black magic (1 Sam. 28:9). The use of "black magic," which is associated with sorcery, applies to all diabolical operations.
6. Diviner, divination (Deut. 18:4; 2 Kings 17:17–18; Jer. 14:14–16). A diviner is one who claims the ability to tell the future based on dreams or by reading and interpreting certain signs called omens. Diviners believe that the spirits or gods are in possession of secret and future knowledge and that they can be induced to impart it to the diviners. Their interpretations of information received are usually based on astrological calculations.
7. Enchantments (Lev. 19:26; Deut. 18:10–12). This involves a charmer, one who by magic predicts the future.
8. Augury; fortune-telling (Deut. 18:10 ASV). A practice of foretelling by signs (stars) or omens (phenomenon or incident regarding a prophetic sign). Similar to divination.
9. Sorcery (Isa. 47:9, 12–13; 57:3; Mal. 3:5). One bound to Satan in return for knowledge and skill in magic. Also used in connection with witchcraft. The word "witchcraft" in Galatians 5:20 is *sorcery*, meaning the use of drugs, charms, or magic words; practicing the arts of magicians and astrologers by which one pretends to foretell events with the assistance of evil spirits (Acts 8:9–11). In a broad sense sorcery is involved in occultism. The Greek word for

sorcery is *pharmakeia,* from which we get our word "pharmacy."

10. Occult/clairvoyance. The whole gamut of astrology—a study and worship of the heavenly bodies, which is commonplace in our society today—is an abomination to the Lord. The *occult,* which embraces all forms of astrology, and *clairvoyance* (mind-reading) are on the increase today. Mailing lists for the occult publications alone number nearly 9 million. Most buyers are women, but men are closing the gap. Marketing skills and persuasive sales are being used to entice a much larger number in our population. Astrology also leads the cult of "prophets" who claim to have ESP (extrasensory perception).

A good example of the way the astrologers propagate their false prophecies and prey upon people is seen in material I recently received in the mail. Written on the envelope above my name was an eye-catcher: "Please open this confidential letter immediately! The news it contains *about you* is going to change your life immediately more dramatically than anything you've ever experienced. And it's all going to happen within the next 30 days!" Then came the letter from "Roxanna," who informed me that while she was studying the stars and planets she discovered *Golden Opportunity Days* for *me*, Robert Boyd. As soon as she thanked the stars for this startling discovery, she had to contact me right away. She told me that if I act within the next thirty days of this Golden Opportunity period, my whole life will be changed—not gradually, but dramati-

cally and immediately. Time is limited, so I must send her $19.95 (listed in small print), and if I do, she says there is absolutely no question that within the next two months I would (1) come into a great deal of money, (2) reach a level of success I never even dreamed could happen, (3) find a new and exciting romance in my life, and (4) achieve happiness I've only read about.

So urgent was her letter that she said, "I was compelled to write to you. I simply must let you know all of the truly miraculous things that lie ahead for you. I was driven to tell you all the pitfalls you might encounter and protect you from them. I was compelled to share my knowledge and information with you. I have no choice. Neither do you. You must reply now!"

The initial letters of Golden Opportunity Days spell *GOD*, so according to her, if I join, God will be with me and I can come into unexpected thousands of dollars or even hundreds of thousands of dollars in lotteries. All it will cost is $19.95. To encourage prospective clients, she gives testimonies from people who have made a fortune, such as, "It's amazing, I played the numbers every day but lost. Roxanna's numbers are fantastic, and I'm winning big now." One begins to wonder why she begs for $19.95 when, if what she says is true, she isn't raking in money and winning now from her own predictions?

The child of God must so familiarize himself with the Word of God so as not to be deceived by false prophets such as has been mentioned in the so-called science of astrology. God's children must be aware that Satan can and does give power to work signs and wonders (2 Thess. 2:9–12), and he usually comes as an angel of light to deceive (2 Cor. 11:13–15). Christ alone has the answer for every circumstance, contrary to what Roxanna says. We are told in the Word of God that we have been given everything we need for this life and for godliness, which comes from a knowledge of Him (2 Peter 1:3). No one in astrology has *the* Truth. What they do have is in contrast to a true prophet of God, who is correct in *each* of his predictions.

Reasons for Studying Prophecy

There are many reasons that Christians should study the prophecies in Scripture.

1. To know God's mind (Amos 3:7; Deut. 29:29; 1 Cor. 2:10–13).
2. For our own blessing (Rev. 1:3).
3. That we may grow in patience, hope, and comfort (Rom. 15:4).
4. For the unfolding of Scripture (Luke 24:25; 1 Peter 1:11).
5. For usefulness in God's service (2 Tim. 2:15; 3:16–17).
6. To be knowledgeable in prophetic matters, both fulfilled and unfulfilled (Isa. 53; Rom. 11:25; 1 Thess. 4:13; 2 Peter 3:4–13).
7. That we might be prepared for future events (Matt. 24:36–44).
8. Because of its value as evidence of divine inspiration.
9. That we might be a greater witness of Truth to the unbeliever.

Fulfilled Prophecies

Some fulfilled prophecies are local, some deal with the great nations, empires, cities, peoples, and individuals. Such information is helpful in giving an outline of the political history of the world. These predictions were uttered long before the event described transpired, which prove beyond a shadow of a doubt that they could not have been predicted by anyone but God Himself. God uses fulfilled prophecy as proof that He has spoken in and through His prophets (Isa. 41:22–29). The argument from prophecy, then, may be set forth in clear and simple words. If events of future history were foretold in accordance with the rules of prophecy, holy Christians of old were moved by the Holy Spirit, and the established records can in no way be questioned.

The Nation of Israel

Abraham's Seed

Prediction. God prophesied that He would make of Abraham a great nation (Gen. 12:2). He prophesied that his heir would come out of his loins (Gen. 15:4). Abraham was seventy-five years old when he left Haran, and by the time he settled in Canaan, he was at least seventy-six (Gen. 12:4–6). Ten years later, at the age of eighty-six, his maid Hagar gave birth to his son Ishmael (Gen. 16). Abraham and Ishmael were circumcised when Ishmael was thirteen years old, making Abraham ninety-nine years old (Gen. 17:24–26). But the promised son had not yet been born.

Fulfillment. When Abraham was 100 years old, at least twenty-four years after God made His prophetic statement that Abraham would have an heir from his loins, Isaac was born, the "seed of promise" (Gen. 17:15–19; 21:1–5). Isaac, becoming the one through whom God established His covenant, became a great nation—the children of Israel—the Jewish people of our day. Ishmael, according to prophecy in Genesis 17:20, also became a great nation through Abraham—the Arabs of our day.

One other nation that God established through the fulfillment of prophecy about great nations in Genesis 12:2 is the one made up of those who by faith in Jesus Christ have been born into the family of God. They are of the seed of Abraham—that "holy nation" of which Peter spoke (Gal.3:26–29; 1 Peter 2:9).

The Promise of a Land

Prediction. Israel was chosen by God through Abraham, and prophecy was made to give his seed the land of Canaan, or the Promised Land (Gen. 12:5–7). It was a land of "milk and honey," a land of valleys and springs, of vegetation, and a land out of whose hills they might dig iron and copper (Deut. 8:1–10).

God's promise to give the land
  a. to Abraham (Gen. 15:7, 18–20; 17:8)
  b. to Isaac (Gen. 24:7; 26:4)
  c. to Jacob (Gen. 28:13; 35:9–12)
  d. to Moses (Exod. 6:8; 12:25; Deut. 14:21–22)

God's promise for Israel to inhabit and possess the land was given to Moses in Leviticus 20:24 and Numbers 35:34.

God's promise to go before them and fight their battles in the land was given
  a. to Moses (Deut. 1:10; 3:22; 9:3; 31:3)
  b. to Joshua (Josh. 1:5)

Fulfillment. God's faithfulness to His promises (prophecy).
  a. He fought for them (Josh. 10:42)
  b. He gave them all the land He promised to them (Josh. 11:23; 21:43–45; 1 Kings 8:56; Jer. 9:21–26)

The statement has often been made that Israel did not possess all the land that God promised. The original prediction to Abraham was from the "river of Egypt to the river Euphrates" (Gen. 15:18). The "river of Egypt" is not the Nile, but a "wadi," or a stream in its valley at the border of Egypt, which became a dividing line between the tribe of Judah and Egypt (Josh. 15:4, 47). Joshua said that God fulfilled His Word by giving to Israel "All the land which He swore to give to their fathers; they possessed it and dwelt therein. There failed not ought of any good thing which the LORD had spoken to the house of Israel; all came to pass" (Josh. 21:43–45). True, Israel's settlement did not fully reach up to the Euphrates River, but one can possess land without living in it. If all came to pass as God promised, what more does one need than these verses?

When Solomon dedicated the temple, he testified that "there had not failed one word of all his good promises which the LORD had promised to Israel concerning the land" (1 Kings 8:56). Even Nehemiah, after Israel's exile in Babylon, and upon their return to the land, testified that the land God had promised to their fathers had been possessed (Neh. 9:21–26). God's original promise to Abraham about his seed possessing the land of Canaan was made about 2000 B.C. Under Joshua's leadership, Israel possessed the land about 560 years later.

We need to keep in mind that all is not recorded about possession of the *whole* land, but when we read that

David's dominion was established by the Euphrates River (1 Chron. 18:3) and that Solomon's border was to the border or "river of Egypt," we must conclude that the Promised Land was extended to its fullest. It is wrong to say that Israel never possessed all her land.

Egyptian Bondage

Prediction. When God made an unconditional covenant with Abraham about the Promised Land (Gen. 15:7–21), He stated that Abraham's seed (Israel) would be in bondage in a land not theirs for 430 years but would later return (vv. 13, 16). This prediction by God was made ca. 2000 B.C.

Fulfillment. It is amazing how God engineers circumstances to fulfill His Word. Joseph, who was hated by his brothers, was sold by them at Dothan to merchants and taken to Egypt. He was then sold to an officer of Pharaoh's guard (Gen. 37:13–36). In time, Joseph was exalted and made second only to Pharaoh as a result of his interpretation of Pharaoh's dream (Gen. 41:38–40). Afterward, a famine covered the whole earth, and nations came to Joseph's storehouse to buy corn. When Joseph's father heard there was plenty of food in Egypt, he sent his sons down to purchase some (Gen. 41:56–42:3). Joseph recognized his brothers and revealed himself to them saying, "God sent me before you to preserve you a posterity in the earth, and to save your lives by a great deliverance" (Gen. 45:7).

According to Joseph's statement, it was not God's *permissive* will that placed Joseph in Egypt, but His *direct* will. If Israel were to be the people through whom Messiah was to come, they would have to survive the seven-year famine in which there would be no planting or harvest. God, who foresaw this famine in all the lands, saw to it that His man was in the land of plenty to save His people from annihilation by starvation. Joseph's father, Jacob, and his family moved to Egypt to be with Joseph, and for some time, even after Joseph's death, Abraham's seed enjoyed the benefits of Pharaoh's kindness.

But after Joseph's death, there arose a king who knew not Joseph, and Israel was put in servitude (Acts 7:17–19). The first twelve chapters of Exodus give a vivid picture of Israel's Egyptian bondage until they were finally set free. God's prophecy was given about 2000 B.C., started about 1880 B.C., and was completed around 1450 B.C.

God's Commands for Israel's Kings

Prediction. While Israel was still in her wilderness journey, God, about 1430 B.C., gave specific commands for Israel's future kings. Although these instructions were not in the form of direct predictions or prophecy, they were given to warn their kings of failure if they did not write these laws in a book and read them often as a reminder to obey them. Three commands for a king were given in Deuteronomy 17:14–20: (1) Do not multiply unto himself horses from Egypt; (2) do not multiply unto himself wives; and (3) do not multiply unto himself silver and gold (vv. 16–17).

Fulfillment. Solomon, 500 years later, ignored these commands, did that which was right in his own eyes, and multiplied unto himself horses from Egypt, took in an abundance of gold and silver, and multiplied unto himself wives (1 Kings 10:26–28; 11:1–3). As a result, the kingdom of Israel was divided, which finally resulted in the fall of both the Northern and Southern Kingdoms. Solomon's reign was brought to shame by his failure to observe Deuteronomy 17:14–20.

Israel's Idolatry

Prediction. God gave Israel a command in Leviticus 18 for Israel not to do as the Canaanites did in their abominable sins of adultery, homosexuality, human sacrifice, and bestiality (vv. 3, 6–30). He also made a prediction that once they got into the Promised Land they would break His covenant and serve other gods (Deut. 31:16, 20), and that if they did not drive out the inhabitants, the Canaanites would teach them their ways and would become "pricks" and "thorns" in Israel's side (Deut. 7:1–5; 20:17–18). He also said that in failure to drive them out He would do to them what He said He would to the Canaanites (Num. 33:50–56).

Fulfillment. After Israel entered their land, defeated the enemy, and rested from war, the tribes received their living portion in Canaan. They enjoyed rest during all the days of Joshua and served the Lord until the elders who outlived Joshua died (Josh. 24:31).

Soon afterward Israel began to *walk by sight*, not faith, and was unable to defeat the inhabitants they had failed to drive out (Judg. 1:19, 28, 34; 2:2–3). Joshua had disobeyed the Lord in making a covenant with the Gibeonites, letting them live (Josh. 9:14–15) as God had commanded them not to do in Deuteronomy 7:2. They did evil in the sight of God and turned to the strange god Baal, which involved embracing a vulgar, sensual religion.

In this they forgot and forsook God (Judg. 2:11–12; 3:7). They intermarried with Canaanites when they were commanded not to (Deut. 7:3–4 with Judg. 3:5–6). They worshiped Baal's idols when they had been commanded to destroy them (Deut. 7:5 with Judg. 3:7; 8:33; 10:6). In their desire to be like other nations, they dethroned God, denouncing a theocratic form of government, and embraced a monarchy, having demanded a human king (1 Sam. 8:5–7, 19–20).

Several centuries later they had stooped so low in sin that they were doing more evil than all the nations round about (2 Kings 21:9). Psalm 106:34–40 and Jeremiah 19:4–5 tell us that they were even offering their own sons and daughters as burnt offering (human) sacrifices to the god Baal. God's prophecy in Deuteronomy 31:16 and 20 literally came to pass. Had it not been for a faithful remnant who remained true to His Word, God would have done to His people what He did to Sodom and Gomorrah (Isa. 1:9). Israel became so sinful that God called them the rulers of Sodom and the people of Gomorrah, as well as the "sister" of Sodom (Isa. 1:10; Ezek. 16:48). Israel's sins made Sodom's look righteous (Ezek. 16:52).

King Jeroboam's Altars Destroyed

Prediction. When the united kingdom of Israel was divided after Solomon's death, King Jeroboam took ten tribes to form the Northern Kingdom of Israel. In rebellion against the house of David and worship of the true God of Israel, he erected two altars, calves of gold—one at Bethel and the other at Dan—where pagan sacrifices were offered (1 Kings 12). A prophet of God prophesied that a future king of the Southern Kingdom of Judah, Josiah by name, would break down and destroy these altars. This prophecy was stated ca. 930 B.C.

Fulfillment. About 300 years later, when Josiah was king, he repaired the temple which had been deteriorating. Inside the temple the Book of the Law, which had been neglected, was found. Josiah had it read, a revival broke out, and he was responsible for many reforms. Among his actions to clear the land of idolatry, he broke down and destroyed the altars of Jeroboam (2 Kings 22:1–23:20).

A Famine of the Word of God

Prediction. Out of the nineteen kings of the Northern Kingdom, all did evil in the sight of the Lord! Only eight of those of the Southern Kingdom did that which was right in the eyes of the Lord. Sin was rampant. Amos was sent by God to reprimand His people for disobeying His Word. Amos predicted a famine, not of bread and water, "but of hearing the Word of God" (8:11–12).

Fulfillment. Isaiah said of Israel, "Therefore as the fire devoureth the stubble, and the flame consumeth the chaff, so their root shall be as rottenness, and their blossom shall be as the dust: because they have cast away the law of the LORD of hosts, and despised the Word of the Holy One of Israel" (5:24). By despising their Scriptures, they have a weird way of interpreting it to suit their fancy. They have ideas about certain things, make up their own laws and regulations so that hearing what God says, they hear not, and seeing, they see not. Isaiah had made mention of this (6:9). At the time of

Christ the Jews acknowledged God with their lips but their heart was far from Him (Matt. 15:8). They refused to worship God on *His* terms—on the basis of His Word—simply because they were "in the famine" of which Amos spoke. They had substituted their Scriptures for the traditions of their fathers (Matt. 15:3, 6b–8). Even though they *could* have believed because they knew who Jesus was, confirmed by the miracles He did, they would not and were blinded to the point where they *could not* believe on Him (John 1:11; 11:47–53; 12:37–40). It is amazing how totally ignorant of their Scriptures many Jews are today.

Fall and Captivity of the Northern Kingdom

Prediction. Due to Jeroboam's sin, God said He would smite Israel and take her out of the land (1 Kings 13:33–34; 14:15–16). This prophecy was stated ca. 910 B.C.

Fulfillment. Several Assyrian kings invaded Samaria prior to her downfall, such as Pul (Tiglath-pileser) and Shalmaneser (2 Kings 15). Shalmaneser besieged the city for three years (2 Kings 17:1–5). According to Scripture, this king started the final siege of Samaria, but Assyrian records indicate that he died and Sargon actually captured the city. Scripture does not list the conquering king, simply that "they took it," and that "Israel was carried away out of their own land to Assyria" (2 Kings 18:9–10; 17:23). The Northern Kingdom fell in ca. 722 B.C., about 188 years after the prophecy of its fall was given.

Interestingly, a record was found in the ruins of Sargon's palace that he carried into captivity 27,290 Israelites.

Having left many Israelites in the land, he repeopled it with Assyrians, who intermarried with the Israelites. He even returned an Israelite priest to teach the people about the true and living God (2 Kings 17:24–28). As the result of intermarriage, this new race of people was called "Samaritan"—a person of Assyrian and Jewish descent. We read much about them in the New Testament.

Fall and Captivity of the Southern Kingdom of Judah

Prediction. Isaiah (39:5–7) and Micah (4:4, 9) prophesied of Judah's downfall and that Babylon would be the place of their captivity. These prophesies were made about 740 to 736 B.C.

Fulfillment. Jeremiah informs us that these predictions were fulfilled when king Nebuchadnezzar conquered Jerusalem, 586 B.C. (52:27–30; 2 Chron. 36:17).

Israel's Seventy-Year Babylonian Captivity

Prediction. All the nations round about Israel were gross sinners. They did not have the light of God's Word. Israel had been entrusted with God's sacred oracles, and the light in her had become darkness. Manasseh had seduced them to do more evil than all the nations round about. As a result, she became the most sinful nation. She made her temple religion an object of false security, the Law a mockery of justice, turned separation into a curse, made circumcision a fetish, used the Holy Land for unholy practices, exalted her past, sinned in the present, and ignored future judgment leveled at her through the prophets (2 Kings 21:9; 2 Chron. 36:14–16). There are at least four reasons why Israel (Judah) was taken into Babylonian captivity:

1. Ungratefulness. God had been faithful in bringing her into her land, had supplied her need and fought her battles, but she broke His covenants, dethroned Him for a human king, constantly walked contrary to His Word, and trampled underfoot sacred things. Isaiah accused them of being more stupid than dumb animals and labeled them as the "rulers of Sodom and the people of Gomorrah" (1:2–3, 10). He said if it had not been for a faithful remnant among the people, God would have done to them what He did to Sodom and Gomorrah (1:10 with Gen. 19:1–29).

2. Idolatry. Having forsaken God for Baal, Israel practiced this sex religion. Symbols of sex and fertility were erected throughout the land and in the house of God (1 Kings 14:24; 2 Kings 21:7; 23:6–7). Incense was burned to the brazen serpent that Moses made in the wilderness, and they offered their children as burnt offering sacrifices to the god Baal (2 Kings 18:4; Jer. 19:4–5; Ps. 106:34–40). Much of this was due to unfaithful priests (2 Chron. 36:14).

3. Touching God's anointed. Israel had been commanded not to do God's prophets harm (1 Chron. 16:22). To touch God's anointed is to touch God. To fight against or murmur against God's servant is to murmur against and fight God (Exod. 16:8). Israel had been guilty of doing this for many generations (2 Chron. 36:15–16a).

4. Failure to keep the Sabbatical year. Israel was instructed to till the soil for six years and then let the land rest the seventh year to enjoy her Sabbaths (Lev. 25:1–7). If she disobeyed, God prophesied that He would

make their cities waste, bring their land to desolation, and would take them out of their homeland (Lev. 26:27–35).

This prediction was made about 1475 B.C. Isaiah prophesied that because king Hezekiah made a mistake in showing Babylonian visitors the treasures of the temple and his house after he had been healed, they would be taken captive to Babylon (Lev. 39). Hosea also predicted that Babylon would be the place of Israel's 70-year captivity (4:9–10). Jeremiah, in about 600 B.C., prophesied that Israel would be captive for 70 years (25:9–12). This was due to Israel's not having kept the Sabbatical year for 490 years. By dividing 7 into 490, we get 70, the number of years Jeremiah predicted.

After king Hezekiah had been miraculously healed and his life extended fifteen years, the king of Babylon desired to visit him regarding his sickness and recovery. Instead of witnessing to him about the goodness of the Lord, Hezekiah proudly showed him the priceless wealth of the temple and royalty. Isaiah took him to task for doing this and predicted about 690 B.C. that this valuable treasure would be taken to Babylon.

Fulfillment. Because of Israel's habitual disobedience, God's patience ran out and "the wrath of the Lord arose against His people until there was no remedy" (2 Chron. 36:16). As a result, He brought upon them the king of the Chaldeans about 900 years after His first warning in Leviticus 26.

Nebuchadnezzar came up against Jerusalem, destroyed the city, showed no mercy to both young and old in slaying them, took the priceless vessels of the temple and palace as Isaiah had predicted, burned the temple and all the palaces, broke down the city walls, and took survivors as prisoners to Babylon "to fulfill the word of the LORD by the mouth of Jeremiah, until the land had enjoyed her Sabbaths: for as long as she lay desolate she kept Sabbath to fulfill threescore and ten [seventy] years" (2 Chron. 36:16–21). Israel's final deportation to Babylon took place in 586 B.C.

Israel's Release from Captivity by King Cyrus

Prediction. Some 120 years plus, before the exile of the Jews to Babylon and about 150 years before he was born, God, through the prophet Isaiah, said that a man named Cyrus would come upon the scene and deliver Israel from her Babylonian captivity. He would give them permission to go back to their holy city Jerusalem and rebuild it and their temple.

What a remarkable prediction! Isaiah also stated in this prophecy that God called this heathen king "My Shepherd" and "My Anointed" and that he would perform all My pleasure (Isa. 44:28–45:6). These designations indicate that all rulers are subject to God—"the powers that be are ordained of God" (Rom. 13:1).

Fulfillment. Sometimes it is difficult to come up with an accurate date about ancient history, but after consulting several Bible dictionaries and commentaries, we have come up with the following regarding Isaiah's prophecy concerning Cyrus and his release of Israel from Babylonian captivity. [See "Cyrus" in Index.]

Jeremiah prophesied that Israel's captivity would last seventy years (35:11 with 2 Chron. 36:21). Nebuchadnezzar first started besieging Jerusalem in about 605 B.C., at which time king Jehoiakim, Daniel, the three Hebrew boys, and others were taken captive to Babylon (2 Chron. 36:5–7; Dan. 1:1–7).

The second invasion of Jerusalem by Nebuchadnezzar was about 597 B.C., at which time Jehoiachin, Ezekiel, and others were taken to Babylon (2 Chron. 36:9–10). Nebuchadnezzar's final invasion and complete victory over Jerusalem (and the Southern Kingdom of Judah) was in 586 B.C., when the able-bodied who survived the sword were taken captive to Babylon (2 Chron. 36:17–21).

The seventy-year captivity started in 605 B.C. with Nebuchadnezzar's first invasion of Jerusalem. Cyrus, in fulfillment of Isaiah's prophecy, came upon the scene and conquered Babylon in 537 B.C. He issued his famous "Declaration of Independence" for Israel to return to Jerusalem and rebuild her temple and city (Ezra 1:1–4). One year later, 536 B.C., 43,000 Israelites, with 7,337 servants and maids, returned to Jerusalem with Zerubbabel (Ezra 2:1–2, 64–65). When we subtract 536 from 606, we get seventy years for the Babylonian captivity.

Israel's Promised Messiah

Prediction. There are any number of Old Testament prophecies foretelling the coming of Messiah, not only for the Jews, but for Gentiles as well. They are too numerous to mention in this volume, but a few will suffice.

1. The "seed of the woman" who will defeat the cause of sin, namely Satan (Gen. 3:15). In most instances in the Bible it is always the male seed which is mentioned, but since Messiah was to be born of a young woman who was a virgin, fathered by the Holy Spirit, Messiah was prophesied to come through the "seed of a woman."

Fulfilled. (Gal. 4:4, 5; Matt. 1:18–25).

2. Messiah was to be the "Star out of Jacob," a "Scepter shall rise out of Israel" (Num. 24:17).

Fulfilled. (Rev. 22:16; Matt. 2:2).

3. Messiah was prophesied to be like the Prophet God would raise up like to Moses, and to Him should they hearken (Deut. 18:15).

Fulfilled (Acts 3:22–23; 7:3).

4. Messianic Psalms. These have to do with the coming Messiah. Although locally voicing the cry of King David under varying circumstances, they give a complete and perfect illustration of David's Greater Son, the Lord Jesus Christ. There is probably a more complete picture of Christ in the Psalms than we find in the Gospel accounts. In the Gospels we find He went out to pray; in the Psalms we have His prayer. The Gospels tell us of His crucifixion; Psalms give us insight into His heart while being crucified. The Gospels tell us that He went back to be with His Father; Psalms show us Christ seated in the heavens with His Father. In at least nineteen Psalms Christ is portrayed in five general characters:

a. as the suffering Messiah (18:1–17; 22, 69). Fulfilled (Acts 2:22–23)

b. as the Son of Man (8, 20, 23, 40). Fulfilled (Luke's Gospel account).

c. as the Son of God (2, 16, 118). Fulfilled (John's Gospel account).

d. as the Eternal Priest (11). Fulfilled (Heb. 1:3; 4:14–17; 7:25).

e. as the reigning King (future) (2, 18:18–50; 21, 24, 45, 72, 89, 97, 101, 132).

5. Time of Messiah's coming— First Advent. One prophecy in particular should have compelled the Jews to pinpoint His coming, and that is Daniel 9:24–27. Six things are found in verse 24 which must be accomplished in a seventy-week period of time. (See also Luke 4:16–19.)

1. finish the transgression of Israel
2. make an end of sins
3. make reconciliation for iniquity
4. bring in everlasting righteousness
5. seal up the vision and the prophecy
6. anoint the Most Holy

The above prophetic accomplishments certainly refer to the finished work of Christ at Calvary.

Two questions are raised in reference to this prophecy:

1. What is the meaning of "seventy weeks"? The phrase "seventy weeks" is a symbolic prophetic expression coming from the Hebrew word *shib'im*. It does not mean a period of seven days to a week as we think. It means "weeks of years," or *heptads*. Thus, a "week" in prophetic symbolism means *seven years*. Therefore, seventy weeks is a total of 490 years. Out of the seventy weeks or 490 years, we are concerned with the first sixty-nine weeks, or 483 years: "From the going forth of the commandment to restore and build Jerusalem unto the Messiah, the Prince, shall be seven weeks [forty-nine years] and three score and two weeks [sixty-two weeks or 434 years]," making a total of sixty-nine weeks or 483 years.

2. When did the seventy-week period start? The decree of Cyrus ca. 536 B.C. simply gave Israel permission to return to her land and rebuild her temple and city after her seventy-year captivity. Upon her return one year later, the Jews started to rebuild the temple. Haggai (chap. 1) informs us that they neglected work on the temple to build their own houses, and after they were rebuked for this sin, they completed it in ca. 516 B.C.

The decree or command of which Daniel speaks is a vastly different one from that given by Cyrus. The Jews were content to maintain their houses without completing the building of the wall around the city. This left them defenseless. Nehemiah was much concerned about Jerusalem's protection and finishing the work of rebuilding. Upon pleading with king Artaxerxes to allow him to return to the Holy City and rebuild the walls, permission was granted. The king wrote a letter or command for him to have authority to return. This was written about 445 B.C., "in the month of Nisan [March/April], in the twentieth year of Artaxerxes, the king" (Neh. 1:1–2:9).

Daniel's prophecy (9:25–26) to restore and build the city of Jerusalem is based on the commandment or letter of Artaxerxes given in 445 B.C., making it 483 years between this commandment until Messiah, the Prince, would come.

Fulfillment. The Jews recorded time by the lunar (moon) system—360 days to the year. By multiplying 360 days by 463 years, we arrive at the spring of the year, A.D. 32, 173,800 days later. Some scholars have calculated the last day fell on April 6, A.D. 32. This would be the day Christ, according to Luke 19:28–38, made His triumphal entry into Jerusalem and fulfilled the prophecy of Zechariah, "Rejoice greatly, O daughter of Zion; shout, O daughter of Jerusalem: behold, thy King cometh unto thee; he is just, and having salvation; lowly, and riding upon an ass, upon a colt, the foal of an ass" (9:9). A few days after this event, Messiah, the Prince, "put an end to sin" when He was offered once and for all as God's Lamb upon the cross, fulfilling Daniel's prophecy sixty-nine weeks, or 463 years, later (9:24–27).

There have been several changes in the calendar. Pinpointing dates has been difficult because of the dating of events by both the solar and lunar systems. For years such scholars as Dr. C. I. Scofield and others accepted Ussher's chronology giving Adam's date of creation as 4004 B.C. This has proven to be wrong. Some put Christ's birth at zero—ending B.C. and starting A.D. Some say we date Christ's birth as 4 B.C., some say 6 B.C. We can be relatively safe in saying that Daniel's prophecy is a part of God's inspired Word, and no matter what calendar we use or what date we use, the 69 weeks or 483 years *were fulfilled.* Christ did it when He made reconciliation for iniquity and brought in everlasting righteousness.

Israel's Rejection of Messiah

Prediction. The fifty-third chapter of Isaiah is a perfect picture of Messiah's coming to suffer and bear the sins of all who have gone astray, although Isaiah is speaking primarily to Israel. "He [Messiah] is despised and rejected, . . . he is despised and we esteemed him not" (53:3). The psalmist also said, "The Stone [Messiah] which the builder [Israel] refused is become the headstone of the corner [church]" (Ps. 118:22).

Fulfillment. When Christ presented Himself to His own people, they received Him not (John 1:11). Although the Roman government carried out the act of crucifying Christ, it was at the instigation of the Jews. By their own cry, "Crucify Him," they, by association, "by wicked hands had crucified and slain Him" (John 19:6; Acts 2:22–23). In refusing or rejecting their Messiah, they rejected the "Chief Cornerstone" (Ps. 118:22 with Eph. 2:20; 1 Peter 2:6–8). It is unfortunate that they substituted the tradition of their fathers for their Scriptures and missed what Simeon and Anna the prophetess recognized because they knew what the Scriptures said about Messiah (Matt. 15:3, 6b; Luke 2:25–38).

Note that many other prophecies relating to Christ (Messiah) will be listed in the section dealing with "Fulfilled Prophecy in Christ (p. 125ff)."

Israel's Worldwide Dispersion

Prediction. In Deuteronomy 28, God unfolds to Israel what His blessing to them will be if they obey Him (vv. 1–14). Verses 15–68 give us prophetic statements concerning God's judgment upon His people if they fail to keep His commandments. Among many judgments that would come their way, one was, 'The Lord shall scatter thee among all people, from one end of the earth even to the other" (v. 64). God said He would "bring a nation against thee from far . . . as swift as the eagle; a nation whose tongue thou shalt not understand" (v. 49). [See "Fall of Jerusalem" in Index.]

Fulfillment. We noted previously, under the heading "Israel's Failure— Her Idolatry," that Israel was a very sinful, disobedient nation. She lost her national status because of this and was taken out of her land into Babylonian captivity. After her seventy-year exile, she was under Gentile domain except for the period of time during the Maccabeans (ca. 165–63 B.C.). From 63 B.C., under Roman rule, there was much friction between the Jews and the Roman rule. In A.D. 70, Titus brought in the Roman army and destroyed Jerusalem, which began a worldwide dispersion or scattering of the Jews.

Rome was the nation God brought in whose language (Latin) Israel could not understand, and as God said, Rome came in as a swift eagle. How interesting—Rome's insignia was an *eagle!* How well Israel could have been blessed by God, but in her rebellion against Him, as Deuteronomy 28 prophesied, she was scattered, she became a by-word, her life was constantly in danger, and she found no rest throughout the nations of the world (vv. 63–67). History verifies this prophecy—literally fulfilled (see Deut. 29:22–28).

Destruction of the Temple

Prediction. Jesus, about A.D. 33, prophesied that the temple would be destroyed and that no stone would be left on top of the other (Matt. 24:1–2). Usually, when a building was destroyed during war in those days, battering rams would knock down walls but always some stones at the base or foundation would be left on top of each other. But Jesus predicted that "there shall not be left one stone upon another that shall not be thrown down." Quite an odd prediction, wouldn't you say?

Fulfillment. Stones in temples were usually held together not with mortar but with gold or silver bars fitted into grooves to hold them together and in place. The Roman soldiers knew this, and "to the victor belongs the spoil."

Titus' soldiers literally took one stone off top the other to "pocket" the precious metal, thus fulfilling Christ's prophecy. [See "Destruction of Jerusalem" in Index.]

Israel to Be Few in Number (Deut. 28:62)

Fulfillment. According to Josephus, as the result of the sieges against the land of Palestine and the destruction of Jerusalem, 1,356,000 Jews were slaughtered and 101,700 were taken captive. Many preferred death to capture and slavery.

Prisoners Taken Captive to Egypt in Ships (Deut. 28:68)

Fulfillment. Josephus also tells us that after Titus completely destroyed the Holy City, tens of thousands of Jews who were not slain were deported to Egypt in ships to work in their mines night and day, lashed to their work without intermission. They received horrible treatment—far worse than their ancestors had suffered in Egyptian bondage many centuries before.

Desolate Land; Waste Cities (Lev. 26:32–35; Deut. 28:15–18)

Fulfillment. A few Jews were able to remain in the area of Jerusalem after Titus's victory. Still rebellious under Roman rule, these remaining Jews were scattered in A.D. 135 under orders by the emperor Hadrian, and their land was sold to Gentiles. God's prophecy came to pass, which resulted in the Jews' losing their Promised Land. Over the centuries, and under the Turks and British until 1948, much of the land lay idle, was trodden down, became parched by the sun, and its cities were laid waste.

No King, No Priests, No Sacrifices (Hos. 3:4)

Fulfillment. After the worldwide dispersion under Titus and Hadrian, the Jews had no place to worship and offer sacrifices. They built synagogues and observed some feasts, had Rabbis, and offered chickens on the Day of Atonement. But they were a wandering, scattered people until Israel became a nation in 1948. They still have no king, no temple, no scriptural sacrifices, and no priests. And Hosea predicted this over 2,700 years ago.

Israel Regathered

Prediction. God promised the land of Canaan to Abraham and his seed forever (Gen. 17:8). On two occasions, due to Israel's sinful lifestyle, she was driven out—in Babylonian captivity in 586 B.C. and her worldwide dispersion in A.D. 70 under Titus. But the land is still hers, and God said through Ezekiel, "Behold, I will take the children of Israel from among the heathen, whither they be gone, and will gather them on every side, and bring them into their own land" (37:21). He predicted that Israel, as dry bones in a grave, would be raised to go back home (37:1–13). This has to do with Israel going back to her homeland in unbelief. Isaiah prophesied that "they shall build the old wastes, they shall raise up the former desolations, and they shall repair the waste cities, the desolations of many generations" (61:4). Isaiah also prophesied the "desert would blossom as a rose" (35:1).

Fulfillment. Beginning in 1775, some Jews from Russia, and later from Poland, Germany, and other European countries, immigrated to the ancient land of their fathers up through the late 1800s. They did two things to acquire property: (1) they purchased it, and (2) they homesteaded. This was done under the Turks.

After World War I, the Turks lost the land, and the British were given the mandate over Palestine. Under the Balfour Declaration, the Jews were given a "national homeland-freedom" to move there and purchase land and settle. But due to Arab opposition, the British issued two "White Papers," one which said that anyone who was born in the land since 1921 was a "Palestinian." The other, issued in 1931–32, divided the land in such a way that many Jews lost their property and could purchase no more. Immigration was curtailed.

After World War II, Britain lifted the mandate over Palestine and pulled out. This left about 600,000 Jews at the mercy of hundreds of millions of Arabs. The United Nations, sensing a problem, partitioned the land in 1947, giving so much to the Jews and so much to the Arabs (called Jordan). The Palestinians, plus other Arab nations, vowed the Jews had no right to any of the land, and when war broke out, it was the determination of the Arabs to drive the Jews into the Mediterranean Sea. After a bitter struggle the Jews won, and in 1948, for the first time since Nebuchadnezzar of Babylon captured Israel in 586 B.C., Israel became a full-fledged nation. There have been several wars since, but Israel has won them all and she's still *at home.* Ezekiel's prophecy has been fulfilled.

What about Isaiah's prophecy— rebuilding the old wastes, raising up the former desolations? Isaiah also predicted that the "land shall blossom as the rose" (35:1). When Israel became a nation, her people went to work to make the fallow ground productive. Many more Jews immigrated, so new cities were built. Finding that the soil had been baked by the sun for centuries and in places had become as hard as cement, modern machinery was used to dig in. The British had written off the Negev desert as uninhabitable, but Israel had to expand, so trees were planted to help keep moisture in the ground. Five-and-a-half-foot pipes channel water from the Jordan River into the desert for irrigation. Grain and citrus trees now grow in abundance. As one visits the whole land of Israel today, immediately Isaiah's prophecy is seen—"the desert is blossoming as a rose."

Bible students recognize the truth that Palestine belongs to Israel. Since the world does not recognize Israel's biblical right to the land, does Israel, in their eyes, have any right? The answer is yes. It is hers by right of purchase and conquest. When any nation conquers another nation, she possesses the loser's territory, whether it be Russia, America, England, France. This is a fact of history.

- Israel won Palestine from the Palestinians and other Arabs.
- Britain won Palestine from the Turks.
- The Turks won the land from the Byzantines.
- The Byzantines took it from the Romans.
- The Romans took it from the Greeks.
- The Greeks took it from the Medo-Persians.
- The Medo-Persians took it from Babylon.
- Babylon took it from Israel.
- Israel took it from the Canaanites.

Now the Jews are back where they were when Joshua led them into Palestine (the Promised Land) in the late 1400s B.C. It is a pity that the United Nations and all the governments of the Arabs and Palestinians cannot see history in all this. Why can they not see that Palestine is now Israel's by purchase and conquest? One reason is that those who have vowed to drive Israel into the sea, as descendants of Ishmael, are called "wild men" (Gen. 16:21). What a tragedy when Abraham's wife, Sarah, told him to go lie with her handmaid Hagar. As a result, Ishmael was born. This is the cause of the turmoil in the Near East today—the problem between the natural seed of Abraham, Ishmael (the Arabs), and Abraham's seed of promise, Isaac (the Jews).

Israel has done what any nation has done down through the centuries. She has fought wars and won. The territory is hers. She has every right to defend herself and the land. And it is hers because God said so!

Landmarks of 4,000 Years of Jewish History

2100 B.C.	Abraham settled in Canaan
1446	Exodus from Egypt
1406	Fall of Jericho
1000	David captured Jerusalem
966	Solomon began building the temple
931	United Kingdom of Israel divided
722	Fall of Northern Kingdom of Israel
586	Fall of Southern Kingdom of Judah (Babylonian captivity)
536	First return from Babylonian captivity. Israel no longer a ruling nation—now under Gentile rule
332	Alexander the Great conquers Palestine

285–247	Translation of Hebrew O.T. into Greek—the Septuagint
168	Desecration of temple by Antiochus Epiphanies
165	Maccabean Revolt against Greece and Grecian culture
142	Hasmonean Period. Jews possessed land; Maccabeans assumed role of priesthood and political rule
63	Pompey of Rome conquered land; Jews now under Roman rule
40	Herod the Great named king by Roman Senate
37	Herod the Great captured Jerusalem
6–5	Birth of Messiah
4	Death of Herod the Great
A.D. 29–30	Crucifixion of Christ
66	Beginning of first Jewish Revolt
70	Fall of Jerusalem to Titus of Rome
73	Fall of Masada
132	Beginning of second Jewish Revolt
135	Fall of Jerusalem to Hadrian
200	Completion of Mishna (oral interpretation of O.T. ordinances)
500	Completion of Babylonian Talmud (collection of writings that constitute the Jewish civil and religious law. In two parts: *Mishna*, the text, and *Gemara*, the commentary)
614	Invasion of Persians
636	Fall of Jerusalem to Arabs
1099	Fall of Jerusalem to Crusaders
1187	Fall of Crusader Kingdom
1517	Conquest of Palestine by Ottoman Turks
1882	First Aliya—organized immigration of Jews to Palestine
1896–97	Theodore Herzl's Zionist Movement
1909	Tel Aviv founded; Degania, first kibbutz founded
1917–20	Balfour Declaration of Britain giving Israel right to homeland in Palestine; Britain given mandate over Palestine, having liberated land from Turks in World War I
1921	British "White Paper," stating anyone born in mandated territory was a "Palestinian." This is why Yassar Arafat organized the PLO and claims the land belongs to the "Palestinians."
1931–32	British "White Paper" limited purchase of land by Jews and curtailed their immigration
1939–45	World War II. Jewish Holocaust in which Nazi Germans under Hitler slaughtered over 6 million Jews
1947	Britain lifted mandate and left Palestine. War of Independence began for Israel against Arabs
1948	Israel victorious. United Nations partitions land, giving part to Israel, part to Jordan. Proclamation of State of Israel, first time as full-fledged nation since 586 B.C.
1949	Chaim Weismann elected first president. Armistice agreement signed with Arab states. Israel admitted to United Nations
1950	"Law of Return" passed, giving any Jew right to "come home."
1956	Sinai Campaign
1962	Execution of Adolf Eichmann, chief Holocaust exterminator.
1967	June (Six-Day) War
1973	October (Yom Kippur) War
1977	Sadat, President of Egypt, spoke in Jerusalem to Knesset
1979	Camp David Accord signed by Sadat of Egypt and Begin of Israel
1982	Israel's attack on the PLO in Lebanon
1990–91	Israel threatened by Saddam Hussein of Iraq
1993	Israeli/PLO get together for land settlement

Egypt

It may come as a surprise that Egypt is mentioned at least 601 times in the Bible, and the term "Egyptian(s)" is mentioned at least 120 times, making a total of 721 times this country and its people are referred to—second only to Israel. Her past culture, sciences (medicine, arithmetic, architecture), religions (over 2,500 deities), and wealth (King Tut's fabulous treasures) are second to none. She was an ancient world power, an industrious people with some skills that cannot be equaled in our day and scientific age. Yet God predicted the decline of this mighty nation through Isaiah (ca. 750 B.C.) and Ezekiel (ca. 590 B.C.).

To Become the Basest of Nations; No More Rule over Other Nations

Prediction. This prediction was made by Ezekiel, also saying that God would diminish them . . . and the pride of power shall come down (29:14–15; 30:4–6).

Fulfillment. For centuries after these predictions were made, all continued to go well for Egypt. However, God's reckoning day came to pass, and in the seventh century A.D., things began to happen. From about 638 A.D. to World War I, God's Word was fulfilled, and Egypt became the basest of kingdoms. The abject condition of the peasantry was appalling. Her villages were mud brick huts, her people became the poorest of the poor, there was child labor, primitive threshing floors, disease, primitive water wheels for irrigation (even today in outlying areas some customs are the same as they were in Abraham's day). Egypt existed as a nation but simply had no power and influence as the once proud and mighty nation had in ancient times. She had become what God said she would be—the basest of kingdoms. There was nothing but mere existence—squalor, filth, and depression.

Unemployment; Outsiders Cause Egypt to Err in Every Work

Prediction. One of the thriving industries of the Egyptians was their work in fine linen and the weaving of cotton. They could weave linen so finely that a mummified body could be wrapped in as much as 600 yards! There were 540 threads to the inch and the knots and breaks were not discernible even when held to the light. Isaiah made mention that there would come a time when the weavers would become ashamed of their work and lose hope in what they were doing (19:9). He also mentioned the absence of Egypt's wise men, that outside influence would seduce them, that the Lord would mingle a perverse spirit in her midst, causing her to err in every work (lose the art of originality), as a drunk man staggers in his vomit, resulting in no work—idleness (19:9, 14–15).

Fulfillment. When one visits the tombs of the ancient Pharaohs and sees artistic work as though it had been painted yesterday, seeing garments colored with dyes, noticing the architectural style of structures still standing, mummified bodies, metal objects, surgical and dental tools, colored glass and porcelain objects, and then looks at what Egypt has to offer today, we can vouch for Isaiah's prophecy being true. All these things have become a lost art. Objects painted 5,000 years ago look like they were painted yesterday. We can't even make paint that will last twenty years! [See "Sciences in Egypt" in Index.]

The result of Egypt's becoming the "basest of kingdoms" led them into this economic depression mentioned by Isaiah. Having sought advice from others, she was constantly led astray. A good example, even in our day, is her having been deceived by Russia, which resulted in the 1967 "Six-Day" War, in which the Jews soundly defeated the Egyptians. The Aswan Dam is the result of bad advice, and the Nile River is not as productive as it once was nor is the land as fertile.

The Paper Reeds Shall Wither; No More Fish

Prediction. Paper reeds refer to the papyrus which grew by and in brooks and the Nile. It grew in abundance and helped give life to bodies of water. Ancient tomb paintings show royalty hunting and fishing among papyrus. Its leaves were split, laid parallel, and pressed with ooze from the Nile, producing a linen paper. It was so plentiful that the rich and poor used it. Some of our New Testament manuscripts were written on papyrus. Isaiah predicted that this "paper reed" would wither—vanish (19:7).

Isaiah (19:8) also predicted that the fishermen would mourn and languish as they sought to catch fish for a living. Tomb paintings show spear-fishing, and records relate a tax revenue that one Pharaoh received from a very prosperous fishing village—$1,000,000 in taxes. Yet Isaiah prophesied that fishing would cease.

Fulfillment. Over the centuries the papyrus died out. When vegetation is lost in water, fish lose their breeding grounds. Egypt even lost the lotus plant, the national flower of ancient Egypt. The only papyrus Egypt has today is what she imports and what is grown at a Papyrus Museum in Cairo. There are no fish of commercial value today in the Nile. Both the lack of papyrus and fish confirm Isaiah's prophecy. Since Egypt had to get fish from the Mediterranean Sea for many centuries, the government today is establishing fish-breeding farms near the Aswan Lake. One farm alone is expected to yield 1,000 tons of fish a year, and refrigerator cars, each carrying thirty tons, will supply the fish markets of Cairo.

The City of Luxor (Thebes) or No

Prediction. Luxor, or No, was probably the largest city in ancient Egypt (Nah. 3:3). The street which led to the city was called "The Avenue of the Sphinxes," since it featured sphinxes in the form of animals with the figure of a small man standing between the animal's front legs. The avenue led into a huge temple area. The "Hypostyle Hall" of the temple is one and three-quarters miles in circumference. Over 100 columns still stand. It takes seven men joining hands to encircle a single column. Obelisks standing 100 feet high were erected in many places. Any number of other temples had been built by Pharaohs' erecting them in honor of their god or gods. There were sacred pools for people to bathe and have their sins washed away. It was a magnificent city, but Ezekiel said that judgment would be executed upon it and it would be broken up (lie in ruins: 30:14, 16).

Fulfillment. As one visits Luxor (No) today, 2,570 years after Ezekiel prophesied, the ruins (though many have been preserved), are mute evidence of the truthfulness of this prophecy. Looking at this city that was "rent asunder," having had more than a million inhabitants, one's heart is encouraged to know that God never lies, but always keeps His Word.

City of Memphis or Noph

Prediction. Egypt was probably the most polytheistic nation that ever existed. Over 2,500 gods and goddesses in the form of idols representing man and animals and creeping things were venerated and worshiped. Some idols were half human and half animal, some were all animal and creeping things, reminding us of Romans 1:21–25.

Israel was familiar with the god Apis, a sacred cow or bull, and while in her wilderness journey made a molten or golden calf, fashioned after Apis, and worshiped it. God predicted through the prophet Ezekiel, saying, "I will destroy the idols and will cause the images to cease from Memphis, . . . and she shall have distresses daily" (30:13, 16). As one reads Ezekiel 30:1–19, attention is drawn to the fact that cities throughout Egypt would be under God's judgment.

Fulfillment. Noph is the biblical name for Memphis (Jer. 46:19). It was a much older city than No. Nearby is the oldest pyramid, the Step Pyramid, built around 2600 B.C. This city suffered God's wrath because of her idolatry, and was so completely destroyed that as late as a century ago, its location was in dispute. Archaeologists dug beneath twenty feet of sand and mud to find it. All that was left was a colossal statue of Rameses and a granite sphinx. When a tomb was found in the vicinity, it was thought at first to be that of a Pharaoh. It turned out to be a tomb containing twenty-nine sarcophagi, each preserving the mummified body of a sacred bull, each sacred to the god Apis, god of the sun, the god of creation. They had been worshiped, fed the best of food, bathed daily, and upon death had been given a royal funeral at a cost of between $25,000 and $35,000 per bull.

Because of such idolatry, the land had become impoverished. Only by divine revelation could Jeremiah and Ezekiel have predicted that the sin of idolatry would bring about the destruction of No and the annihilation of Noph.

Foreign Rulers over Egypt; Desolation

Their Land to Be Sold

Prediction. Ezekiel prophesied that "the sword would come upon Egypt, and that God would "sell the land into the hand of the wicked . . . by the hand of strangers [foreigners]" (30:4, 12).

Fulfillment. In losing her power, influence, and wealth, Egypt has been under the rule of many foreign nations—all strangers. History records Egypt has been under subjection to the Persians, Macedonians, Romans, Arabs, Turcomans (tribes east of Iran and west of Afghanistan), Mamelukes (Arabic slaves who became a military caste), Turks and Mongols, and British. Even Israel's history under foreign masters has been one of continuous oppression. Thousands of natives were cruelly slaughtered by Diocletian in 296 B.C. The barbarous cruelty of Mohammedan leaders in Egypt is almost beyond description. Of 40,000 Egyptians conscripted to build a canal 40 miles long and 200 feet wide, having no tools but their hands, 23,000 died. Surely Egypt had been sold (surrendered and occupied) into the hands of strange, wicked men just as God had said she would be.

Egypt and Neighboring Countries Desolate

Prediction. Ezekiel made a sad prophecy concerning Egypt's becoming desolate. But to make the prophecy all the more effective, he said that Egypt would be desolate "in the midst of the countries that are desolate!" This means that these neighboring countries could be of no help to Egypt (30:7–8).

Fulfillment. On the northwest, the province of Barca in Tripoli was once a place of wealth and busy cities of splendor, retaining their prosperity even up to the time of Christ. Today, only two or three cities are left.

Fezzan, in southwest Libya, was repeatedly conquered. Practically all trade of the past vanished, and today fewer than 26,000 people live there in poverty.

Ethiopia was a nation formerly characterized by strength, civilization, and order. Mohammedans sapped its strength and the country was finally divided into small states. Today there is disorder and famine caused by communism.

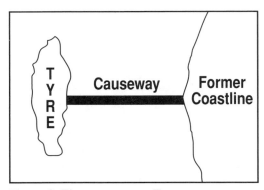

Figure 2. The causeway at Tyre

City of Tyre

Prediction. Isaiah prophesied against Tyre (chap. 23). Ezekiel prophesied its doom (26:1–14). It was a mighty, well-fortified, impregnable, proud city. Ezekiel said its stones, timbers, and dust were to be laid in the midst of the waters (Mediterranean Sea). It would never be rebuilt; it would be a place for the spreading of fishing nets.

Fulfillment. When the Assyrians came to power in the 700s B.C., Sennacherib failed to conquer it after several years of war. Later, after Nebuchadnezzar of Babylon was enthroned, he besieged the city for thirteen years and failed to gain victory. However, he destroyed the mainland. The citizens of Tyre fled to an island half a mile off shore for security. Since Nebuchadnezzar had no fleet, he left. The new city of Tyre was rebuilt on the island and it lasted until Alexander the Great approached it in 332 B.C. When his demand for surrender was refused, he ordered his men to take the rubble from the old city and build a causeway to the island (see fig. 2). Marching his troops over this bridge, he conquered and destroyed Tyre. Ten thousand Tyrians were slaughtered, and 30,000 became slaves for resisting Alexander. The city has never been rebuilt, and today fishermen spread their nets to dry on the stones that remain of Alexander's causeway.

How true the Word of God, even in such small details as fishermen drying their nets (v. 14; see fig. 3). The Tyre of which Ezekiel spoke was "Palae-Tyre," the continental Tyre. It is the Tyre from which people came to hear Jesus (Mark 3:8), and is the same Tyre that Paul visited (Acts 21:3). This Tyre has about 7,000 inhabitants today.

City of Sidon

Prediction. In order for Sidon to recognize that God is Lord, Ezekiel prophesied that God would execute judgments against her by sending pestilences and war. Blood would run freely in her streets, and the wounded would be judged in the midst of her by the sword (28:20–23).

Fulfillment. Sidon was a Phoenician city, and the Phoenicians were warlike people. Her history has been one of violence and bloodshed. She had a bad name in Scripture as a hotbed of idolatry. Ashtoreth was the goddess of the Zidonians (Sidonians), the goddess Solomon went after (1 Kings 11:5).

Since the Zidonians did not recognize God as God, He said He would see to it that they were judged during the course of their history. Down through the years she fell under the power of Assyria, Babylon, Persia, Greece, and Rome. History shows that Ezekiel's prophecy came true. Although Ezekiel prophesied judgment and bloody war, he did not pronounce doom as he did for Tyre. Even though it was bombarded by the Turks and British as late as World War I, it still stands today in southern Lebanon with a population of about 27,000. They live in fear of militant Arabs and invading Jews as they have for many centuries.

City of Nineveh

Prediction. The book of Nahum gives a vivid prophetic picture of Nineveh's doom. Their savage atrocities, wicked violence, arrogant pride, and idolatry were causes for God's wrath and actions against them. The following predictions were made for her utter destruction:

Figure 3. Stone columns on a beach at Tyre used for drying fish nets

1. Opening gates of the river, waters running wild, overwhelming flood, palace dissolved (1:8; 2:6, 8)
2. While its leaders are drunk, they shall be devoured as stubble (1:10)
3. Their enemy shall be like chariots of flaming torches (2:3–4)
4. In drunkenness they shall seek to prepare their defenses (2:5)
5. To be leveled: become empty, void, and waste (2:10; 3:7)
6. Her chariots shall be burned in the smoke (2:13)
7. Fire to destroy her strongholds (3:13)
8. No hope for survival. God "will make an utter end of the place" with "no hope healing in thy bruises" (1:8; 3:19)

To summarize, "The LORD hath given a commandment concerning thee, that no more of thy name be sown; out of the house of thy gods will I cut off the graven image and the molten image; I will make thy grave, for thou art vile" (Nahum 1:14).

Fulfillment. The prophecy God leveled against Nineveh doesn't sound much like the action of a God of love. Nahum reminded them that God is "slow to anger" (1:3). He had sent Jonah to preach repentance toward God, and they did. Their turnabout did not last long, and about one hundred years later, they had rebelled and were back to their old way of life. She was like those who rebel against light, and when light becomes darkness, how great is that darkness (Job 24:13; Matt. 6:23b). Nahum (3:8–10) used the illustration of God's destroying No and other cities in Egypt, hoping, no doubt, that this would wake them up, but to no avail (see Jer. 46:25; Ezek. 30:14–16). The Egyptian cities fell in 663 B.C. Nahum's prophecy was made soon after.

Nineveh got off to a bad start. It was built some time between the flood and the building of the tower of Babel by either Nimrod or his descendants (Gen. 10:11). Nimrod means "rebel," one who rebels against the divine order of things—a self-willed man. The whole of Mesopotamia, or the Assyrian Empire, became known as the land of Nimrod (Mic. 5:6). He was a ruthless tyrant who captured, tortured, and enslaved people.

The Ninevites (Assyrians) of Nahum's day lived up to the name of the city's founder. They, too, were brutal, murderous tyrants. Archaeological discoveries show that the heinous, barbarous treatment inflicted upon prisoners of war as well as some of its citizens were gruesome. Some would have their arms and legs spread out and staked on the burning sand; some would have their eyelids cut off and were made to stare at the sun until blinded. Others were skinned alive and their skin wrapped around building pillars to dry out for drums and leather products. Some were impaled; poles were rammed into their stomachs and then erected as the victims screamed in agony (see fig. 4). Some were forced to march into flaming pits to be burned alive. Eyes were gouged out, ears were cut off, legs and hands and other extremities were chopped off, and many had their tongues torn out by the roots. Pregnant women would have their abdomens ripped open with swords. This gives some idea of Assyrian brutality. (Keep in mind that modern Iraq is ancient Assyria.)

In spite of God's being slow to anger, He must judge sin, so He predicted He would make full end of this wicked adversary, Nineveh (1:8). At the time of Nahum's prediction, Nineveh was at its height of fame and fortune. The city was about 60 miles in circumference, and its walls were about 100 feet high and 25 feet thick. The walls were strengthened by 1,500 towers and were wide enough for three chariots to ride abreast. The city stood on the left bank of the Tigris River, and the side not protected by the river was surrounded by a moat. The oldest aqueduct in the world was constructed to bring fresh drinking water for its inhabitants. Many magnificent palaces of the Assyrian kings mentioned in Kings and Chronicles, such as Sennacherib, Esar-haddon, Pul (Tiglath-peleser), and Sargon, were wonders to behold.

In 612 B.C., the kings of Babylon and Persia joined forces to invade Nineveh. Demolition experts destroyed the aqueduct and diverted the river. This dual engineering project caused a flood of water to pour into the city, fulfilling Nahum 1:8; 2:6, and 8. Torches were set to buildings standing above

Figure 4. A depiction of Assyrians impaling prisoners

the water as Nahum had said (2:13; 3:13). Nahum was right: "Wasted is Nineveh, she shall be no more heard" (3:7; 2:13).

In less than 300 years after its downfall and destruction by the Babylonians and Medes, Alexander the Great took an expedition over the site and was ignorant of the fact that he was walking over the ruins of one of the mightiest empires that ever existed.

The prophet Zephaniah (2:13–15) said that after its destruction, "flocks shall lie down in the midst of her." Although the government has been rebuilding parts of its wall and gate entrances as a tourist attraction, one sees today on its ruins just what Zephaniah said: "grazing flocks of sheep!"

Edom

Prediction. In about 585 B.C. three prophets made predictions against the people of Edom, who lived in Seir, southeast of the Dead Sea. Isaiah said these people were cursed of God to judgment (34:5, 12). Ezekiel said God would cut off man and beast from Edom and that Israel would "do in Edom according to My fury, that they shall know My vengeance" (25:12–14). Obadiah prophesied Edom's doom because of Esau's violence against Jacob; because of pride and exaltation of themselves (vv. 3–4, 10–14).

Fulfillment. The biblical Edomites were originally the descendants of Esau, Jacob's brother (Gen. 25:24–26; 36:1). Esau's mother plotted to have Jacob deceive their father Isaac to

Figure 5. Buildings at Petra

receive the blessing. On the surface it appeared that Esau forgave his brother, but underneath he held a grudge (Gen. 28; 31:1–16). Esau married many heathen women and became the head or father of the Edomites (Gen. 36:1, 43). Over the next few centuries the story of Jacob's getting the birthright from Esau by deception caused the descendants of Esau to become perpetual enemies of Jacob's descendants. One illustration of this animosity was the Edomites' refusal to let the children of Israel pass through their land in their wilderness journey (Num. 20:18–21). Another illustration occurred when Nebuchadnezzar captured Jerusalem and took the Israelites captive. The Edomites gloated over their defeat (Obad. 10–14). Ezekiel had prophesied that Edom's doom would come at the hands of Israel (25:12–14). This was fulfilled in the Maccabean Period.

Judas Maccabeus, a Jew, in 164 B.C. defeated the Idumeans (as the Edomites were called then—1 Macc. 5:1–5).

After the Romans sacked Jerusalem in A.D. 70, the Edomites disappeared. Their stronghold had been in the mountains of Seir, but all that one sees today is rugged terrain. One famous spot in the place where the Edomites dwelt in the clefts of the rocks is the uninhabited city of Petra, called the "Red Rose City, Half as Old as Time" (see fig. 5). Facings of buildings carved out of the sides of rock mountains by the Nabateans in the second century B.C. have become a tourist attraction in the country of Jordan today. It was called "Sela" in Old Testament days (2 Kings 14:7). The silence today in this old Edomite area is a testimony to God's prophecies coming to pass just as He predicted centuries ago.

Babylon

Prediction. The once mighty capital of Nebuchadnezzar's kingdom was doomed to become like Sodom and Gomorrah—utterly destroyed (Isa. 13:19). Isaiah also predicted that it would be perpetually uninhabited. Just doleful creatures would live there and no Arabian would pitch his tent there (13:20–22). Jeremiah also had prophetic remarks to make about this mighty city. He foretold of the appearance of its ruins as "heaps" (51:37). He foretold the process of its destruction (50:24–46), and that Babylon's land of Chaldea was to become desolate (50:23; 51:43). [See "Fall of Babylon" in Index.]

Fulfillment. When we consider the strength and beauty of this city, which was called the "Lady of Kingdoms" by Isaiah (47:5), it almost seems impossible that such a mighty city would fall and be utterly destroyed. These predictions were made ca. 750 B.C.

The ancient historian Herodotus said that Babylon's wall was 60 miles in length, 15 miles on each side, 300 feet high, and almost 80 feet thick. Over 2,550 pillars (monuments), from 50 to 250 feet high, had been erected to her warlords. In the center of the city were 150 pillars, 88 feet high and 19 feet in diameter, supporting a chapel of solid marble. It contained an image to the god Bel, 40 feet high and overlaid with solid gold. Surrounding this temple were twelve other beautiful temples dedicated to various gods. Gorgeous palaces extended for several miles along the banks of the river Euphrates, and there were the hanging gardens containing plants and trees of all kinds, watered by an ingenuous system of machinery. Fields produced abundant crops to support inhabitants in case of a siege, and huge gates of bronze, beaming in the sun, defied any enemy. Seemingly, there was not one chance in a million that Babylon would ever be captured, let alone be destroyed. It was described by Isaiah as "the glory of kingdoms, the beauty of the Chaldees' excellency" (13:19). Nebuchadnezzar called it "this great Babylon" (Dan. 4:30).

Babylon was still mighty when captured by Alexander the Great in the 330s B.C. At the beginning of the Christian era only a small part was inhabited, mainly by Jews. By the twelfth century A.D. Babylon had become an utter desolation. It had become "heaps" as described by Jeremiah. Archaeological expeditions have unearthed many wall foundations, giving evidence of their magnitude. The region, located between the Tigris and Euphrates rivers, was once fertile, but when a new trade route was found to India, it met its commercial doom. Today it is just desert. Bedouins graze their flocks on what little growth there is near the rivers, but none will pitch their tent on the site of Babylon. They regard the ruins with superstitious dread. Among the ruins dwell bats, owls, creeping things, and wild beasts, just as Isaiah foretold.

Four Gentile Kingdoms

Nebuchadnezzar's Dream

Prediction. Nebuchadnezzar had a dream which none of his wise men could interpret. As a result, he threatened to slay them. When word of this threat spread through Babylon, Daniel knew this included him. But God revealed the secret to him, which turned out to be a prediction concerning four Gentile nations. During the days of these kingdoms, God would set up a kingdom that would never be destroyed, one not left to people, one that would stand forever (Dan. 2).

Fulfillment. In Nebuchadnezzar's dream he saw a great image of a man (see fig. 6). His head was of fine gold, his breast and arms were of silver, his waist and thighs were of brass (bronze), his legs were of iron, and his feet were part iron and part clay (2:31–32).

1. The head of fine gold was Nebuchadnezzar himself, who represented the first Gentile kingdom of Babylon, ca. 606/5–536/5 B.C. From the time of his dream until Babylon's downfall was seventy years. Possibly gold is mentioned because Babylon used gold extensively in overlaying buildings, walls, images, and shrines.

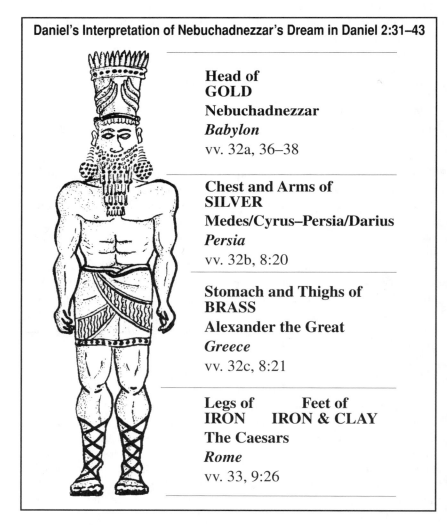

Daniel's Interpretation of Nebuchadnezzar's Dream in Daniel 2:31–43

**Head of
GOLD
Nebuchadnezzar**
Babylon
vv. 32a, 36–38

**Chest and Arms of
SILVER
Medes/Cyrus–Persia/Darius**
Persia
vv. 32b, 8:20

**Stomach and Thighs of
BRASS
Alexander the Great**
Greece
vv. 32c, 8:21

**Legs of   Feet of
IRON   IRON & CLAY
The Caesars**
Rome
vv. 33, 9:26

Figure 6. Nebuchadnezzar's image of four nations

Even the ninety-foot high and nine-foot wide image that Nebuchadnezzar made to be worshiped was of gold (3:1).

2. The silver breast and arms became the Medo-Persian Empire (2:32b, 39). The Medo-Persians defeated Babylon in 536/535 B.C. (chap. 5) and ruled for 204 years until 332 B.C. To the Medo-Persians, silver stood for their medium of exchange. This kingdom became known for their widespread tax system (Ezra 4:13).

3. The brass (bronze) waist and thighs represented Greece. Later, under Alexander the Great, the Greeks would conquer the then-known world (2:32c, 39b). Persia fell to the Grecians in 332 B.C., and Greece ruled until 145 B.C. They used bronze extensively in their weapons, which helped Alexander's soldiers to defeat their enemies.

4. The iron legs and iron and clay feet represent the Roman Empire. The two legs represent the Western Empire with Rome as its capital and the Eastern Empire with Constantinople (Byzantium or Istanbul) as its capital (2:33, 40). Rome conquered Greece in 146 B.C., and her power lasted until A.D. 476, about 662 years (some historians make this figure lower).

Iron is a good designation of Rome. It was used in Roman implements of war, and as a much stronger metal, was able to crush gold, silver, and bronze. Rome was strong enough to crush and shatter the world of her day by her military strength.

The iron and clay feet represent the futility of earthly kingdoms to exist forever, shown by the impossibility of iron being mixed with clay (2:41–43). The importance of Daniel's interpretation is to show that God alone, the true God of heaven, is forever and forever and knows the end from the beginning. No matter how powerful earthly kings are, God's wisdom and might change the times and seasons. He removes or destroys and sets up kings and kingdoms according to His sovereign will and purpose. Furthermore, according to Daniel, He is to establish a kingdom *during* the days of these kings which shall never be destroyed, a kingdom not left to other people, but a kingdom not of this world that will overcome all other earthly kingdoms and stand forever (2:17–22, 44–45).

Fulfilled Prophecies Relating to Christ

There are no fewer than 333 Old Testament prophecies concerning the Messiah that were fulfilled in Christ as recorded in the New Testament. Only a partial list will be given here, stating the prophecy, where it is recorded, and where its fulfillment is found in the New Testament.

1. Advent—for Jew and Gentile alike (Gen. 3:15; Num. 24:17; Deut. 18:15; Isa. 9:6 with Gal. 4:4–5).
2. Born of a virgin (Isa. 7:14a with Matt. 1:22–23; Luke 1:30–33).
3. Divinity—Immanuel, God with us (Isa. 7:14b with 2 Cor. 5:19).
4. Born in Bethlehem (Mic. 5:2 with Matt. 2:6; Luke 2:11 [see "Bethlehem" in Index]).
5. Adored by great persons (Ps. 72:10 with Matt. 2:1–12).
6. Herod's slaughter of innocents (Jer. 31 :15 with Matt. 2:16–18).
7. Flight into Egypt (Hos. 11:1 with Matt. 2:13–15).

8. Dwelling in Nazareth that He might be called a Nazarene (Matt. 2:23).

9. Ministry of John the Baptist (Isa. 40:3 with Matt. 3:3; Luke 1:76).

10. Anointed by the Holy Spirit (Isa. 11:1–2 with Matt. 3:16; John 1:33).

11. Galilee, place of public ministry (Isa. 9:1–2 with Matt. 4:12–17).

12. Taking our infirmities (Isa. 53:4 with Matt. 8:16–17).

13. Working miracles (Isa. 61:1–2 with Luke 4:16–19; John 2:11).

14. Spirit of Elijah in John the Baptist (Mal. 4:5 with Matt. 11:10–14).

15. Servant for Gentile salvation (Isa. 42:1 with Matt. 12:15–18).

16. Meekness and compassion (Isa. 42:2–3 with Mark 1:41; Matt. 11:29).

17. Speaking in parables (Isa. 6:9–10 with Matt. 13:13–14, 34).

18. Purification of the temple (Ps. 69:9 with Luke 19:45–46).

19. Riding into Jerusalem upon an ass (Ps. 118:26; Zech. 9:9 with Mark 11:1–11).

20. The Rejected Stone (Ps. 118:22–23 with Matt. 21:42; Luke 20:17).

21. Betrayal by a friend (Ps. 41:9 with Matt. 26:47–50; Luke 22:47–48).

22. Sold for thirty pieces of silver (Zech. 11:13 with Matt. 26:14–16).

23. Disciples forsaking Him (Zech. 13:7 with Matt. 26:31; Mark 14:27, 50).

24. False witnesses against Him (Ps. 35:11 with Matt. 26:59–60).

25. Potter's Field purchased with betrayal money. (This allusion is to Jeremiah 18:1–4; 19:1–3, but more directly to Zechariah 11:11 with Matthew 27:3–10.)

26. Opened not His mouth (Ps. 38:13; Isa. 53:7 with Matt. 27:13–14).

27. Dishonored and shamed (Ps. 69:19 with Matt. 27:18, 29; Mark 15:16–20).

28. Smitten and visage marred (Isa. 50:6; 52:14; Zech. 13:7 with Mark 14:27).

29. Falling beneath the cross (Ps. 109:24 with Matt. 27:32; Luke 23:26).

30. Crucified in prime of life (Ps. 89:45). He entered His ministry at the age of thirty; died three years later.

31. Messiah cut off—hands and feet pierced, wounded for our transgressions (Mic. 5:1; Isa. 53:5–6, 10 with Matt. 27:35a; Mark 15:22; Luke 23:33; John 19:16–18). Christ was crucified in the customary Roman manner—hands and feet being pierced by huge spikes which fastened the body to a wooden cross (Ps. 22:16 with John 20:25–27). [See "Christ, Crucifixion of" in Index.]

32. His death voluntary (Ps. 40:6–8 with John 12:27–33).

33. Casting lots for His garment (Ps. 22:18 with Matt. 27:35; John 19:23–24). How exact is this prophecy! The garment was to be *parted* (torn and divided) among them, but the vesture was to be awarded to *one* by casting *lots*. These are statements that would appear contradictory unless explained by the record of this scene at the cross.

34. Prayer for His enemies (Ps. 109:4; Isa. 53:12 with Luke 23:34).

35. Stared at upon the cross (Ps. 22:17 with Luke 23:35a, 48).

36. Crucified between two thieves

(Isa. 53:12 with Matt. 27:45; Mark 15:28).

37. Mocked by the crowd (Ps. 22:7–8; 109:25 with Matt. 27:39–43).

38. Darkness at the crucifixion (Amos 8:9–10 with Matt. 27:45, Mark 15:33).

39. Forsaken by God (Ps. 22:1 with Matt. 27:46; Mark 15:34).

40. Given vinegar to drink (Ps. 69:21 with Matt. 27:48; John 19:28–29).

41. Friends stood afar off (Ps. 38:11 with John 19:31–36).

42. Committed Himself to God; His death (Ps. 31:5; Isa. 53:12 with Matt. 27:50; Mark 15:37; Luke 23:46; John 19:30).

43. Not a bone broken (Ps. 34:20 with John 19:31–26).

44. His side pierced (Zech. 12:10 with John 19:34, 37).

45. His grave with the rich (Isa. 53:9 with Matt. 27:57–61; John 19:38–42).

46. In the grave three days and three nights. This is not an Old Testament prophecy. When the Jews asked Him for a sign, Jesus referred them to Jonah's being in the great fish for three days and three nights, and that He would be in the earth for that same period of time (Matt. 12:39–40). This we note fulfilled in Matthew 27:57–61 and John 19:38–42.

47. Sabbaths to cease (Hos. 2:11 with Matt. 28:1).

48. The resurrection (Ps. 16:10 with Matt. 28:1–6; John 20:1–12).

God's Everlasting Kingdom

When John the Baptist first started preaching and then introduced Christ, both of them began with this message: "Repent, for the kingdom of *heaven/God* is at hand" (Matt. 4:17; Mark 1:14–15). This is the same spiritual kingdom of which Jesus spoke to Nicodemus when He said no one could enter unless he had been born again (John 3:3, 5, 70).

These two kingdoms are one and the same, as we note in such cross-references as Matthew 13:11 with Mark 4:11 and Luke 8:10. This is confirmed in Matthew 19:23 mentioning the difficulty of a rich man's entering "the kingdom of heaven" and verse 24 saying the same thing about a rich man's entering "the kingdom of God."

This is the "kingdom" of which Christ spoke to Pilate, saying "My kingdom is not of this world" (John 18:36), the "kingdom" the "God of heaven" set up during the Roman period (Dan. 2:44). During this time Christ, the "Stone," who was born to die, finished the transgression, made an end to sins, made reconciliation for iniquity by being crucified, dying, rising from the grave, and bringing in everlasting righteousness to become King of Kings and Lord of Lords (Rev. 13:8; Dan. 9:24; Rom. 4:25; 1 Cor. 15:3–4; 1 Tim. 6:15; Rev. 19:16).

This kingdom, set up from the stone cut out from the mountain without hands, one that no earthly kingdom can stand against, is the one Luke mentions that will have no ending (Dan. 2:44–45 with Luke 1:30–33). This cannot be the millennium (the thousand-year reign of Christ) because that kingdom has an end.

Prophecies Relating to Christ's Return

1. We have already discussed Israel's prophecy from Jerusalem's fall in A.D. 70 to the present time. [See "Israel" in Index.]

2. "But as the days of Noah were, so shall also the coming of the Son of man be, for in those days they were eating and drinking, marrying and giving in marriage" (Matt. 24:37–38). In his day "God saw the wickedness of man was so great in the earth and that every imagination of the thoughts of his heart was only evil continually" (Gen. 6:5).

This is the picture of the world today, especially in America— violence, crime, murder, permissive sex, perilous times, covetousness, crooked politicians, blasphemers, homosexuality, traitors, lovers of pleasures. Leaders in our country "have a form of godliness" but favor immorality (2 Tim. 3:1–5).

3. "Likewise also as it was in the days of Lot . . ." (Luke 17:28). How sinful were they? Sodom's lifestyle was so sinful that she was linked as "sister" with Israel. The city was guilty of pride, self-satisfied (no concern for those less fortunate, the poor and needy), abundance of idleness, haughty, and indulged in abomination, which is sodomy or homosexuality (Ezek. 16:48–52). When the two men came to warn Lot and his family to flee Sodom, the men of the city wanted these two men "that we might know them" (Gen. 19:5). Sodomy or homosexuality was the city's besetting sin—her abomination.

Is not this being fulfilled in our day at home? Political officials condone such activity. They favor permissive sex, even passing out condoms in our high schools, and our former Surgeon General wanted to educate second- and third-graders in sex by teaching them at an early age how to use condoms. She said this was like "taking out insurance like you do on a car or house, it's there in case you need it."

Glorifying sex has become the major cause for the deadly disease AIDS. Say what you will, Christ's prophecy regarding the days of Noah and Lot are sure signs of His prophetic return.

4. What shall be another sign of Christ's return for His own? "Many shall come in my name, saying I am Christ [Messiah], and shall deceive many" (Matt. 24:5). False religions are springing up everywhere in our day. Rev. Moon of Korea is a self-proclaimed messiah, having millions of followers. David Koresh of Waco, Texas, claiming to be Jesus Christ, had many followers who were seduced by him. Even a branch of Jews had an elderly rabbi they claimed to be the messiah.

Many people can easily become brainwashed to accept false teachings. Consider all those who committed suicide under the leadership of Jim Jones. There is no doubt this prophecy of Christ is being fulfilled in our day.

5. Jesus also predicted "wars and rumors of wars—nation shall rise against nation . . . and there shall be famines and pestilences, and earthquakes in various places . . . but the end is not yet" (Matt. 24:6–7). All one needs to do is read the newspaper and listen to the news on TV to see and hear of all this coming to pass on a fast scale. We often hear of earthquakes in South America, Turkey, India, Japan, and California, but as recently as late 1993 there have been some in Lancaster and Reading, Pennsylvania, unusual spots for such a catastrophe.

Think of all the countries in the world today pitted against each other in Europe, Israel and the Arabs,

China, India, South America, the racial hatred in America and Germany. Killing each other seems to be the norm throughout the world—wars and rumors of war.

Think of the pitiful deaths of those in many lands due to famine and starvation. Countless millions have died, and the end doesn't seem to be in sight. Much of it is caused by hatred on the part of government officials, but it is a part of Christ's prediction of events that relate to His soon return.

6. Spiritual death. Paul speaks of a "falling away," Peter makes mention of "false" prophets/teachers, and Jude tells of "deniers" of God and the Lord Jesus Christ, all coming upon the scene prior to Christ's coming to rapture His bride (2 Thess. 2:3; 2 Peter 2:1–3; Jude 4). Modernism and liberalism have done more to lull church members to sleep, teaching "man's opinion" of the Scriptures rather than "Thus saith the Lord." Truths are flatly denied, error has been substituted in its place, and works are now predominant over faith in Jesus Christ for salvation. Fundamentalists are looked upon as those who belong to the dim ages of the past, and to multitudes, churches have become more like social clubs than "soul-saving stations." Pity the pastors who have become "blind leaders of the blind," but what the writers of the Bible said about the last days *is* coming to pass.

Summary

None can dispute the prophetic statements whose fulfilled evidence supports the authenticity of the Scriptures. Since God alone can predict the future and see to it that His prophecies are brought to pass, it is sheer folly to deny Him and ignore His Word. In Christ we have a "more sure word of prophecy, whereunto ye do well that ye take heed, as unto a light that shineth in a dark place, until the Day Star arise in your hearts" (2 Peter 1:19).

SECTION THREE

Archaeology and the Bible

1

The Romance of Archaeology

The subject or science of archaeology, especially as it relates to the Bible, is a valuable tool in giving us living messages from a buried past. It helps to correct mistaken concepts regarding biblical history, which critics have often questioned. Our Western minds, ignorant of Eastern biblical customs, find archaeology helpful in illuminating many portions of Scripture by providing abundant material to give us a better perspective of life and events. Numerous artifacts and objects discovered by the pick and spade of the archaeologist have helped to confirm or verify the historical accuracy of the Word of God.

Too often this subject is presented in technical and lofty language. Technical terms and multiple footnotes cause many people to become frustrated and bogged down, and they don't end up learning anything. While such documentation is vital and necessary, this subject can be made interesting when presented in understandable terms. This we will do in this section.

You will read here of many discoveries, information that will delight you as you open your Bible and read as the Scriptures take on new meaning. With your Bible in hand, imagine the thrill of making your way to a buried city in the land of the Bible. It looks like a hill or mound of dirt to you, but to the trained eye, it is a buried city about to be resurrected! And *you* are going to find something that reveals life as it was centuries ago. At this site (called a "mound" or "tell"), you may unearth any number of clay tablets. There will be recorded business transactions, legal matters, domestic problems. You might even find a tablet or an inscribed stele (monument or pillar) that pinpoints a person or event that happened in a period of history or is mentioned in the Bible itself. You may discover a tomb in which skeletons and personal belongings buried with the deceased unfold life in a given age. You will find countless "potsherds" or "sherds" (broken pieces of pottery from vessels) and cooking utensils. A fairly large piece may have served as a dipper, or if darkened by smoke, it might have been used as a lamp or to carry live coals of fire from one place or house to another. Among the thousands of potsherds unearthed at your dig, you might discover an ostracon, an inscribed pottery fragment often used to scribble a message, give instructions, serve as a receipt or delivery bill, or even deliver a secret message in war, such as was found at the site of Lachish, written when King Sennacherib of Assyria was attacking this city (2 Chron. 32:9). The texture of a sherd and how it was fired helps in giving the approximate time of the finding.

Broken pottery may remind you of Job, who found comfort in scraping his boils with a potsherd (2:8). Potsherds can remind you of our being at enmity with God, without strength, constantly at strife with our neighbors, and alone (Ps. 22:15; Isa. 45:9). Every broken piece will also be a reminder of a sinner's heart—broken and beyond human repair, forgotten like a broken vessel (Prov. 26:23; Ps. 31:12). You may, however, find an unbroken vessel, and that will remind you of a vessel molded by the Potter, one that is useful and ready for the Master's use.

The purpose of this section is to make biblical archaeology so interesting that the Christian can use it as a tool in verifying the truth of the Word of God. As the written Word takes on life, it reveals the Living Word, even Jesus Christ Himself, who is the theme of the Bible and who is God's answer to man's age-old problem—*sin.*

Believers do not need this external proof to accept the Scriptures—they do it by faith—but unbelievers need to see something themselves to arouse their interest, so while God is pleased to "make stones cry out," and to cause "Truth to spring out of the earth," we must use this evidence *now* (Luke 19:40; Ps. 89:11).

2

Basic Archaeological Information

For years critics scoffed at Christians for their faith in the Bible. These unbelieving scholars said we had no proof for historical statements found in the Old Testament. They claimed that many kings and nations mentioned there never existed, that fictitious names were used, or the bulk of such narratives were Jewish tales or folklore.

Discoveries relating to the Bible are too numerous to list in a volume of this nature, but the bulk of what will be mentioned will relate to the historical accuracy of Scripture.

Deciphering Clay Tablets and Inscriptions

Ancient records would be meaningless if scholars could not decipher records found in buried sites. There are two discoveries that came to light that enable scholars to decode ancient languages, thus enabling the world to understand what has been written. The reader should understand that a true archaeologist *does not* excavate to find something that will prove the other fellow wrong. One never knows what will be found.

When our astronauts went to the moon, scientists said they would either find life or that life had previously existed there. Their minds were made up, but moon dust and rocks proved them wrong. Some archaeologists dig to prove the Bible wrong, but so far no discovery that relates to the Bible has done this.

Found in 1799 by one of Napoleon's soldiers at Rosetta, Egypt, the Rosetta Stone is a stone slab about 4 feet high, 2 feet wide, and about 1 foot thick. It is now in the British Museum, London (see fig. 7). Its message had been decreed by priests honoring Ptolemy V (203–181 B.C.). It was written in three languages—Egyptian hieroglyphics in the top section, Egyptian demotic, a written form of hieroglyphics, in the middle section, and Greek in the bottom section.

Scholars could easily read Greek and soon found some of the demotic expressions were "Greekish." In the demotic there were some identifiable places and names of kings in the frames of the hieroglyphics that enabled scholars to break the code of the hieroglyphical symbols.

Figure 7. The Rosetta Stone

Inscriptions of ancient Egypt can easily be read today. The equivalent to our alphabet is shown in figure 8.

In 1835 a British army officer in Persia was attracted to a smooth surface on the side of a rock mountain about 390 feet above the valley, the Behistun Rock (see fig. 9). Climbing up the mountainside at the peril of his life, he discovered there were messages carved in three different languages. The size of the inscribed area is about 12 by 65 feet. The monument above is about 10 by 36 feet and is of King Darius who helped defeat Babylon. He is mentioned ten times in Ezra and once in Nehemiah. The inscription was a record of Darius's deeds and exploits, in which he often praised himself. The languages were ancient Assyrian cuneiform (see fig. 10), old Elamite, and old Persian. Following the same manner in which the Rosetta Stone was deciphered, scholars went

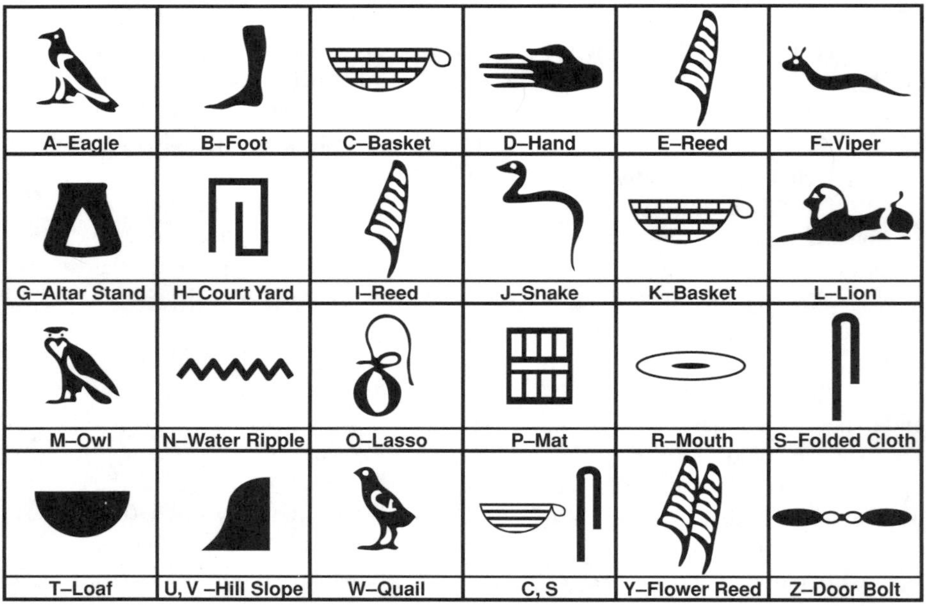

A–Eagle	B–Foot	C–Basket	D–Hand	E–Reed	F–Viper
G–Altar Stand	H–Court Yard	I–Reed	J–Snake	K–Basket	L–Lion
M–Owl	N–Water Ripple	O–Lasso	P–Mat	R–Mouth	S–Folded Cloth
T–Loaf	U, V –Hill Slope	W–Quail	C, S	Y–Flower Reed	Z–Door Bolt

Figure 8. Samples of Egyptian hieroglyphics

Figure 9. A sample of Assyrian cuneiform

Figure 10. The Behistun Rock

from Persian to Elamite to cuneiform and found the message was the same in each. This enabled them to read cuneiform, so that today scholars can easily make known ancient inscriptions found in Mesopotamia.

How Cities Become Buried

Now that we have found out how scholars can go about deciphering ancient writings—Egyptian hieroglyphics and Mesopotamian cuneiform symbols—one other question should be answered before we unearth some discoveries that confirm many portions of Scripture.

How do archaeologists know where to dig? It might come as a surprise to some that drifting sand is but a small factor in the burial of an ancient city. In the desert regions this might be true, but the main reason is the repeated destruction and the rebuilding of a city on the same site (see fig. 11). The original city was built on a hill. This was for protection, since a soldier in a tower on the city wall could see the approach of an enemy from any van-

tage point. Cities were built near springs or waterholes, and houses, buildings, and temples were erected with stones and mud bricks.

Many factors could lead to a city's destruction. Disease, fire, earthquake, and war would cause its citizens to abandon the site. Over a period of time the walls of houses and buildings would collapse, fences would fall down, stray animals would uproot soil, terraces would disintegrate, sand and debris would clog up wells and springs, and winds would pile up debris and refuse in the streets.

Figure 11. The Dothan mound

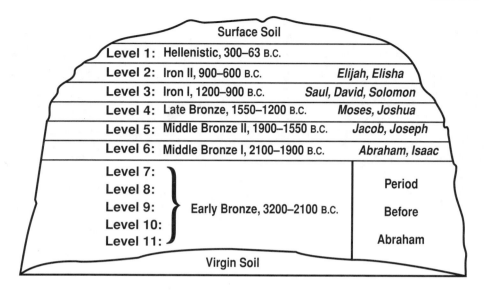

Figure 12. Levels in the Dothan mound

When a nomadic group would later pass by and decide to settle, their custom was to rebuild a new city on the old site, salvaging what stones and material were usable. The chief reason for continuing on the old site was not necessarily the ease with which this could be done or because the water supply was there already, but the desire to follow, wherever possible, the outline of old buildings, particularly temples, to earn the protection of the gods and spirits that previous inhabitants had pacified.

Over a period of centuries numerous cities were built on the same site (see fig. 12). The first city, built on virgin soil, occupied the largest amount of territory. The second city was smaller, and so on, until it was no longer practical to build another city. Over the centuries the last city was covered by debris. The rebuilding of numerous cities on the same site

results in the erection of an artificial mound. It becomes terraced, showing where each city was rebuilt, and looks like an inverted cone. When the Old Testament site of Dothan (Gen. 37:8–17) was excavated, archaeologists went through eleven cities or periods of civilization.

Jerusalem is a good example of a city being destroyed and rebuilt on the same site. The city had been partially destroyed over twenty times. A complete destruction came at the hands of Nebuchadnezzar in 586 B.C. When Israel returned from Babylonian captivity, Ezra and Nehemiah directed the rebuilding of the city—its walls and the temple on the same site. This layer of occupation came more than seventy years after its destruction by Babylon's king, and some of the artifacts of the old level differed from those the children of Israel brought back from Babylon. In A.D. 70, Rome, under Titus, completely destroyed this city again. Jerusalem's site has been the same for centuries. Recent excavations have shown that the Jerusalem of Christ's day is about twenty feet below its present level. This was revealed by the steps leading into the temple area just outside the present southern wall. There is every reason to believe these were the same steps Christ walked up as He approached the temple.

Helpful Definitions

Archaeology

Archaeology is the scientific study of the remains of populated centers, written materials, artifacts, and monuments of the past, both historic and prehistoric. It is an investigation of ancient things that were lost but are now found. Archaeology does not seek to prove anything—it just works with facts, the evidence at hand.

Biblical Archaeology

From a Christian viewpoint, the aim of archaeology is to learn everything possible about life and lands in biblical times. It is interested in geography, for history has its roots in the soil. It reveals how natural barriers protected nations, or became sources of disunity and isolation, what bearings natural resources (water, pasture land, ore, climate) or lack of them had on people, and how livelihood was affected by distance from or nearness to trade routes on land and on sea.

Archaeology supports the historical claim of God's own people and of nations and kingdoms related to Israel's past. Its findings confirm passages of Scripture and illuminate numerous customs.

Tell

A tell is the site to be excavated—an artificial mound or hill formed by successive layers of human occupation, resulting from trash disposal, the ruins of old buildings, houses, city walls, and accumulated dust or sand. [See "Buried Cities" in Index.]

Excavation

An excavation is the scientific uncovering of past civilizations at a given site, often called a *dig*.

Expedition

An expedition consists of an organized team of skilled experts and assistants on a given project. Expeditions are usually conducted by historical societies, universities, museums, or countries.

Surface Soil

The surface soil is the current topsoil of the tell or mound.

Virgin Soil

Virgin soil is the topsoil of a natural hill upon which the first city was built. The archaeologists can tell when they hit virgin soil when they no longer find any evidence of a buried civilization.

Occupational Level

The occupational level is a single level in a tell, or the level of the city at any given time during its existence. It is sometimes called a *strata*.

Potsherds or Shards

Potsherds are broken pieces of pottery. They are important in helping to date a particular level due to type of clay, clay mixture, the way it was fired or baked, painted designs, style, and the signature of the designer.

Ostracon

An ostracon is a pottery fragment upon which a message has been inscribed in ink. The plural of ostracon is ostraca.

Epigraph

An epigraph is writing on a wall, statue, or other surface.

Stele or Stela

A stele is an upright stone slab or monument bearing a sculptured design or an inscription.

Insitu

Insitu is the actual location in which an artifact is discovered.

Artifact

An artifact is anything discovered that has been made by human skill. Artifacts are sometimes called *objects*.

ARCHAEOLOGICAL PERIODS OF THE MIDDLE EAST		
Period Name	**Age**	**Date**
Mesolithic	Middle Stone Age	ca. 10,000 B.C.
Neolithic	New Stone Age	ca. 8000–4300 B.C.
Chalcolithic	Copper Age	4300–3200 B.C. (early/late)
Early Bronze		ca. 3200–2050 B.C. (four periods)
Middle Bronze		ca. 2050–1550 B.C. (two periods)
Late Bronze		ca. 1500–1200 B.C. (two periods)
Iron I		1200–900 B.C.
Iron II		900–600 B.C.
Exilic Period		600–530 B.C.
Persian Period		530–332 B.C.
Hellenistic (Grecian) Period		332–63 B.C. (Ptolemaic/ Seleucid/Hasmonean)
Roman Period		1st century B.C.–5th century A.D.
Late		1800s to present

Chart 1. Archaeological periods of the Middle East

3

Archaeological Tidbits in the Old Testament

When Nineveh was excavated, thousands of clay tablets were discovered that made up the library of King Ashurbanipal of Assyria who reigned from 668 to 626 B.C. He was mentioned by Ezra as Asnappar (4:10) and was quite a history buff. His hobby was collecting old clay tablets. Over 22,000 were found in his palace ruins.

The Creation Tablets

A set of seven tablets, called the Creation Epic, lists six days of creation and one day of rest, which corresponds with our biblical account (see fig. 13).

Another account of creation was found called the Babylonian Creation Account, which also mentions an account corresponding to Genesis 1. In the mid-1950s another creation tablet was found at ancient Ebla in northern Syria. All of these tablets were written centuries before Ashurbanipal and show that the ancients did not believe they evolved but that they were created.

An early Egyptian monument shows their god Khun at a potter's wheel fashioning the shape of a human from soft clay. When he finished, another god stepped up, blew breath on this form of clay, and the human came to life. This corresponds to God's making man out of the earth and breathing into his nostrils the breath of

Figure 13. A Creation tablet

life. While they attribute creation to many gods, yet there is some truth in the accounts. The question is raised, where did they get such information that relates to the biblical account of creation? There can be only one answer: they received it by word of mouth—one generation telling another. This is not as reliable as writing it down, but enough truth was retained to inscribe what they believed about their being divinely created. [See "Creation, Clay Tablets of" in Index.]

Adam and Eve Seals

Also found at Nineveh was a clay impression depicting a man and a woman seated beside a tree with a ser-

Figure 14. A seal of Adam, Eve, and serpent

Figure 15. A seal of a dejected Adam and Eve

pent standing erect behind the woman. This seal shows the main features of the biblical story of the temptation of Eve by a serpent (Gen. 3:1–6; see fig. 14). Another seal shows the impression of a man and woman in a dejected position being driven out of a paradise (see fig. 15), which agrees with their expulsion from the Garden of Eden (Gen. 3:16–24).

The Flood

We have already mentioned evidence supporting the worldwide flood recorded in Genesis 6:11–8:14 [see "Flood, Worldwide" in Index]. There have been several scientists who have made trips up the mountains of Ararat. Some have said there were sightings of an outline of a huge boat, but so far the ark has not been discovered. However, from the library of Ashurbanipal has come a clay tablet called the Gilgamesh Epic, which records the account of the Babylonian flood. Utnapishtim (Mesopotamia's Noah; see fig. 16) relates his version of the flood as that the gods were determined to destroy humankind with a flood and gave warning to such. Instructions were given to build an ark and take into it the seed of all living things. The ark was built, a family was taken inside, and the flood began at the appointed time. Later the ark came to rest on Mount Nisir, and Utnapishtim sent forth a dove, a swallow, and a raven. The dove and the swallow returned, but the raven saw that the waters were abated and did not return. All left the ark, and sacrifices were offered to the gods by Utnapishtim.

The Gilgamesh Epic may be gauged by its impact upon other nations, for as early as 2000 B.C. it was known in at least four other languages.

A fragment found at Megiddo in northern Palestine in 1955 reveals the Epic was known there in the fourteenth century B.C. Although the records do not agree in every detail, at least it appears that archaeological discoveries of the Babylonian account of the flood and the biblical account of the flood refer to the same one. The pictures show impressions from clay seals of people and animals entering Utnapishtim's ark.

Archaeology has produced no fewer than thirty-three separate tablets of this gigantic flood that may be consulted among peoples and races living today. Of this large number of independent witnesses, only two, the Egyptians and Scandinavians, fail to coincide with the biblical account of the flood. In these records, twenty-eight mention an ark as the method which rescued the remnant, thirty mentioned that the ark rested on a

Figure 16. A Babylonian account of Noah

mountain, twenty-nine state that birds were sent out to bring back the good news that the waters were receding, thirty mentioned the divine favor which dwelt upon the survivors, and thirty-one mention an act of worship as the survivors left the ark. A comparison

COMPARISON OF BIBLICAL AND ARCHAEOLOGICAL FLOOD ACCOUNTS

Genesis Records	Archaeological Records
There was a deluge	There was a deluge
because of sin	because of human failure
A warning was given	The remnant was warned
An ark was built	A boat was made
A remnant was saved	A select few were saved
A divine act enabled escape	There was a divine escape
Animals were preserved	Animals were spared
Race of man destroyed	Race perished
Ark under divine care	Boat saved by the gods
Ark settled on mts. of Ararat	Boat settled on mts. of Armenia
Remnant offered sacrifice	Remnant worshiped with sacrifice
God promised not to destroy man again	Gods repented and pledged peace
Sign was given—a rainbow	A sign was given
Remnant repeopled the earth	All men came from these few

Chart 2. Comparison of biblical and archaeological flood accounts

Figure 17. The Weld-Blundell Prism

the end of this "pre-flood" list of kings, the record says that the flood swept over the earth. A line is drawn which divided the account of the pre-flood kings. Truth certainly has sprung out of the earth in defense of the flood and the Word of God (Ps. 85:11).

The Tower of Babel

The account of the building of this tower is recorded in Genesis 11. According to Genesis 6, people had become so evil that God sent a flood to destroy them all, except Noah and his family.

After the flood, in due time, people sought to build a tower to heaven to make a name for themselves (see fig. 18). They may have thought that another flood would come upon the earth and such a tower would be an avenue of escape. While they were building, God came down, detected the purpose of their work, and confounded their tongues. Since groups could not understand one another, the work came to nothing, and they were scattered.

of the creation accounts is show in the chart (see fig. 16).

The Weld-Blundell Prism, a clay record (see fig. 17) found in 1923 in lower Mesopotamia and written about 100 years before Abraham, lists eight kings who ruled before the flood. At

An interesting archaeological

Figure 18. Ziggurat (tower) at Ur

discovery came to light from secular history to confirm this portion of Scripture. A monument discovered in this particular region of Ur mentions king Ur-Nammu, who received orders from his gods to build a ziggurat (tower). The record, a monument, or stele, is nearly 10 feet high and 5 feet wide. At the top stands the king in an attitude of prayer. He is setting out a compass, pick and trowel, and mortar baskets to begin construction. In panels beneath him are men working, scaling ladders as the tower rises (see fig. 19).

A clay tablet was unearthed that gave the account of the building of this tower. The gods were highly offended and in a single night they destroyed what had been built and impeded their progress. They were scattered abroad and their speech was strange. This tablet account confirms Genesis 11:1–9.

The City of Ebla

The Mardikh mound in northern Syria was excavated in 1964, and the buried city, according to an inscription, was identified as Ebla. Over 17,000 clay tablets were found, dating the city to ca. 2450 B.C. The tablets are in two languages, which make it easier for scholars to decipher. There are such subjects as tariffs, treaties, tributes, judicial proceedings, and religion.

Of significance to the Christian was the discovery of a creation account, which ties in closely with our Genesis record. A flood account was also unearthed. One tablet mentioned the names of Sodom and Gomorrah—the earliest mention of these cities outside the Bible.

This is good evidence from secular history as to the existence of these cities, which some scholars had denied. Of special interest is the name "Urusalima" (Jerusalem), this being the earliest known reference to this city. Reference to a god whose name has the same root as the Yahweh of the Old Testament is significant, showing that many in that day were monotheistic. Names like Eber of Genesis 10 (Abraham's ancestor), Adam, Israel, Saul, and David appear hundreds of years before such names were written down in Scripture. *Time* (October 18, 1976) quoted a high-ranking university scholar as saying that he thought of ancestors like Eber as symbolic. He didn't believe that they should be regarded as historic, at least not until these tables were found.

It is thought provoking that finding such tablets as those at Ebla consistently support the Bible as a thoroughly

Figure 19. Stele of Ur-Nammu

accepted record. And there's more to come as tablets are deciphered.

Ur of the Chaldees and the Hittites

Abraham, the man of faith, came from Ur of the Chaldees, located in southern Mesopotamia. Humans were thought to be ignorant in Abraham's day, but excavations at Ur in 1923 revealed that civilization was highly advanced at least 1,000 years before Abraham's day.

Craftsmanship in gold was second to none, as tombs revealed. Children in Abraham's day were taught mathematics and writing skills. One tablet contained a multiplication table of nine (9 x 1 to 9 x 9). Also included in their curriculum was geography and, of all things, ancient history.

Discoveries revealed much sordid paganism, which ties in with Abraham's father's serving other gods (Josh. 24:2). Ur was a city filled with sin and great wickedness, as evidence shows. Fire, the stars, and the forces of nature were worshiped. Religious prostitution, sodomy, and licentious ceremonies were common in his day. But we see the grace of God in singling out one man who served the true God, and God called Abraham out of the land with great promises—a land and "in thee shall all the nations of the earth be blessed" (Gen. 12:1–3).

When God called Abraham from Ur, He promised him a land comprised of many nations, one of which was the Hittite (Gen. 15:18–21). No evidence from secular history had ever indicated these people ever existed. For this reason critics of the Bible ridiculed the historical accuracy of such a statement in the Bible.

Hittites are mentioned at least forty times in Scripture. In 1870 evidence began to come to light. The Tel el-Amarna tablets (which will be mentioned later) were found in Egypt. They mentioned the activities of a Hittite army in Palestine. These letters hinted that the Hittite people were based north of Palestine in Asia Minor. In the early 1900s in Boghazkoy, central Turkey, God produced "dead Hittite stones" with living messages. As the archaeologists excavated, inscriptions on massive stone buildings showed that the Hittite Empire flourished in Abraham's day and that it formed a worthy third with two other empires of importance—Babylonia-Assyria and Egypt.

Groups of Hittites were settled in Palestine, just as some Chinese are settled in California and French in Canada. When Abraham lived in Canaan he met some Hittites and purchased the cave of Machpeleh in Hebron from them for a burial place (Gen. 23). When God gave assurance to Moses that He would fight Israel's battles for them, He said He would drive out the Hittites (Exod. 23:28). Joshua met opposition from Hittites when he invaded Canaan (Josh. 9:1–2). King David had an affair with the wife of a Hittite (2 Sam. 11:3–4). Hittites were real people and this nation was a fact of history.

An inscription was found in Egypt showing the defeat of a Hittite king before a victorious Pharaoh. Between the two was the Hittite's daughter, being given as a tribute. Daughters or wives were often given as a peace treaty among nations (see fig. 20).

Who knows what kings brought gifts to Solomon? They often gave him wives and princesses because of his fame and power. This might explain how he got so many heathen women who turned his heart against God (1 Kings 11:1–8). The Hittites clearly *did* exist, and Solomon got at least one of them for a wife (v. 1).

The Nuzi Tablets

When these tablets were discovered in northern Syria, they were traced back to the days of the patriarchs. Some of the biblical accounts find reflection in many Nuzi laws. One law stipulated that if a married couple did not bear children, the wife would permit her husband to lie with a handmaid to produce a child. This will help us to understand why Sarah told Abraham to have relations with Hagar.

The law also stated that if friction arose between the wife and the mistress, the wife could order both the mistress and the child to leave. Sarah followed both these laws (Gen. 16:1–6). We find the same law applying to Rachel, Leah, and Jacob (Gen. 30:1–9). The selling of one's birthright was also a common practice under Nuzi law, which might explain why Esau thought nothing of selling his to Jacob (Gen. 25:29–34).

Teraphim (Family Gods)

When God commanded Jacob to leave his uncle Laban and go back to Bethel, his family packed their belongings and left. Rachel stole the family gods of her father and hid them in the camel's furniture or saddle (Gen. 31:3, 17–18, 34). When Laban discovered that his gods were missing, he spent several days chasing after Rachel and Jacob. He searched among Jacob's goods but found nothing, and Rachel would not get off the camel for him to search its furniture. Laban had to go back home without his teraphim (see fig. 21).

Figure 20. Depiction of a Hittite princess being given as a peace offering

What was the significance of these gods or images? Under Nuzi law, they not only represented a family's religion, but served as title deeds to one's possessions—lands, houses, livestock, and servants. And why did Rachel steal them? She knew that one of the Nuzi laws stated that the one in possession of the images could go to court, and in the presence of witnesses, state they were his, and these family gods and what they represented then belonged to the one who presented them as his. Possibly Rachel was trying to get even with her father so she could give them to Jacob. Her father had promised her to Jacob, but after Jacob worked seven years for her, Laban gave him Leah and he had to

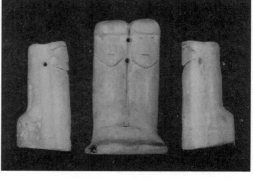

Figure 21. Examples of teraphim (family gods)

work seven years more for Rachel. Laban gave Jacob all the bad cattle and kept the best. He changed Jacob's wages ten times. Rachel figured her father did not treat her husband right, and by her stealing these gods—title deeds—she could get even with Laban, and Jacob could lay claim to all his father-in-law possessed.

We have no record that Rachel told her husband about this matter, but it is quite possible she did, for when they were near Bethel, Jacob made all in his group cleanse themselves and told them to put away all the strange or foreign gods. He buried a fortune simply because God meant more to him than material possessions (Gen. 35:1–7).

Figure 22. A depiction of taskmasters

Joseph in Egypt

The story of Joseph's being sold by his brothers at Dothan, taken to Egypt and sold as a slave, becoming a servant of an Egyptian officer named Potiphar, later imprisoned due to false charges made against him by Potiphar's wife, interpreting a dream of Pharaoh, and then being elevated to second in command of Pharaoh is told in Genesis 37; 39:1–41:44.

Archaeological finds show that Asiatic groups began filtering into Egypt about 1900 B.C. and finally gained control of the land. They were known as "shepherd kings" and were the rulers when Joseph was given his high position. Being Semites, they acted kindly toward other Semites (of which Joseph was one) and Bedouins (nomadic people). They introduced the horse-drawn chariot, the bow and arrow, and cultural ideas during their rule in Egypt.

Since foreigners, not native Egyptians, ruled Egypt at that time, it is interesting to note that Moses called Potiphar an Egyptian (Gen. 39:1). If the Pharaoh had been an Egyptian, to say simply that Potiphar was an officer of the Pharaoh would imply he was a hired native—an Egyptian. A Hyksos would not be obligated to hire an Egyptian as a bodyguard, but this he had done. The expression becomes perfectly clear because it reveals the local conditions at that time.

When Joseph's family came to Egypt to live, Joseph gave some peculiar advice to his father. As recorded in Genesis 46:34; 47:3, they were to tell the Pharaoh they were shepherds, in spite of the fact that all shepherds were an abomination to the Egyptians. To tell an Egyptian king that they were shepherds would be to prejudice themselves immediately, but to tell this to a Hyksos king was the same thing as saying, "We are nomads or shepherds the same as you." They were welcomed as allies and given choice land in Goshen (Gen. 47:1–11).

Israel in Egyptian Bondage

Under the Hyksos rule the family of Jacob grew and multiplied and were treated kindly. Sometime after Joseph's death, Egypt regained her land and there arose a king who knew not Joseph (Acts 7:17–19). Fearing the multiplied masses of the Israelites, this king, believed by some to be Ahmose, put burdensome tasks upon them and made their lives hard with bondage "in mortar and in brick." Two cities built by the Israelites were Pithom and Rameses (Exod. 1:11–14). These sites have been excavated and house and wall foundations reveal bricks, some with and some without straw. Pharaoh gave orders to the taskmasters (see fig. 22) that straw should be withheld from them in making bricks (Exod. 5:6–11; see fig. 23).

An ancient document found in Egypt called the Papyrus Anastasi relates the complaint of an Egyptian officer whose duty it was to supervise construction in the land of Goshen. "Work stopped on all projects," he said, "because I do not have any materials. . . . I do not have any straw." A huge monument was found in the ruins of Rameses showing Rameses receiving praise from his god for having built the cities of Pithom and Rameses (see fig. 24). At the base of this monument are carvings of Semite slaves who built these cities and could well represent Israelites. Pictured is a pharaoh representing a taskmaster.

Figure 23. Straw in bricks

Figure 24. Stele of Ramsses

Figure 25. A statue of Hatshepsut

Moses in Pharaoh's Palace

Based on various archaeological discoveries, it appears that Moses was born at the beginning of the reign of Thutmose I whose daughter, Hatshepsut (see fig. 25), was most likely the princess who found Moses in the bulrushes (Exod. 2:1–10). Moses was raised in the palace and schooled in all the wisdom and sciences of the Egyptians until he was forty years old (Acts 7:17–23). Hatshepsut later became queen of Egypt and was known as the "Female King." She had no legal heir to the throne and wanted Moses to be called "the son of Pharaoh's daughter" (Heb. 11:24). This would fit him for any office in the government, even the throne.

He became familiar with court life, the military, their sciences and litera-ture, their law, and the grandeur and pomp of the religious life. At this time in ancient history, Egypt was unsurpassed in civilization by any other peoples, and what Moses acquired during his tenure in the palace groomed him for leadership of the Israelites for the Exodus.

The Riches of Egypt

An interesting archaeological discovery has given us the answer to the riches of Egypt mentioned in Hebrews 11:26. The world could only imagine what this wealth was until Howard Carter discovered King Tutankhamon's tomb in the valley of the kings, located on the west side of the Nile River opposite Thebes, about 500 miles south of Cairo. Pharaohs would have their tombs hewn inside rock mountains. The longer they lived the more rooms were hewn. Their religious beliefs taught them to prepare for eternity, so personal belongings were buried with them to have and use in the hereafter.

Tut's tomb was the first to be discovered that had not been plundered. His mummified body was found inside a solid gold coffin, which was inside two other gold coffins. His body was bedecked with 143 gold and jeweled ornaments and his face was covered with a gold mask. The weight of the three coffins was about 2,000 pounds. By today's gold standard of $370.00 per ounce, the total value of these three coffins would be almost $12,000,000.

His furniture was gold overlay; there were numerous gold statues depicting activities of his life, alabaster vases and precious stones with an estimated value of tens of millions of dollars. Keep in mind that these were the riches of just *one* pharaoh!

Had Moses chosen to be called the son of Pharaoh's daughter, he could have been in line for Egypt's throne, he would have been an Egyptian god (each pharaoh was considered a god), and he could have been worth more than the mind could imagine. He chose rather to have the riches of Christ than the treasures in Egypt, so by faith he forsook Egypt and endured as seeing Him who is invisible (Heb. 11:24–27).

Moses didn't know the verse as we do, but he knew that it would profit him nothing if he gained the whole world and lost his own soul (Mark 8:36). He cared not what others might say about his stand for God; he just wanted to be linked with those who had their eyes on the Lord. Moses taught us that it takes courage to stand up and be counted, but that it also takes more courage to keep standing after one has been counted.

Plagues in Egypt: Israel's God vs. Egyptian Gods

One of the best accounts of salvation in the Old Testament is found in Exodus 6. Archaeological evidence shows God's judgment in chapters 7 through 11 before He provides redemption in the Passover in chapter 12. Israel was in bondage with no avenue of escape apart from God's deliverance. This shows people's bondage to sin and God's deliverance through Christ. In Exodus 5:1 "Moses and Aaron went in and told Pharaoh, thus saith the LORD God of Israel, Let my people go . . ." Because Pharaoh defied God, the Lord said, "Now shalt thou see what I will do to Pharaoh" (Exod. 6:1).

God executed the ten plagues to bring Pharaoh to his knees. Were the plagues miracles performed by God, or were they events that "happened" as phenomenons, based on *natural reasoning*, as the critics of Scripture say? God had prophesied Israel's bondage in a land not theirs. This prophecy was fulfilled in Israel's tenure in Egypt, and the time of their stay was coming to a close. Judgment was to befall this nation, and Israel was to leave with great substance (Gen. 15:13–14). Pharaohs had practically ground the Israelites into such a position that escape was impossible. To be delivered, God must intervene. Judgment was pronounced upon the Egyptian gods to show this pharaoh his helplessness in opposing God and His people (Exod. 12:12).

The Ten Plagues were an attack against Egypt's pantheon. It has been said that at one time Egypt had approximately 2,500 gods and goddesses. These plagues were against the so-called power of such gods and particularly against the power the pharaohs were supposed to wield.

Pre-plague Snake (Exod. 7:9–12)

The cobra was a symbol of ruling power. The crowns of the pharaohs had the head of the cobra, ready to strike. When Moses' rod became a snake as did the magicians' rods, Moses' rod ate theirs. This miracle of God in destroying Pharaoh's magicians' snakes was a symbol of overcoming Pharaoh's power. This helps explain why God said, "Now shalt thou see what I will do to Pharaoh" (Exod. 6:1). The serpent goddess was Wadjet, demon prefect of the underworld.

Plague One: The Nile River Turned into Blood (Exod. 7:14–25)

This miracle was against the god Hapi, supposed spirit of the Nile during flood season, fertilizing the land and "giver of life to all men." The annual inundation was called "the arrival of Hapi."

The Nile was the transformed lifeblood of Osiris. Turning the Nile into blood was also an affront to another of Egypt's chief gods. The fish god, Hatmeyt, was helpless to prevent all the fish in the Nile from dying. Critics of this miracle simply say that the red color of the Nile was due to red clay sweeping into the river from the southern highlands.

Plague Two: Frogs (Exod. 8:1–15)

The frog-headed goddess, Heqet, played a part in creation. She was the head of Egypt's oldest fertility cult. With the land being filled with frogs, Heqet was helpless to control the rapid multiplication of these "gods," which became objects of loathing and created a stench throughout the land.

Plague Three: Lice (Exod. 8:16–19)

In a book on the gods of Egypt by Wallis Budge, there is no mention of a god of lice in the pantheon. However, since Pharaoh's magicians could not give answer for the lice upon the people and beasts, they informed Pharaoh that this "is the finger of God," which caused Pharaoh to harden his heart. Some have suggested that the lice were gnats.

Plague Four: Flies (beetles; insects: Exod. 8:20–32)

Since "flies" is in italics in the King James Version, in all probability this plague was against the god Khephera, god of resurrection or recreation. This was a scarab-headed god under Atum or Ra. It could be against

the "fly god," which was related to sorcery. No name has yet been found for this god. As a symbol of bravery, soldiers were decorated with a golden fly. Uatchit has been suggested as the "fly god."

Although God at times used nature to perform miracles to confound the enemy (e.g., Josh. 10:11–14), natural reasoning says that the red clay contaminated the Nile River, choking the fish. The fish in turn moved to the swamps where the frogs lived and infected them. This caused the frogs to move out on land and invade people's houses. The frogs died without water, and flies and lice began feeding on their carcasses.

Plague Five: Murrain, or anthrax (Exod. 9:1–7)

This plague primarily attacked cattle, the bull god Apis, which was the sacred cattle of Hathor, the cow-headed love goddess. Murrain, or anthrax, was an infectious disease common to cattle. It appeared as malignant pustules—a type of skin cancer—and was often transferred to humans. Actually, this plague was against Pharaoh, who worshiped Hathor.

Other gods associated with cattle (and animals) were Ptah (creator of gods) and Amon (god of life and reproduction).

A grave was discovered by archaeologists near the Pyramids with twenty-nine sarcophagi (stone coffins) containing the mummified bodies of sacred bulls. These animals were bathed daily, and the preparation for burial with oils, spices, and ointments cost as much as $30,000 for each. Four-footed beasts were considered gods by the Egyptians (Rom. 1:23).

Plague Six: Boils (Exod. 9:8–12)

This plague was against the god of healing, Im-Hotep. Although Im-Hotep was a nobleman, he was not deified at the time of the Exodus but was revered as a god.

The goddess Sekhet (or Sekhmet) was also known for her healing powers. However, she was helpless because the boils were also directed against the priests or magicians using their craft to protect Pharaoh.

How does the critic explain the plagues of the cattle and boils? The red clay poisoned the Nile River and its floodwaters poisoned the soil, which gave rise to a pestilence that affected animals feeding on grass and grain. Because people were closely associated with domestic animals, especially cattle, people became infected from meat and the symptoms resulted in boils.

Plague Seven: Hail (Exod. 9:13–15)

Nut was the sky goddess, "mother of the sun-god Ra whom she swallowed in the evening and gave birth in the morning." She was to protect houses and lands from any destruction which descended from the heavens, but hail brought devastation and Nut was helpless.

The gods Reshpu and Qetesh were to control the natural elements except for light, and Set was supposed to be in charge of winds and storms, but neither could control the storm of hail. Exodus 9:31 mentions that flax and barley were destroyed. This helped to cause a food shortage as well as a shortage of flax, which was used for clothing and the wrapping of mummies.

Plague Eight: Locusts (Exod. 10:1–20)

The locust-headed god was Senehem. During this plague, the locusts were so thick that the "eye of the earth" was darkened (v. 5). One of the epithets of the sun-god Ra was "the eye of Ra." By causing darkness while the sun was shining, Ra was discredited. The plague of locusts was also directed against Geb, the god of vegetation, and Min, the fertility god who ripened grain.

Natural reasoning, denying God's miracle-working power, says that while hail is practically unheard of in Egypt, probably unusual atmospheric conditions resulted in such a storm. Since hail ruined foliage and crops, locusts, or grasshoppers, swarmed the land looking for food.

Plague Nine: Darkness (Exod. 21:27)

Next to Pharaoh, the greatest god was the sun. The sun-god Amon-Ra was the principal deity of the pantheon. He made possible all growth in humans, animals, and plants. Pharaoh called himself "son of the sun." With three days of only darkness upon the Egyptians, the principal deity was scorned.

Tragically, the critic of the Bible says that a dust storm, which blew in from Libya, caused the darkness over the land.

Plague Ten: Death of the first-born (Exod. 11–12)

Pharaoh's right to rule rested in his divinity. Each Pharaoh was believed to have been begotten by the sun god Amon-Ra. The last plague was not only against the supreme god of Egypt, Pharaoh himself, but against the future

Pharaoh, his son. This prophetic plague was that the firstborn of man and beast were to die, and the Bible answer was fulfilled (Exod. 12:12–13, 29–30).

Since none of the Israelites died because of their obedience in sprinkling blood upon the doorposts, the unbeliever is left without a word. Even if God used nature in connection with His miracles, He was not only showing the futility of the Egyptian gods but revealing to Israel that He is the God of gods and the Lord of Lords—the God over all gods.

Israel acted out her faith and escaped death in the family. Pharaoh could have saved his firstborn, but his act of faith would have destroyed the Egyptian system of gods, since he would have acknowledged that the God of Israel is God and his were false.

Why didn't Pharaoh believe? As a god he would have lost his divinity. But God hardened his heart. Why? If Pharaoh had let Israel go when God said, "Let My people go," all the gods of Egypt would have retained their greatness in the eyes of both the Egyptians and the Israelites. The people had to suffer the plagues to demonstrate that all gods but God (Yahweh) were nothing.

Moses' father-in-law, Jethro, gave good testimony that God had delivered Israel out of the hand of Pharaoh saying, "Now know that the Lord is greater than all gods. Yes, in the [very] thing in which the Egyptians dealt proudly, God showed Himself infinitely superior to all other gods" (Gen. 18:10–11 *The Amplified Bible*).

Summary of the Plagues

In the section on prophecy, mention was made about the idolatry of the ancient Egyptians leading to the destruction of the city of Memphis or Noph. Archaeology has given us the information necessary to learn about the gods of the plagues that wrought havoc with Pharaoh and his religious beliefs. As each plague struck a god, judgment befell an object worshiped by the people. The Nile River becoming blood exposed the helplessness of this "god" to give its worshipers a flood to fertilize the land. A sudden increase in the number of animals and insects who were considered deities, and the disease and death inflicted on them, was God's way of showing the Egyptians how helpless their gods were to deliver themselves. There were gods of nature, but hail and darkness proved that Israel's God was Master over nature. When boils afflicted the people, even the beasts they worshiped could not cure them.

Figure 26. A golden calf idol

Ultimately it took the death of Pharaoh's firstborn to make him realize he and his gods were helpless. This brought him to his knees and Israel was set free (Exod. 7:14–12:32).

The Golden Calf in the Wilderness

Solomon began to reign about 970 B.C. During the fourth year of his reign, 480 years had lapsed since the Exodus (1 Kings 6:1). This would date the Exodus at about 1448 B.C., putting it in the reign of Amen-hotep II, the Pharaoh before whom Moses and Aaron appeared (Exod. 7:7).

Having been granted permission to leave, Israel gathered her meager belongings, received jewels of gold and raiment from the Egyptians, and left. God's miracle of opening the Red Sea delivered His people but destroyed Pharaoh's army (Exod. 14:5–31).

Arriving at Mount Sinai, Moses ascended the mountain to receive the Ten Commandments, or the Decalogue. The Israelites persuaded Aaron to fashion a molten calf from the gold earrings they received from the Egyptians. They began to eat, drink, and be merry and worship the calf (Exod. 32:1–6).

The calf was probably fashioned after one of Egypt's gods, as shown in figure 26. Archaeologists have found a number of these figurines. A silver one was recently discovered at Ashkelon, the capital of the ancient Canaanite kings. It was dated at about 3,500 years old.

When Moses learned of Israel's frivolity and idolatry, he flung down and broke the tablets of stone (Exod. 32:15–19). Calves were again used by Jeroboam in the Northern Kingdom of Israel in opposition to worship of God

Figure 27. Copper looking glasses on shelves with potsherds

in the Temple at Jerusalem (1 Kings 12:25–29).

Looking Glasses

Archaeological discoveries have shed some light on the looking glasses the women of Israel gave as material for use in the tabernacle (Exod. 38:8). In giving a list of the material used in the tabernacle, glass is not mentioned. When the Israelites left Egypt and were given what they required from the Egyptians (Exod. 12:31–36), this must have included looking glasses. A number of them have been found in tombs. They are copper mirrors, shaped like modern vanity mirrors (see fig. 27). When highly polished, they gave an excellent reflection.

The Code of Hammurabi

The discovery of the Code of Hammurabi in 1901 in Shushan (Persia) revealed a series of several moral laws and customs of the Patriarchal Age. This code was written about three centuries before Moses. King Hammurabi is

Figure 28. The Code of Hammurabi

shown receiving laws from the sun-god Shamash, the god of justice. As he stands before Shamash in an act of worship, he is given a ring and a rod, and in turn he attributes to Shamash the inspiration he received to gather laws of justice in a code.

The basalt stele, which contains 282 laws, is 8 feet tall and about 2 feet in diameter (see fig. 28). The laws dealt with three classes of people—upper class free, middle class free, and slave. Fees and wages were set for each group. The laws touch on nearly every phase of life—marriage, property rights, rights of children, and divorce. Many of the laws correspond to biblical laws. The prohibition against sorcery corresponds with Deuteronomy 18:10, false testimony with Deuteronomy 19:18–19, theft with Exodus 22:1–4, kidnapping with Exodus 21:16, adultery and incest with Leviticus 20:10, 17, striking a parent with Exodus 21:15, 17, and murder with Exodus 21:15, to name a few.

Violations of many laws were punishable by death, but mutilation was imposed for crimes which did not warrant death. Among these were cutting off the tongue at its roots, severing the ear, hand, or breast, or blinding. For a son who struck his father, his hand was severed. If a physician did not succeed with a patient's operation and had to "bury his mistake," he too was buried. If the patient suffered loss of a hand or eye, so did the doctor. Whatever one did to another physically, they reaped the same. It was an eye for an eye and a tooth for a tooth.

When critics of the Bible learned that such laws predated Moses, they said that Moses copied these and other laws. For some time they appeared successful, but after a careful comparison of Hammurabi's laws with those of Moses, it was found that Hammurabi, under the approval of his sun-god Shamash, permitted degrees of immorality. The Mosaic Law, far superior to Hammurabi's, condemns the practice of sin, demonstrating that the Hebrew laws dealing with morality and holiness were not derived from other sources as the critics claimed.

Israel's Wilderness Journey

After Israel left Sinai, they journeyed northward to Kadesh-barnea (Deut. 1:2). Sending spies to get firsthand information about the land of Canaan, the majority reported the cities were well fortified (see fig. 29), and there were giants in the land. This caused Israel to fear, and she turned back to roam in the wilderness for another thirty-eight years (Num. 13:1–14:39). Moses sought permission to pass through the land of the Edomites but was forbidden and had to go south to the Gulf of Akaba (Red Sea) and turn on the east side of the mountains of Seir [See "Edom, City of" in Index]. Archaeologists have discovered the ruins of a number of well-fortified cities that caused Israel to encircle that region.

The Fall of Jericho

The account of Israel's defeat of Jericho is found in Joshua 6. Critics often said such stories as the walls falling flat were nothing more than folklore, old maids' tales, and Jewish mythology, especially since the walls came tumbling down at the blowing of trumpets and shouts from the Israelites. In the late 1920s, Professor Garstang of the Palestine Exploration Fund excavated the city and found the walls had fallen exactly as the Bible states. Usually in ancient wars battering rams and other engines of war were used to force the stones to fall inward. But the stones on Jericho's wall foundation

Figure 29. A depiction of a fortified city

indicated they had crumbled—fallen flat and rolled outward. All Israel had to do was climb over the stones and invade the city. Not only that, but there was sufficient evidence to show they had burned the city (Josh. 6:24). Even though many houses were of stone, there was much wood to burn— roof beams, doors, and furniture.

Kathleen Kenyon of the British Archaeological School excavated the site again in the 1950s and tried to discredit Garstang's findings. However, in a recent article in *Archaeology and Biblical Research* titled "Uncovering the Truth at Jericho," Bryant Woods reveals there is sufficient evidence to show that Jericho was destroyed as the Bible records, and that it was done in the late 1400s B.C.

The Tel el-Amarna Tablets

In 1887, a woman was rummaging through rubbish at a place called Tel el-Amarna south of Cairo, Egypt, and found a number of clay tablets. Since they were in cuneiform, not in Egyptian hieroglyphics, they were suspected to be forgeries. Upon close examination they were found to be written by officials and "kinglets" of

Figure 30. Merneptah (Israel) Stele

the Canaanite cities of Palestine pleading for help from Egypt because of invasions and hostilities by the *HA-RI-BU*, believed to be a code name for Israel. They date from the time of Joshua's invasion of Canaan.

One of the letters said, "The Haribu plunder all the lands of the king. If archers are here this year then the lands of the king, my lord, will remain. But if the archers are not here, then the lands of the king, my lord, are lost. All the lands of the king, my lord, are going to ruin."

Another inscription had been written to an Egyptian official, Harmhab, informing him that their Canaanite cities had been burned, that they had barely escaped with their lives, and that during their flight from their homeland they had lived like beasts of the field. Since this episode had taken place during the time of Israel's invasion of Canaan, it is plausible to identify these people as those who had been defeated under Joshua and escaped with their lives.

Joshua's Altar at Mount Ebal

In Deuteronomy 27:4–8, God told Moses that the children of Israel were to erect an altar on Mount Ebal when they entered the Promised Land. Part of the Israelites were to ascend Mount Gerizim and pronounce the blessings of God if they obeyed Him, and the other half were to ascend Mount Ebal and pronounce the judgments of God if they disobeyed Him (Deut. 11:29). After a number of victories in the land, Joshua obeyed the commandment given by God to Moses and built an altar for a sacrifice on Mount Ebal (Josh. 8:30–33).

In the mid-1980s an Israeli archaeologist discovered a huge stone altar on Mount Ebal, believed to be the one built by Joshua. It measures 25 x 30 feet and is several feet high. Nine hundred forty-two bones of 50 to 100 animals—goats, sheep, cattle (oxen)—were found in the debris, the only animals permitted in biblical sacrifices. There is sufficient evidence in pottery and artifacts to show that this altar dates back to the days of Joshua, about 3,400 years ago.

The Merneptah Stele

A question is often raised why there is no mention of Israel on any record in Egypt, especially since Joseph held an important position second to Pharaoh, and why there was no mention of Israel's being in bondage. The answer lies in the fierceness of national and kingly pride.

Nations in those days would record only what would enhance their position among other nations and how one king would outdo the other. To record anything about the Hyksos rulers would be demeaning to the Egyptians.

Many times a succeeding king, out of jealousy, would destroy monuments left by his predecessor. If any records had been left by the Hyksos mentioning Joseph or Israel, they could have easily been destroyed. Hatshepsut, for example, could have constructed a monument recounting Moses' deeds, but her brother hated her so much that when he succeeded her he may have defaced many of her monuments.

Merneptah, a pharaoh who ruled Egypt from about 1224–1214 B.C., left an inscribed monument on which we have the first mention of Israel (see fig. 30). It refers to his exploits against foreign powers, such as sea peoples in Phoenicia and the Israelites in Canaan. The enlarged line in the picture states: *"Israel is laid waste, his seed is not; Hurru [i.e., Syria] is become a widow for Egypt."* This does not imply that Israel does not exist. The expression "his seed is not" refers to Israel as a designated people in Canaan who were not yet regarded as a settled political unit such as they became later under the kingship rule of Saul.

Ruins of the City of Hazor

Much evidence has come to light from the pick and spade of the archaeologist showing the destruction of cities during Israel's invasion of Canaan. The city of Hazor, located northeast of the Sea of Galilee, is a good example. Excavations were conducted there in the late 1950s. Joshua had destroyed the city about 1400 B.C. The Israelites never occupied it, and in due time, the Canaanites who had not been driven out as commanded by God moved back and rebuilt it.

It wasn't until the period of the Judges that Jabin of Hazor oppressed Israel for twenty years. Deborah and Barak struck back, and once again, about 1235 B.C, Hazor was destroyed (Judg. 4–5).

Much evidence was unearthed to substantiate the fact that Canaanite culture permeated the city and that the Canaanites had occupied both cities, the one of Joshua's day and the one of the period of the judges. All evidence among the ruins showed there had been great battles with much violence and destruction.

Chariots of Iron

God had promised Israel He would fight their battles for them and that in so doing, Israel was to drive the inhabitants out of the land (Deut. 1:30; 7:1–5). Israel failed to do her part, and by the time we get to the period of the judges, natives of that land had forced the Israelites into the mountains, keeping the fertile valleys for themselves (Judg. 1:19, 34).

Israel's problem was the same as when she accepted the report of the spies at Kadesh-barnea—she walked by sight instead of by faith. The Israelites of this period no doubt had

Figure 31. A plate depicting a chariot of iron

Figure 32. A grindstone similar to Samson's

been told of the fragile wooden chariots of the Egyptians, but when they faced chariots of iron (Judg. 1:19), their hearts melted and the enemy got the upper hand. The carving in figure 31 shows a chariot of iron, a potent weapon in that day.

Walking by sight seemed to be Israel's problem throughout the period of the judges. Living an "elevator life," she was up one time and down another, coming under oppression by surrounding peoples seven times.

"Without faith, it is impossible to please God," and "whatever is not of faith is sin" (Heb. 11:6; Rom. 14:23). If Israel had only obeyed the Lord, she wouldn't have "done that which was right in her own eyes" (Judg. 21:25).

Samson and Delilah

"Samson Love Letter Spurs Lively Talk Over Dead Sea Scrolls" was a headline in the *Times Union* newspaper, Albany, New York. John Strugnell, head of a twenty-two-member team of scholars with exclusive access to most of the unpublished Dead Sea Scrolls found in 1947, said he recently found a fragment containing nine words and three lines of a copy of a letter sent by Samson, probably to his Philistine

mistress, Delilah. He suggested it may be a love letter because it fit into the context of "erotic and sapient literature" that developed in the early Jewish period. Since no other information was given except that it was without question from Samson, we will have to wait for further research.

The story of Samson is told in the book of Judges (chaps. 13–16). His victories for Israel were stopped by Delilah, who seduced him and learned the secret of his strength. By cutting his hair while he was asleep, Delilah accomplished what thousands of Philistines couldn't. Samson awoke to find his strength gone and that the Lord had departed from him. He was easily overtaken by the Philistines; they blinded him, bound him with fetters, and made him grind grain in prison (Judg. 16:15–21). Figure 32 shows a grindstone of his day. Samson avenged himself in death, but what an awful price to pay when one sows his wild oats (Judg. 16:22–31 with Num. 32:23 and Gal. 6:7).

Baal Worship

God gave Israel a picture of the awfulness of sin in the land of Canaan while she was still in her wilderness wanderings as recorded in Leviticus 18. In verses 6–20, He warned that the norm of the people was fornication and adultery; in verse 21 they offered human beings as sacrifices to their gods; in verse 22 they practiced homosexuality (sodomy) and lesbianism; in verse 23 they practiced sex acts with animals (bestiality); and in Deuteronomy 32:17, 31, they worshiped the Devil or demons. God warned them the land was defiled and that all these practices were an abomination to Him (Lev. 18:24–30).

In Deuteronomy 7:1–5, God instructed Israel to smite and utterly destroy these people, make no covenant with them, do not intermarry, and destroy all their altars and images (idols). Before Israel entered the Promised Land, God said, "Do not do after the doings of the land of Canaan, neither shall ye walk in their ordinances" (Lev. 18:1–3).

Is there any proof that such conditions existed in Canaan at this period of time? In 1929 the ancient city of Ugarit (Ras Shamra) in northern Syria was excavated. Archaeologists found a set of clay tablets that confirmed all these degrading acts were a part of Baal worship (see fig. 33). They were found in a library between a temple to Dagon and a temple to Baal. Also found were the ruins of a school for priests of Baal. The tablets revealed that priests and prostitute priestesses would perform sex rites and acts at altars which gave license to the worshipers of Baal to fulfill their lustful desires. Baal and his sister, Anat, would perform sex rites and acts with each other and with animals. Sodomites and lesbians performed publicly. Children were offered as human sacrifices to gods (see fig. 34). The picture shows the skeleton of an infant offered to Baal, found at the Old Testament site of Dothan. A number of silver and stone-carved snakes were discovered, tying in with their worship of the Devil and demons.

The great tragedy of all this is that Israel, in failing to drive out the people of Canaan, also failed to heed God's warnings and commands against "learning the ways" of the Canaanite inhabitants (Deut. 20:17–18). They erected groves at their altars in violation of Deuteronomy 16:21–22. Groves

Figure 33. The god Baal

Figure 34. The skeleton of a child that was offered in sacrifice to Baal

at altars were "sex symbols." In their failure to drive out the inhabitants, Israel served Baal and the idols, forsook God, intermarried with these pagans, and forgot God (Judg. 2:2–3, 11; 3:5–7). They dethroned God and chose a "man king that they might be like other nations" (1 Kings 8:19–20). Solomon hit the skids spiritually after marrying pagan women. He even had idols put in the house of God to ap-pease his idolatrous wives (1 Kings 11).

This played a large role in the dividing of the nation into two kingdoms—the Northern Kingdom of Israel and the Southern Kingdom of Judah. Jeroboam became king of the Northern Kingdom and began an idolatrous worship of calves (1 Kings 12:25–33). Soon after Rehoboam became king of the Southern Kingdom, he built high places for images and groves, and sodomites (homosexuals) were in the land, doing according to the abominations of heathen nations round about (1 Kings 14:21–24).

By the time we get to king Manasseh of Judah, he had "seduced Israel to do *more* evil" than all the Canaanites (2 Kings 21:9). They were offering their own sons and daughters as burnt offering sacrifices to the god Baal (Jer. 19:4–5), and, as if this were not enough, they were "inventing sins" and worshiping devils (Ps. 106:34–40). In their worship of demons, they were burning incense to the brazen serpent which had delivered their ancestors in the wilderness (2 Kings 18:4). God likened His own people to those of Sodom and Gomorrah and said if it had not been for a faithful remnant, He would have destroyed them as He did those two cities (Isa. 1:9–10 with Gen. 19; see also Ezek. 16:48–52).

The Jebusite Gutter

When David decided to leave Hebron and make Jerusalem his capital, the Jebusites, who possessed Jerusalem, put the sick and the lame at the gates of the city, hoping David's soldiers would show sympathy and not invade. David knew of a shaft, or gutter, that had been drilled like a well inside the city centuries before by the Canaanites to secure water flowing from the Spring of Gihon. His men secretly stole up the gutter and took the city by surprise. This gutter or shaft was discovered when excavators found the conduit of King Hezekiah, which will be discussed later.

King David

Several archaeological findings have surfaced which shed light on events relating to the life of King David.

The Cup of the Twenty-Third Psalm

By every spring or well in the Holy Land a stone "cup" was placed for sheep to drink from (see fig. 35). They usually measured about 30 inches long, 18 inches wide, and 18 inches deep and were hollowed out. The shepherd would scoop up water and pour it into the cup. He never would let the sheep drink it dry and then refill but would continually keep pouring water in the cup. As the shepherd poured in more than the sheep could drink, the sheep could testify, "my cup runneth over" (Ps. 23:5b).

Slaying Goliath

Israel was fighting the Philistines in the valley of Elah (1 Sam. 17). The Philistine giant, Goliath, had put fear in Israel's defenses, and defeat seemed

Figure 35. The "cup" of Psalm 23

Figure 36. A depiction of a Philistine soldier

near. David volunteered to tackle the giant. When King Saul realized David meant business, he offered him his armor. David refused and chose rather to trust in the Lord for victory.

Selecting five smooth stones from the brook in the valley, he faced the enemy, put a stone in his sling, and hit Goliath in the forehead. The giant fell, and David took Goliath's sword and killed him. The Philistines fled and Israel came forth as victors. The picture of the head of a Philistine soldier (see fig. 36) may well represent Goliath.

Playing the Harp

David often played the harp to soothe King Saul (1 Sam. 10:23; see fig. 37).

Tear Bottles

David made mention of God putting his "tears in a bottle" (Ps. 56:8). An ancient custom during the time of heartache and sorrow was to hold tear bottles beneath one's eyes to catch the tears of grief. When filled, they were sealed and put in a conspicuous place in the home. At first these bottles were made of dried skin; later they were made of thin glass. At death, they were buried with the owner as their most sacred possession. The ones shown vary from three to six inches tall (see fig. 38). When David said, "My sin is ever before me," he could

Figure 37. A relief of a harp player

Figure 38. Tear bottles

quite possibly have had in mind his tears of remorse and repentance in a bottle—a reminder of his sin of adultery with Bathsheba and his responsibility for having Bathsheba's husband murdered (2 Sam. 11:1–24). The "sword" never departed from David's house; he reaped what he had sown (2 Sam. 12:1–12; Gal. 6:7).

Interestingly, we note in Luke 7:38 that a woman washed the feet of Jesus with her tears. Is it possible for someone to cry enough to wash someone's feet with their tears? This woman was branded as a sinner, and no doubt had cried many a night, seeking a solution to ease her guilty conscience. Catching such tears in bottles, she finally found the answer to her sin problem, and in meeting Christ, pouring out her tears to wash His feet was symbolic of confessing her sins to the only One who could forgive her.

The City of Megiddo

This city, in northern Palestine, was located on a hill overlooking the Plain of Esdraelon (Jezreel), where many believe the battle of Armageddon will be fought. The scene, described in Revelation 16:16, is comparable to Ezekiel 38 and 39, where a foe from the north comes "against the mountains of Israel." The plain measures 15 miles wide and 20 miles long. Several passes enter into it which give easy access to military forces. Through the centuries a succession of conquerors passed Megiddo—Egyptians, Canaanites, Philistines, Israelites, Assyrians, Persians, Greeks, Romans, Turks, and even the British in World War I.

Megiddo was of interest to Joshua, who effected a temporary victory over its king (Josh. 12:21). It was assigned to the half-tribe of Manasseh (Josh. 13:7). It became a famous city when Solomon rebuilt and fortified it during the tenth century B.C. and made it one of his chariot cities (1 Kings 9:15). Several excavations have revealed ruins of 40,000 stalls for his horses and chariots (1 Kings 4:26). Numerous sheds, hitching posts, and mangers (feeding troughs) were lined for these animals. Solomon had disobeyed the Lord in going to Egypt for horses (Deut. 17:16 with 1 Kings 10:28a).

A secret tunnel had been chiseled through stone beneath the city to supply water so that besieging armies would not be able to cut off its supply. The tunnel was 300 feet long and a shaft of 100 feet was drilled to reach the tunnel. Levels of occupation show there had been at least twenty-two cities of Megiddo built on the same site. It is perhaps the most thoroughly excavated site in the biblical world.

Each ancient city had a secret passage in and out of its city wall. This

Gold

was to allow the city's soldiers to sneak out to spy on their enemy and return safely. Walls were constructed so that a stone could be slipped out to allow men to crawl through. Strangers on the outside could not tell which stone concealed the secret entrance. The book of Judges tells of spies from Israel's army at Bethel seeking a secret passage. They asked a man outside the city wall, "Pray, show us the way into the city, and we will deal kindly with thee" (1:24). The man did and the Israelites slipped into the city. A secret passage afforded an avenue of escape when Nebuchadnezzar attacked the city of Jerusalem: "The king with all his men of war fled by night by the way of the gate between two walls . . ." (2 Kings 25:4).

Solomon and His Gold

David had desired to build the temple but because he was a man of war, God prohibited him from building it and the job was given to his son Solomon (2 Sam. 7; 22:6–11). David had accumulated much material for its building, among which were 108,000 talents and 10,000 drams of gold, and much silver, bronze, and iron (1 Chron. 19:4, 7). A talent was worth about $30,000 and a dram about $5, making a total of $3,240,050,000 in gold alone.

In the construction of the temple, Solomon used pure gold for chains before the sanctuary and gold to overlay the altar, the cherubim, the table of showbread, the inner sanctuary, the floor, and the doors (1 Kings 6). Even in building his palace, he spared no expense. The temple was no doubt the most magnificent structure that ever existed. The glitter of gold must have been eye-catching—a dazzling sight to behold.

Quite possibly it was such a sight that caused Solomon to disobey God's commandment in amassing such a storehouse of gold (Deut. 17:17). It became an obsession with him, and his love of luxury helped to contribute to his downfall. On one occasion King Hiram of Tyre sent him 120 talents of gold valued at $3,600,000 (1 Kings 9:14). Hiram brought Solomon another 420 talents, valued at $12,600,000.

In 1 Kings 10 we notice the amount of gold that came to him in one year alone—666 talents, valued at $19,980,000 (v. 14). Merchants, kings, and governors brought him gold (v. 15). The 200 gold bucklers (chest protectors) were valued at 600 shekels each. A shekel was worth about 60 cents, or $360.00 each—total $72,000 (v. 16). There were 300 shields of gold, each weighing 3 pounds. At today's standard of $370 per ounce for gold, 48 ounces x $370 = $17,760 x 300 shields = $5,328,000. His throne and the steps leading up to the throne were overlaid with gold (vv. 17–19). All his drinking vessels were pure gold (v. 20). He had ships coming in every three years bringing gold (v. 21), and all who visited him brought vessels of gold (v. 24).

One of his visitors was the queen of Sheba. Among her gifts to him were 120 talents of gold, valued at $3,600,000 (1 Kings 10:10). Sheba is a part of Ophir where Hiram got his gold. Most scholars are of the opinion that Ophir is south of the land of Edom off the shore of the Gulf of Akaba (Red Sea). Archaeological records, especially some inscriptions on ostraca (pieces of pottery), verify mining of gold in this region. These records support the visit of the queen of Sheba to Solomon and how he managed to get so much gold from Ophir.

King Rehoboam and King Shishak of Egypt

King Rehoboam was the first king to rule over the Southern Kingdom of Judah after the death of his father, Solomon. For three years he walked in the way of David and Solomon when they lived as they should (2 Chron. 11:17). Second Chronicles 12 gives us an account of Rehoboam's reign for the next two years. He established the kingdom, he strengthened himself, he forsook the law of the Lord—and he dragged Israel down with him (v. 1). As a result, God raised up Shishak (Sheshonk), king of Egypt, to invade Judah, conquer cities, and arrive at Jerusalem "because they [Rehoboam] had transgressed against the Lord; they had forsaken the Lord" (vv. 2, 5).

Figure 39. A wall in Shishak's temple

Although God granted them some deliverance, Shishak took away the treasures of both the temple and the palace—even the shields of gold which Solomon had made—*he took all* (vv. 7–9).

When Shishak built a temple at Karnak, about 500 miles south of Cairo, it was erected to honor his god. He had carved on the side of the stone temple the exact same thing we find in 2 Chronicles 12 (see fig. 39)—his taking fenced (walled) cities, his robbing the temple and palace, and his taking prisoners back to Egypt.

As a result of losing the shields of gold, Rehoboam made shields of brass, or bronze (vv. 9–10). Bronze, highly polished, will give a good reflection, like the bronze looking glasses the women of Israel gave for material in the tabernacle, but highly polished bronze does not glitter and glow like gold. Gold represents a testimony that glows and glitters for the Lord. Bronze, a substitute, stands for hypocrisy. It may look good from a distance, but up close, one can tell it is not gold.

Rehoboam lost all in the end because he did evil in the sight of the Lord (v. 14). And the monument of Shishak in Egypt stands until this day as a "billboard" advertising Rehoboam's and Israel's having forsaken the Lord. The world sees us for what we are. If we have a testimony that glows for the Lord, they don't say much, but let us stumble and fall like Rehoboam and the world will advertise our hypocrisy.

Seals and Signet Rings

A number of signet rings (seals) have been discovered. The word *seal* is a term used to describe a device for making an impression and for the impression itself. The use of a seal to authenticate a document was an old Bible custom. It corresponds to our Western usage of one's signature.

When Ahab sought to buy Naboth's vineyard and was refused, his wife, Jezebel, deceivingly wrote letters to the elders of Naboth's city for him to be slain so Ahab could get his vineyard. She wrote these letters in Ahab's name, using his seal, thus making her murder plot "official" (1 Kings 21:1–16).

Archaeologists at Megiddo discovered the seal of "Shema, the servant of [King] Jeroboam." The word *servant* means minister, the equivalent of "Prime Minister" or "Secretary of State." The seal of King Jotham (2 Chron. 27:1–9) was found when excavations were conducted at the Red Sea port city of Ezion-geber (see fig. 40). This is the only seal yet discovered of Israel's kings. Both Shema's and Jotham's seals have the figure of a lion, the symbol of Judah. Christ is referred to as the "Lion of the Tribe of Judah" (Rev. 5:5).

After Nebuchadnezzar captured Jerusalem, he made Gedaliah ruler over the Jews who were left in the land. His seal has been found with these words: "To Gedaliah who is ruler [governor] over the house." He was later murdered by Ishmael, whose seal has also been found (Jer. 40:5 with 2 Kings 25:22–25). [See "Seals" in Index.]

The Moabite Stone

After the capital of the Northern Kingdom of Israel was moved to Samaria, King Omri made Mesha, king of Moab, pay tribute to him. Part of the tribute was sheep's wool. According to biblical critics, Mesha was supposed to be a fictitious char-

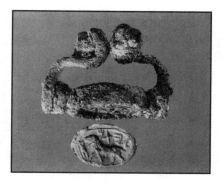

Figure 40. King Jotham's seal

acter and Moab was too barren to graze sheep. In 1868 a monument was found at Dibon in Moab. It is 2 feet wide, 1 foot thick, and about 4 feet high. It was labeled the Moabite Stone (see fig. 41). Part of the inscription reads, "I, Mesha, king of Moab, made this monument to Chemosh [Moabite god] to commemorate my deliverance from Israel. . . . Omri, king

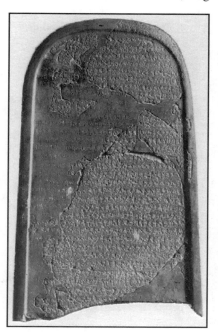

Figure 41. The Moabite Stone

of Israel, oppressed Moab and his son [Ahab] after him. I warred against their cities, devoted the spoil to Chemosh, and in Beth-diblathaim sheep raisers I placed." This "dead stone with a living message" shows that Mesha was *not* a fictitious character, he *did* war against Israel, and Moab *did* have good, sufficient grazing land for sheep.

King Ahab and His Ivory Palace

The prophet Amos took Israel to task for not tithing (4:4), for being at ease in Zion, for their trusting in the mountains of Samaria (a natural fortification) instead of God (6:1), for putting away the evil day and causing the seat of violence to come near (6:3), lying upon beds of ivory (6:4a), and eating, drinking, and being merry (6:4b–6). Israel was completely ignoring God with her lifestyle. In robbing God of His tithe, she was spending money on the fad of the day—costly ivory. Their walls, ceilings, and especially their beds were inlaid with ivory. We are told that Ahab's palace was referred to as his "ivory palace"

Figure 42. Examples of Samaritan ivory

(1 Kings 22:39). The ruins of his palace cover between seven and eight acres.

Excavations at Samaria show that Amos was right. Over 10,000 pieces of ivory have been found, some of them beautifully carved figures and panels for decorating furniture and walls. The subjects portrayed in the ivory reliefs include lions, deer, lotus, papyrus, bulls, winged figures in human form, sphinxes, and figures of Egyptian gods, such as Horus and Isis (see fig. 42). These ivories are often thought of as the most charming examples of miniature art ever found on an Israeli site.

Diggings also revealed houses for the rich and houses for the poor (3:15; 5:11). Many house foundations gave evidence of summer cottages with permanent structure, built with hewn stones, while houses of the poor were built with field stones. Artifacts found in the ruins revealed who was rich and who was poor. The ruins also gave evidence of violent destruction, such as Amos predicted (5:11–27).

Assyrian Kings

A number of Assyrian kings are mentioned in the Old Testament— Sargon, Shalmaneser, Tiglath-pileser, Eserhaddon, Asnapper (probably Ashurbanipal), and Sennacherib. All but Sennacherib invaded the Northern Kingdom of Israel at Samaria. He invaded the Southern Kingdom of Judah. Two separate lists of Assyrian kings have been discovered showing that these kings had frequent dealings with Israel's and Judah's kings. Eleven Hebrew kings are mentioned in these records.

Shalmaneser and

King Jehu of Israel

A monument called the Black Obelisk was found at Calah (Nimrud) in the palace ruins of Shalmaneser. It is about 1 foot square and is 6 feet tall. Carvings picture Shalmaneser receiving tribute from defeated foes. In the inscription it tells of King Jehu paying tribute, and a carved picture shows Jehu bowing in the presence of Shalmaneser (see fig. 43), saying, "Tribute of Jehu, son [or descendant] of Omri, gold, silver, golden goblets, and pitchers, golden vases and vessels, scepters from the hand of the king, javelins I received from him." This obelisk bears the only image or contemporary likeness of any Israelite king. One of Shalmaneser's inscriptions refers to himself as "the legitimate King, King of the universe, King without rival, the 'Great Dragon,' the only power within the four rims of the whole earth . . . who smashed all his foes like pots."

Figure 43. "Tribute of Jehu" from the Black Obelisk

North of Beirut, Lebanon, is a pass which crosses the Lebanon mountains, leading southward toward Samaria in Israel. At the top of this mountain are several carved monuments, one of which is of Shalmaneser himself. The inscription tells of his having aligned his armies with an Egyptian army as they go to besiege Samaria.

Tiglath-pileser (Pul)

God stirred the spirit of this Assyrian king to come up against His people (2 Kings 15:29; 1 Chron. 5:26). In his royal annals Tiglath makes a number of references to Old Testament characters, naming Azariah of Judah and King Menahem of Samaria who paid him tribute. He said he replaced Pekah with Hoshea on the throne of Israel during his campaign in Palestine

Figure 44. A depiction of Tiglath-pileser and a straphanger

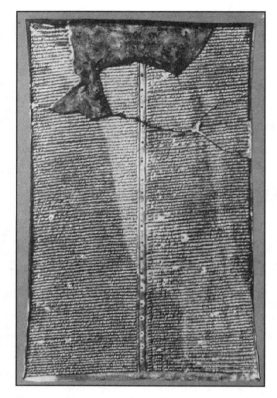

Figure 45. Sargon's captivity count

in 734–732 B.C.

An interesting sidelight as to how archaeology sometimes sheds light on biblical customs is seen in a monument of Tiglath-pileser riding in his chariot with his driver and a third man (see fig. 44). The third man is in the back of the chariot holding on to straps. This is to protect the king in case the horses bolt and the king is thrown backward. This helps explain the portion of Scripture, "the lord [servant] on whose arm the king leaned" (2 Kings 7:2).

Sargon

Critics have said that Sargon never existed, that he was just another fictitious character whose name was thrown in the Bible to add luster to a story. His name is mentioned only once in the Bible, and that in parentheses by Isaiah (20:1). This was a big error, so said these historians.

But a site was excavated in Khorsabad in ancient Assyria. When some inscribed bricks were deciphered, the record said, "I Sargon have built this palace to the praise of mine own glory." God knows just when and how to vindicate His Word! Sargon's palace occupied some 25 acres, and its walls were from 9 to 16 feet thick. Large stone "winged bulls" stood at the gate entrance. The palace courtyard had three temples, a towering ziggurat, luxurious harems, and spacious quarters.

When Samaria was in its final siege, Shalmaneser was said to have begun the invasion. When the city fell, it is said "*they* took it" (2 Kings 18:9–12). According to records found among the ruins of Sargon's palace, Shalmaneser died (killed by his sons), and Sargon actually captured Samaria (see fig. 45). There is no record in the Bible as to how many Israelites he took as prisoners to Assyria, but one of his records was found which showed he deported 27,290 Jews. He rebuilt Samaria and settled Assyrians in cities in the area of the Northern Kingdom. In the intermarriage of Assyrians with surviving Jews, we have the formation of the Samaritan race. References to the Samaritans are common in the Gospels.

Another discovery confirming the accuracy of Isaiah's allusion to Sargon is that of his officer, Tartan, being sent to Ashdod because the king of Ashdod had not been paying Sargon tribute. In the 1950s the Ashdod Excavation Project unearthed an inscription of Sargon's at this site which actually verified Isaiah's statement (20:1). It stated "Ashdod's king, Azuri, plotted to avoid paying me tribute. In anger I marched against Ashdod with my captain, Tartan, conquering." Assyrian kings were most brutal. [See "Assyrian Brutality" in Index.]

King Hezekiah's Conduit

"And the rest of the acts of Hezekiah and all his might, and how he made a pool [of Siloam], and a conduit, and brought water into the city [of Jerusalem]" (2 Kings 20:20). Three hundred years after the Jebusites brought water into the city through a gutter (shaft) to the Spring of Gihon, Hezekiah, realizing the need of water in times of war, had his men dig a conduit through solid rock from the spring to a man-made pool (Siloam) inside the city. Giving his men a blueprint and instructions, he put one group at the Spring of Gihon and another at the Pool of Siloam. Both groups dug toward each other until they were about 4½ feet apart. They called to each other and soon met face to face at the point indicated (see fig. 46).

How do we know Hezekiah had such a conduit built? In 1890, a truant boy was wading inside the conduit at the pool and saw an inscription on the wall (see fig. 47). Written in the Hebrew language, it translates as follows: "This is the history of the excavation. While workmen still lifted up their ax [pick], each toward his neighbors, and while three cubits remain [4½ feet], each heard voices calling one to another. On the day the workmen struck, ax against ax, to meet his neighbors, waters flowed from the [Gihon] Spring to the [Siloam] Pool a thousand and two hundred cubits [1,800 feet]; and a hundred cubits [150 feet] over the

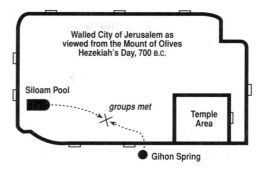

Figure 46. A map of Hezekiah's conduit plan

heads of the workmen." The conduit had an average width of 2½ feet and a height of 6 feet. Evidence of this conduit must leave its former critics speechless.

Sennacherib at Lachish

This king besieged forty-six cities in the territory of Judah, one of which was Lachish, which served as a buffer to help fortify Jerusalem (2 Kings 18:13–16). When archaeologists discovered

Figure 47. Where the pickmen met in Hezekiah's conduit

Sennacherib's palace in northern Assyria (Iraq), a wall relief showed an officer of the Lachish army paying tribute to this Assyrian king (see fig. 48).

Hezekiah also had to pay tribute to Sennacherib, and note was made of this on an inscription. To pay 300 talents of silver and 30 talents of gold, Hezekiah gave him all the silver found in the temple and in the treasuries of the palace, and he had to strip the gold from the doors of the temple and the gold that overlaid the pillars. Sennacherib's record stated Hezekiah paid him 30 talents of gold and 800 talents of silver, while the Bible says 300 talents of silver. A contradiction? Critics shouted in glee, saying "Yes! I told you so; I told you the Bible contained error."

But a later discovery of an inscription showed that 300 talents (weight) of Palestine silver equaled 800 talents (weight) of Assyrian silver.

Sennacherib at Jerusalem

After Lachish was defeated, Sennacherib headed for Jerusalem to subdue king Hezekiah. A note was sent to Hezekiah demanding surrender to the Assyrian. Realizing the Assyrian army greatly outnumbered his men, Hezekiah fell on his face, spread out the ultimatum from Sennacherib, and prayed to God for help. In the night an angel of the Lord came down and smote 185,000 Assyrians, forcing Sennacherib to return "with shame of face to his own land" (2 Chron. 32:21; see fig. 49).

These kings never recorded defeats, and before his death Sennacherib made a record which reveals his campaigns against the cities of Judah as follows: "By assaults of battering rams and the blows of engines, the attack of foot soldiers, sappers [trench diggers], breaches, and axes." Of Hezekiah he wrote: "Hezekiah himself I caged up like a bird in the midst of his royal city, Jerusalem, I shut up." Conspicuously absent was any mention of his army having been destroyed. The best he could say was that for a time before Hezekiah's God came to his rescue, he was bound within his city. The clay prism is the record which Sennacherib inscribed about Jerusalem and Hezekiah (see fig. 50).

Figure 48. A wall carving showing tribute being paid to Sennacherib

Figure 49. A depiction of captives marching to Assyria

Lachish Letters

After Sennacherib's defeat in the days of Hezekiah, Lachish was rebuilt as a fortress to Jerusalem. When king

Nebuchadnezzar of Babylon began besieging the area in and around Jerusalem, it is apparent that only three cities were left standing—Lachish, Azekah, and Jerusalem (Jer. 34:7).

Excavators at Lachish discovered twenty-one potsherds that had been used as writing material to carry military dispatches to Lachish during the last year before Jerusalem's downfall. Possibly potsherds were used to fool the enemy. One of the letters was written at a time when only Jerusalem and Lachish were still in control of the Jews. It stated that "we cannot see Azekah." Another letter mentions a prophet, possibly Jeremiah, because of all his predictions about the downfall of the Southern Kingdom of Judah (Jer. 37:8). This letter accused the prophet of "weakening the hands" of the men of war, which Jeremiah had written when King Zedekiah's court denounced him to the king and asked that he be put to death (Jer. 38:4).

One letter tells us that Nebuchadnezzar had placed Zedekiah on Judah's throne as king, and many of these letters show us how Nebuchadnezzar was tightening the net around the land of Judah before striking his final blow at Jerusalem (2 Chron. 36:10–21). [See "Elephantine Papyri" in Index.]

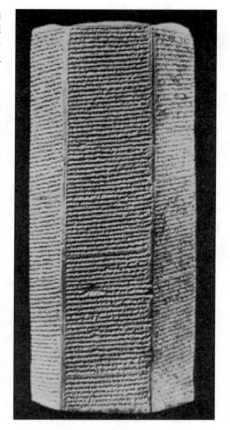

Figure 50. Sennacherib's "prism" mentioning King Hezekiah

Weapons of Warfare

After the discovery of gunpowder by the Chinese in the ninth century A.D., weapons of warfare have become so sophisticated that there is fear today of a worldwide holocaust. But what about weapons in days gone by? Early man used clubs and stones. Flint axes, arrows, and bronze spears soon came on the scene. Added to early arsenals were "sling stones," an instrument of stone or flint so chiseled that it looked like a two-inch stone ball and weighed about three-quarters of a pound (see fig. 51). According to Judges 20:15–17, 700 men of the tribe of Benjamin were skilled in the art of using sling stones. They could "sling stones at an hair breadth, and not miss" (v. 16).

In Old Testament days men who used bows and arrows were called *bowmen* (Jer. 4:29), those who used spears were called *spearmen* (Ps. 68:30), and those who used sling-

Figure 51. A bronze spearhead and sling stones

stones were called *slingers* (2 Kings 25:3; see fig. 52). These "sling stones" are not to be confused with those David used to slay Goliath. He used "smooth stones" he picked up from the brook in the valley of Elah (1 Sam. 17:40).

Engines of War became potent weapons in warfare (Ezek. 26:9). King Uzziah, in the eighth century B.C., made engines of war in Jerusalem to place in towers on city walls and on the bulwarks to shoot arrows and great

Figure 52. A carving of slingers and bowmen

stones (2 Chron. 26:15). Such engines housed a mechanical arm to hurl great stone balls. Twisted rope or strands of leather were wound around levers to create tension, and when released, the stones were hurled at their targets. Other engines were used as battering rams to penetrate city walls, such as the one seen on the wall of Sennacherib's palace (see fig. 53).

The Fall of Jerusalem and Babylonian Captivity

Judah's captivity was foretold by Moses (Deut. 28:36). It was again foretold 150 years before it happened by Isaiah (6:9–12). Babylon was predicted as the place of captivity (Mic. 4:9–10). These reasons brought Israel to the place where she had crossed the point of no return with God. There was no remedy for her now. Jeremiah had pleaded with the Israelites to amend their ways, but they would not heed the plea of God's man, so God had no alternative but to tell Jeremiah He would cast them out. He reminded Jeremiah not to pray for them, for He would not hear him. God further said, "Behold, Mine anger and My fury shall be poured out upon this place [Jerusalem], upon man, and upon beast, and upon the trees of the field and the fruit of the ground; and it shall burn, and shall not be quenched" (Jer. 7:3, 15–16, 20). When God said "vengeance belongeth unto Me, I will recompense," He meant it (Deut. 32:35–36). What a fearful thing to fall into the hands of the living God (Heb. 10:31).

When Jehoiakim became king over Judah, Nebuchadnezzar (see fig. 54), king of Babylon, came to Jerusalem and made him his servant. After three years Nebuchadnezzar bound him in

Figure 53. A depiction of an engine of war

fetters and carried him and the vessels of the temple to Babylon (2 Kings 24:1–5; 2 Chron. 36:5–7). Listed in the first deportation to Babylon was the prophet Daniel (Dan. 1:1–6).

The second deportation took place under the reign of Jehoiachin when the king of Babylon came back and took Jehoiachin and all his mighty men of valor to Babylon. He destroyed the vessels of the temple, which had replaced the ones previously taken, and left the poorest of the people in the land (2 Kings 24:8–16; 2 Chron. 36:9–10). Ezekiel was included in this second group (Ezek. 1:1–2).

The third and final deportation took place under King Zedekiah (586 B.C.). This time Nebuchadnezzar put a blockade around Jerusalem, causing famine. When the people tried to flee he captured them, set fire to the whole city, and broke down its wall. He showed no compassion (2 Kings 25:1–21; 2 Chron. 36:11–21). The final overthrow of the Southern Kingdom of Judah is recorded in these words: "So Judah was carried away out of their land" (2 Kings 25:21), and remained in captivity for seventy-nine long years until the Medes and Persians defeated

the Babylonians (2 Chron. 36:20–23).

The Babylonian Chronicle

This clay tablet records some events in the life of Nebuchadnezzar during the years 605 to 594 B.C. (see fig. 55). It described the great battle of Charchemish (2 Chron. 35:20), mentions the coronation of Nebuchadnezzar, the removal of Jehoiachin and others to Babylon, and lists their rations (2 Kings 25:27–30). It states that Zedekiah was enthroned in Jehoiachin's place (2 Chron. 36:8–11).

Figure 54. A seal of Nebuchadnezzar

Figure 55. A Babylonian chronicle

King Zedekiah Blinded by Nebuchadnezzar

In the fall of Nineveh (see p. 119), we mentioned many of the atrocities of the ancient Assyrian kings. During the heat of the battle against Jerusalem, King Zedekiah and the men of war fled by way of the gate between the city walls. Zedekiah headed toward the plain to Jericho, but the Chaldean

Figure 56. A carving of the blinding of a prisoner

army caught up with him and took him to Nebuchadnezzar. Pronouncing judgment upon him, they first slew Zedekiah's sons before his eyes, and then blinded him, bound him with fetters, and carried him to Babylon.

Figure 56 shows this method of Assyrian torture. With a hook in the jaw, the prisoner is told to look up at the victorious king. If the prisoner does not respond, the king gives a yank of the leash, forcing the prisoner to look up at him, and then he pierces his eyes (see 2 Kings 25:4–7).

The Fall of Babylon

At the end of the seventy-year captivity, Daniel, who had been taken captive to Babylon, prophesied that Babylon would be taken over by the Medes and Persians (2:37–39). It was during the reign of Cyrus, king of Persia, that Daniel calculated Israel would soon be on her way home (10:1–14). His prophecy of Babylon's capture came to pass as recorded in chapter 5 and is also confirmed by history. This chapter gives details of events just prior to its downfall. Belshazzar was having a feast for his lords. Inscribed bricks were numerous on the walls of the banquet hall, but when he saw a finger writing something, he sought wise men to interpret for him. Daniel was able to decipher the message and was promised that he would be the *third* ruler in the kingdom. However, the message stated that Belshazzar, king of Babylon, was found wanting in God's scales and in that night he would be slain. Daniel lists Belshazzar as Babylon's last king.

It was once thought that this was pure fiction on the part of the Bible. The last king of Babylon was known to be Nabonidus, and the name "Belshazzar" was unheard of outside the book of Daniel. Even Herodotus, the Greek historian who wrote the history of Babylon in 450 B.C., had never heard of him.

Inevitably, however, archaeological discoveries began to yield evidence to vindicate Daniel. Clay tablets tell us that Nabonidus entrusted the kingship to his eldest son while he himself lived in Tema. Our English word "Belshazzar" is "Bel-shar-usur" on the Babylonian tablet, and one line reads on what is now called "The Nabonidus Chronicle," "The king was in the city of Tema [Arabia]; the king's son, courtiers, and army were in Babylonia."

This chronicle covers the years of Nabonidus from 557 to 539 B.C. It mentions the ten years he lived in Tema while the crown prince (Belshazzar) ruled and confirms beyond a shadow of doubt Daniel's account.

It is easily understood now why Daniel was made the third ruler in the kingdom. Nabonidus was the first, Belshazzar was the second, and Daniel was offered the one next to the reigning monarch, third (Dan. 5:29).

Israel's Release from Babylonian Captivity by Cyrus

The Medes and Persians brought about Babylon's downfall. Cyrus was the Persian king who claimed Babylon after Darius had marched the troops into the city. Cyrus had been prophesied by Isaiah to be the liberator for Israel (see p. 107). Just as God raised up the king of the Chaldeans (Nebuchadnezzar) to take Israel captive for seventy years (2 Chron. 36:17), so God raised up Cyrus, a pagan king, to release them so they could go back home to reestablish their worship in their holy city (Ezra 1:1–4).

Years ago cynical writers used to scoff at the idea that a Persian king of the sixth century B.C. could be so politically sophisticated as to release captive people and declare religious liberty. This evidently was dismissed simply because the Bible gave the only account of such an event.

But God once again made "truth to spring out of the earth" (Ps. 85:11a). Archaeological discoveries like that of the Cyrus Cylinder have completely silenced all criticism of Ezra's words. This now-famous clay cylinder records how Cyrus marched into Babylon

Figure 57. The decree of King Cyrus

Figure 58. A lion's den

without any resistance and made a decree to free prisoners of war that they might return to their homelands and worship according to their own traditions (see fig. 57). This cylinder is now in the British Museum in London. [See "The Fall of Babylon" in Index.]

Daniel in the Lion's Den

It pleased King Darius to appoint 120 princes to be over the whole kingdom.

Figure 59. Nehemiah (right), the king's cup-bearer

Three were chosen to be presidents, Daniel being the first because of his excellent spirit. Jealousy arose among the other princes and they plotted against him because of his prayer life. They persuaded the king to issue a decree that no one should make a petition to any god except Darius, punishable by being cast into the lion's den. The decree was issued, but Daniel, as was his custom, prayed to his God three times a day. Since the laws of the Medes and Persians could not be altered, Darius had to put Daniel in the den.

The picture shows the ruins of this lion's den (see fig. 58). An inscription was found on the wall that said, "The place of execution where men who anger the king die, torn by wild beasts." (Read Daniel 6.)

Susa (Shushan)—Queen Esther

Susa was occupied as early as 4000 B.C. and survived until A.D. 1200. It shared the honor with Persepolis of being a royal city, where kings of the Persian Empire shared their palaces [see "Persepolis" in Index]. All the events mentioned in the book of Esther revolve around this city. Although Mordecai played an important role in the palace of Ahasuerus (Xerxes), Queen Esther and Nehemiah are the principal figures. Nehemiah (2:11) was the king's "cupbearer" (trusted palace servant; see fig. 59). It was Esther who prevailed upon her husband, the king, to issue a decree to spare the Jews from being massacred due to a former decree. The Feast of Purim was inaugurated to commemorate their rescue. Esther's period of history was ca. 486–465 B.C.

4

The Intertestamental Period

It was during the four hundred silent years between the Old and New Testaments that several groups and sects originated. Archaeological information shows they were especially active during the time of Christ's earthly ministry.

Groups and Sects

1. Samaritans. After the Northern Kingdom of Israel fell in 722 B.C., many Jews remained in the land while others were taken captive. A number of Assyrians moved into Samaria and intermarried with the Jews. Their descendants became known as the Samaritans. During Christ's day "the Jews had no dealings with the Samaritans" (John 4:9). A colony of about three hundred Samaritans live today in northern Palestine in the city of Jenine. They still observe the Passover on Mount Gerizim yearly. Read John 4:1–43.

2. Pharisees. They controlled the religion of the Jews. In their zeal for the Law they had all but deified it and in so doing had became merely external, formal, and mechanical. In their role as custodians of the Law, they took it upon themselves to be the sole interpreters of it, thus making *their* interpretation *the* Law.

According to Josephus, Pharisaism pretended to have a more exact knowledge of the Law, as being the exact sect of the Jews and the most exact interpretation of the Law. In their interpretation of the Law many oral laws were added, which later became known as the traditions of their fathers (Matt. 15:3–5).

These traditions superseded the Scriptures, and the Pharisees became legalists in enforcing them. They were the premier religious hypocrites of their day (Matt. 23). According to Josephus, there were as many as 6,000 Pharisees at the peak of their history, which lasted from the time of the Maccabees (ca. 160 B.C.) to the time of Emperor Hadrian (ca. A.D. 135), almost three hundred years.

3. Scribes. Lawyers: Mark 1:22.

4. Sadducees. Religious leaders; opponents of the Pharisees: Acts 23:6–10. They did not believe in the resurrection.

5. Herodians. Politicians; friends of the Pharisees in plotting to take the life of Jesus: Mark 3:6; 12:13.

6. Zealots. Militant Jewish opponents of Rome who resorted to violence and assassination in their hatred of Rome. Simon the Zealot is distinguished from Simon Peter: Luke 6:15; Acts 1:13.

7. Essenes. The people who hid the Dead Sea Scrolls.

The Dead Sea Scrolls

Alexander the Great conquered the then known world and wept because there were no more worlds to conquer. He died at the age of thirty-three in 323 B.C. After his death a power struggle ensued among his generals. By 198 B.C., Antiochus Epiphanes IV of Syria gained control of Palestine from the Ptolemies of Egypt. He sought to bring the Jews under the sway of Grecian culture and religions. He sent letters to Jerusalem and the cities of Judah demanding that they follow the Grecian laws of the land, set up altars, groves, and idols in the temple, offer swine's flesh and unclean beasts, and not circumcise their children (1 Macc. 1:44–48). These crimes, which Antiochus IV added to his looting and desecration of the temple in 168 B.C., sparked a violent rebellion and war under three Maccabean brothers, which ultimately led to victory in 165 B.C. Jerusalem was liberated, the temple was cleansed, and pure worship was restored.

The Maccabean house usurped the authority of the priesthood but soon became involved in wars and politics. This set the stage for the emergence of those who remained true to the Law. According to Josephus, these proponents of truth were persecuted and dragged from their hiding places, with more than 800 of them having been crucified in Jerusalem.

About 140 B.C. the surviving "fundamentalists" and their families fled the Jerusalem, the City of Blood, to the Qumran, the City of Salt, in the desert near the Dead Sea. A "teacher of righteousness" helped them establish the order that would be known as the Essenes. Their purpose was fourfold: (1) to preserve the purity of the priesthood; (2) to hold to Moses, the Psalms, and the Prophets as their authority; (3) to practice their beliefs daily; and (4) to preserve the Word of God for their posterity by daily copying the Scriptures.

Meanwhile, Grecian power was waning throughout the world, and the fourth great empire mentioned by Daniel soon came to the forefront in 63 B.C. Pompey marched into Jerusalem, and the Roman legions put an end to Jewish political freedom.

Some have speculated that while John the Baptist and Jesus were in the desert, they might have visited the Essenes, but there is no biblical proof for such. By the late A.D. 60s the Jews had such hatred for the Romans that rebellion ran rampant throughout the land. Since every Jew became the enemy of Rome, Rome set out to crush them. This, of course, included the Essenes who were in a "cold war" with the corrupted priesthood in Jerusalem and an impending "hot war" with the legionnaires of Caesar.

As the troops left Jericho after its defeat, Qumran was barely seven miles away. The Essenes immediately hid their scrolls in nearby caves and fled to the hills, hoping to escape death and later return to gather their writings and personal belongings. But Vespasian's army captured their village in A.D. 68 and evidently wiped them out.

In 1947 a shepherd was looking for stray goats near cliffs overlooking the Dead Sea when he noticed an opening over the edge. Throwing a rock into the opening, he heard a noise as the rock found its mark (see fig. 60). Entering the cave he found a number of large jars. Breaking some to find what he thought would be gold, silver, or gems, he saw the ancient scrolls which the Essenes hid when Vespasian invaded their community 1,879 years before. This discovery startled the biblical world, bringing to light portions of Scripture written before Christ's day.

Portions of every book of the Old Testament have been found except Esther. Esther may have been excluded because of the late origin of the Feast of Purim. No writings of the Apocrypha, such as found in the Douay (Roman Catholic) version of the Bible, have been discovered. A scroll containing the complete book of

Figure 60. The Dead Sea caves where the scrolls were found

Isaiah was found (see fig. 61), along with many portions of Daniel, indicating these may have been favorites of the Essenes.

For years, scholars working under

Figure 61. The Isaiah Scroll found in the Dead Sea caves

Israeli leadership have been much criticized for not releasing information of the scrolls to the public. As a result, the Huntington Library in San Marino, California, broke the monopoly by giving qualified scholars free access to its 3,000 photographs of scroll fragments.

A text from a scroll mentioned the execution of a messiah-like leader, suggesting that some ancient Jews shared the Christian concept of the slaying of the Messiah. One fragment has five lines describing a "leader of a community being put to death," mentioning piercing or wounds. The text uses Messiah-related terms such as "the Staff," the "Branch of David," and the "Root of Jesse," which relate to Jesus Christ.

Although the Jews of Christ's day generally expected a Messiah who would restore Israel to political power, the newly released text shows that the Jewish scroll writers had the idea of a Messiah who would suffer and die. The language of the text is close to the Hebrew Old Testament prophecy of Isaiah 53, which speaks of Israel's coming Messiah's being "wounded for our transgressions." The scrolls were written by Jews who were knowledgeable of one who was on the scene to suffer and die. What a discovery to substantiate the historicity of Christianity!

The Effect of These Scrolls on the Christian Faith

Prior to the discovery of the Dead Sea Scrolls, the oldest known Hebrew Old Testament manuscript was dated A.D. 826. We now have portions of the Old Testament Scriptures dating back to 150 B.C., possibly to 250 B.C. Christ read from an Isaiah scroll and read exactly what we read in our Bible (Luke 4:16–21). When we quote the Word of God, we quote the *same* truths Christ did when He referred to the Scriptures. What differences we do find in these biblical scrolls is minute. The KJV says "crooked places straight"; the Isaiah scroll says "hills straight" (Isa. 45:2). The KJV says "Pour down righteousness"; the Isaiah scroll says "rain down righteousness" (Isa. 45:8).

Agreement between the Isaiah scroll, the Hebrew text of A.D. 826, and the text of our KJV shows the care with which the ancient scribes copied Bible manuscripts. Isaiah is still the same book it was when it came from the prophet Isaiah over 2,700 years ago.

For almost two thousand years the silence of the priesthood of the Essenes at Qumran verified the truth that all flesh is as grass and that the glory of man fades away. But out of those Dead Sea caves there has come further demonstration of the fact that, although the grass withers and people die, the Word of God is magnified and will abide forever (Ps. 138:2; Mark 13:31; 1 Peter 1:24–25).

Preparing the World for Christ's First Coming

The apostle Paul said that "in the fullness of time God sent forth His Son to redeem . . ." (Gal. 4:4–5). Christ's coming was to provide a universal salvation for all lost mankind, and for such an event, the world needed to be prepared. By piecing together historical records, some found in monasteries and some discovered by archaeologists, we can see how this came about.

1. Greek influence. The message of Christ was in need of a universal

language. There was classical Greek, which Josephus called a literary language noted for its elegance. There was Attic Greek, used only by the learned, and a dialect of the common people, known as *koine*, written and spoken throughout the Roman Empire by laborers, seamen, housewives, children—everyone but scholars.

The *koine* originated 300 years before Christ when troops of Alexander the Great first started to colonize the known world. It became so popular that international commerce and government documents were forced to adopt it. *Koine* continued as the language of the people of the Mediterranean world right into the New Testament days.

When time came to spread the Gospel to the Roman world, the *koine* was already conveniently accessible and understandable to everyone. How wonderful of God to engineer circumstances in such a way that bond and free, barbarian and noble would have understanding of the message of the kingdom of God through the death, burial, and resurrection of Christ.

The original New Testament books reveal no trace of Attic Greek refinements—only colloquial Greek—*koine*. Although Paul was well educated, he and the writers were not "Atticists." Had they been, Christianity would have been a mysterious or secret religion for the upper class, and the "whosoever wills" would still be in pagan darkness.

Greek philosophy helped destroy older religions, but it still clung to idolatry. Yet it created "free thinking" among all classes. This left many minds open to the "new" religion—the Gospel. Greek literature and history also helped the common people to become concerned about questions of right and wrong and man's eternal future. This contributed in a religious way to make many in the world ready to accept Christianity.

2. Roman influence. Both the Greek and Roman systems of philosophy and religion made a contribution to the coming of Christianity by destroying many of the polytheistic religions and by showing the inability of human reason to reach God. As a result, more people were accustomed to think in terms of sin and redemption. When Christianity did appear, people within the Roman Empire were more receptive to the Gospel and its spiritual approach to life.

   a. Their political stance helped develop a sense of unity throughout their empire.
   b. Roman law was applied to all its citizens.
   c. Rome granted citizenship to non-Romans.
   d. There was free movement in the Mediterranean.
   e. The Romans had developed an excellent road system.
   f. Roman culture helped spread its ideas to other peoples.
   g. Roman conquest led to a loss of belief by many peoples in their gods because their gods had not been able to help them from defeat by the Romans.

3. Jewish influence. The Jewish people, in contrast to the Greeks, did not seek to discover God by human reasoning. They were motivated by the fact that God sought them and revealed Himself to them in the history of their father Abraham.

   a. Judaism existed, not on the generality of pagan gods and

religion, but by its emphasis on monotheism.

b. The Jews knew that Messiah was to come through them. Wherever they were dispersed throughout the world, there was the belief that he would come to bring righteousness to the earth. Even wise men from the East had a knowledge of Him and came to visit Him some time after His birth (Matt. 2:1–12).

c. The synagogue and the Old Testament Scriptures helped propagate an ethical system in sharp contrast to the prevailing systems of that day. It was the "outward" practices of the Jews that helped promote the ethics, not their inward violation of God's law in the heart. It was, however, in the synagogues and the use of the Scriptures in the early Church that enabled the Gospel to spread. The synagogue became the "pulpit" of early Christianity (Acts 13:42–43).

5

Archaeological Tidbits in the New Testament

"And it came to pass in those days, that there went out a decree from Caesar Augustus, that all the world should be taxed. (And this taxing was first made when Cyrenius was governor of Syria)" (Luke 2:1–2).

The Census of Caesar Augustus

Such a census, or enrollment, provided the relevant information (1) for calling up men for military service and (2) for taxation purposes, for without exacting tribute from foreign possessions, Rome would not have been able to afford its luxury, its extravagant lifestyle, its building program, and its sporting activities.

Critics of the Bible have not questioned Rome's tax system but have questioned what they claim are Luke's "errors" in recording this census. They claim that

1. Augustus did not order a census at this time.
2. Cyrenius was governor of Syria at a later date.
3. if a census had been ordered, it was not necessary for a man to go to his own city to enroll, because the tax could be paid where he lived.
4. if the husband went, it was not necessary for any other member of the family to accompany him.

William Ramsey, a noted historian, traveled throughout the Bible lands to prove the fallacy of Luke's historical statements, only to find archaeological proof that Luke was correct in every instance. He found that Quirinius, or Cyrenius, was twice governor of Syria—first when Christ was born and again at a later period. Records show that a census was taken every fourteen years, proving that Rome did indeed have a system of census taking. The cycle shows the approximate time of the one recorded by Luke was 6–5 B.C., which is the calendar date of Christ's birth. The podium from which this decree of Augustus was made still stands in the old Roman Forum.

The following was taken from an ancient document: "Gaius Vibius, prefect [Roman officer] of Egypt. Because of the approaching census it is necessary for all those residing for any cause away from their own districts to prepare to return at once to their own governments, in order that they may complete the family administration of enrollment for each so that they may retain the titled lands belonging to them." It was such a custom of census-taking that necessitated Joseph's taking Mary with him to Bethlehem, where Christ was born in fulfillment of God's Word (Mic. 5:2).

Bethlehem, Christ's Birthplace

"But thou, Bethlehem Ephratah, though thou be little among the thousands of Judah, yet out of thee shall he come forth unto me that is to be ruler in Israel; whose goings forth have been from old, from everlasting" (Mic. 5:2).

Note the amazing accuracy of this prophecy. The Messiah must have a birthplace. There were three continents known to the ancient world—Europe, Africa, and Asia. Asia was chosen, but Asia has many countries. One of them is indicated, a little country we call Palestine—the Promised Land. Here were three districts: Judea, Galilee, and Samaria. It is Judah that is selected, and out of the many villages, the prophet singled out the only Bethlehem Ephratah. Why do

Figure 62. A donkey eats from a manger

they mention this one? Because there were *two* Bethlehems in the Promised Land. The other was located north of Zebulun's inherited land (Josh. 19:15). Micah's Bethlehem was in Judah (Ruth 1:1). The Bethlehem of Christ's day is still an active village, but the other one has not yet been found by archaeologists.

The Manger

While Mary and Joseph were in Bethlehem, "the days were accomplished that she should be delivered. And she brought forth her first-born son, and wrapped Him in swaddling clothes, and laid Him in a manger; because there was no room for them in the inn" (Luke 2:6–7).

A manger is a stone crib or feeding trough where animal food and straw were placed. Figure 62 gives an idea where Mary had to place the babe Jesus. Mangers are still used in Bible lands today.

The Seat of Moses

The seat of Moses was mentioned when Christ berated the Pharisees for being so hypocritical (Matt. 23:2; see fig. 63). This was the chief seat in the synagogue from which the rabbis sat as they taught the people. No doubt Christ sat in such a seat when He spoke in the synagogues, especially after He read from the book of Isaiah (Luke 4:14–28).

The Pharisees were always seeking to sit in the chief seats. There were several seats on both sides of the seat of Moses. While all were important, the ones on the immediate sides of the chief seat were always sought after. The mother of James and John, supposing such seats would be in Christ's kingdom, requested that her sons "may

Figure 63. The seat of Moses

Figure 64. Herod's warning on the temple

sit, one on the right hand and the other on the left in Thy kingdom" (Matt. 20:20–21). Paul also sat in such a seat in the synagogue in Antioch (Acts 13:14–15).

Temple Anti-Gentile Warning Inscription

Jews looked with contempt on Gentiles (Luke 7:24–30). If Jews ever accepted a Gentile, they first had to become a proselyte to Judaism. There was always a Gentile court adjacent to a synagogue in which they could assemble, but in no way would a Gentile be permitted to enter the temple. A warning inscription of Herod's temple has been discovered (see fig. 64), which reads as follows: "No stranger [Gentile] is to enter within the balustrade round the temple and enclosure. Whoever is caught is responsible to himself and for his death, which will ensue."

When Paul made his final visit to Jerusalem, he was persuaded to take some Jews in the temple to perform a vow (Acts 21:15–31). They went well inside the area where only Jews could go. These sacred limits were fenced off by low pillars supporting a handrail with columns at intervals on which inscriptions in Greek and Latin warned all Gentiles against advancing beyond

them upon pain of death. This fence is mentioned by Josephus in a striking passage. After a horrible scene of bloodshed within these sacred limits as Titus was destroying Jerusalem, the Roman leader said: "Was it not yourselves, you wretches, who raised this fence before your sanctuary? Was it not yourselves that set the pillars therein at intervals, inscribed with Greek characters and our characters, and forbidding anyone to pass the boundaries? And was it not we that allowed you to kill anyone so transgressing, though he were a Roman?"

From this it appears that the Jews had full permission from the Romans to kill anyone, even a Roman, if they went beyond the boundaries. It was in this sacred spot of the temple that Paul took these people to purify themselves with them.

Some Jews, who had seen Paul in Asia, accused him of bringing Greeks into the temple. Their uprising almost cost Paul his life, and his arrest finally resulted in his appeal to Caesar and his first imprisonment in Rome (Acts 21:31–40).

Millstones for Capital Punishment

Rome used crucifixion as its method of capital punishment (see

Figure 65. Millstones that were used for capital punishment

fig. 65). The Greek method of capital punishment was to have a millstone tied around one's neck and to be cast into the sea to drown (Matt. 18:1–7). The purpose of Christ in mentioning this Grecian method was to convey the importance of sheep (older Christians) setting a good example before lambs (children). He said that if a proper example were not set, "better for him that a millstone were hanged about his neck and he be drowned in the depth of the sea." If no example were set to lead children to the Lord, it would be tantamount to "the blind leading the blind, and both fall into the ditch" (Matt. 15:14).

'Twas a Sheep, Not a Lamb
It was a sheep—not a lamb, that
    strayed away,
    In the parable Jesus told:
A grown-up sheep that had gone
    astray
    From the ninety and nine in the
    fold.

Out in the meadows, out in the cold,
    'Twas a sheep the Good Shepherd
    sought:
Back to the flock and into the fold,
    'Twas a sheep the Good Shepherd
    brought.

And why for the sheep, should we
    earnestly long,
    And so earnestly hope and pray?
Because there is danger, if they go
    wrong,
    They will lead the young lambs
    astray.

For the lambs follow the sheep, you
    know,
    Wherever the sheep may stray:
If the sheep go wrong, it will not be
    long
    Till the lambs are as wrong as
    they.

So, with the sheep we earnestly
    plead,
    For the sake of the lambs today:
If the lambs are lost, what a terrible
    cost
    Some sheep may have to pay.
                    —Author Unknown

Lamps of the Ten Virgins

Figure 66 shows lamps and an oil cruse, the type which Christ had in mind when he illustrated *readiness* in the parable of the Ten Virgins (Matt. 25:1–13). These lamps fit easily into the palm of the hand. Many scholars interpret this parable as a reference to the Jews in the Tribulation period. The five wise virgins are a type of the remnant of Israel for the millennium with an extra supply of oil in the oil cruse—oil being a type of the Holy Spirit. The five foolish virgins, who did not have an extra supply of oil, were not accepted. Not all who say they are of Israel are true believers (Rom. 9:6–8).

The Two Jerichos

While Jesus was in Jericho on one occasion, He healed the blind.

Matthew tells us this healing took place as Christ *departed from* Jericho (18:29–34). Luke tells us this healing took place as Christ *came nigh* unto Jericho (18:35–43). These two portions of Scripture were ridiculed as an apparent contradiction.

However, in 1907–9, the German Oriental Society conducted excavations at Jericho and learned in Jesus' time that Jericho was a *double* city. The old Jewish city was about a mile away from the new Roman city.

Matthew was speaking of the Jewish city which Christ had left; Luke was speaking of the Roman city which Christ was about to enter. Thus, on the way from the old city to the new, Christ met and healed blind Bartimaeus. This archaeological discovery shows both Matthew and Luke referring to the same event, and there is no contradiction.

Boat (Ship) of Christ's Day

Jesus often used boats on the Sea of Galilee, sometimes to take a trip to the other side (Matt. 15:39), and sometimes as a pulpit to preach to the multitudes (Mark 4:1–2). In the mid-1980s, there was a severe drought in this region, and people could wade on the bottom of the sea quite a distance. The outline of a boat was seen in the mud, and archaeologists rescued it. The carbon 14 method of dating showed it to be from the period of 120 B.C. to A.D. 40. Much pottery found also confirmed this date. The boat measured 26 ½ feet long, 7 ½ feet wide, and 4 ½ feet high. The style was certainly common to the day of Christ, probably the type of ship He and His disciples used, and the type Peter, James, and John used for fishing.

How many people could a boat of

Figure 66. Lamps and oil cruse

this size hold? Josephus tells of ten men of Tiberius who were in a single fishing boat. With a crew of five, the total was fifteen. Skeletons of this period show that Galilean males were about 5 feet 5 inches tall and weighed approximately 140 pounds. A ship of this size could easily accommodate Jesus and His twelve disciples.

While excavating the ship, the waters of the Sea of Galilee began to rise due to rain. The boat was covered in a polyurethane "cocoon," then floated again after 2,000 years. It has been placed in the Yagan Museum at the Kibbutz Gannosar. With the polyurethane removed, one can see much of the wooden ribs of this ancient boat.

Pontius Pilate

Pontius Pilate, who was appointed Roman governor of Palestine by Caesar Tiberius, ruled from A.D. 26–36. He was anti-Jewish. Coins minted in his honor displayed religious symbols which were offensive to Jews

Figure 67. Pilate Stone and coins

(see fig. 67). Josephus and Philo of Alexandria tell us much about his person. They describe him as "an extortioner, a tyrant, a blood sucker, and a corruptible character." He was cruel and his hard heart knew no compassion. His day in Judea was a reign of bribery and violence, robbery, oppression, misery, executions without fair trial, and infinite cruelty. That Pilate hated the Jews was made unmistakably plain to them from time to time.

When Jews protested the abuse of temple funds being misappropriated by Pilate, he had his soldiers club them to death. He slaughtered and imprisoned a number of Samaritans who had gathered on Mount Gerizim. Luke (13:1) tells us of his slaying certain Galileans as they offered their sacrifices. Such acts of tyranny finally led to his removal from office by Tiberius. Legend states that he either committed suicide or was executed under Tiberius or Nero, while others say that he died as a penitent Christian.

Pilate is mentioned fifty-six times in the New Testament. Yet some critics have claimed he was only a fictitious character. In 1961 an Italian archaeologist found what is called the "Pilate Stone" at the amphitheater at Caesarea. The text says: "Tiberium [a temple dedicated to the worship of Tiberius by the Cesareans], Pontius Pilate, prefect of Judea [has erected]." Of interest to Bible students is that he refers to himself as "prefect," a high-ranking official of ancient Rome who exercised powers of the Caesars during their absence. This shows that he had absolute authority in his jurisdiction as "governor." Such a temple built in Tiberius's honor shows himself to be a *friend* of Caesar (John 19:12).

Although Pilate was Caesar's friend, the Jews who were enemies of Jesus knew his weaknesses. They instigated Christ's death and forced Pilate to release Barabbas and crucify Christ, in spite of the fact that he found Him innocent on three occasions (Luke 23:4; John 18:38; 19:4, 6). Under Roman law, this was tantamount to three acquittals. The battle of Pilate for the life of Christ finally terminated in his capitulation to the Jews when he called for water and a basin and washed his hands (Matt. 27:24).

Only Pilate could authorize the death penalty. When he saw that the Jews demanded that he release Barabbas and crucify Christ, he gave in and ordered His crucifixion, but in doing so, he "took water and washed his hands before the multitude, saying, I am innocent of the blood of this just person; see ye to it. Then answered all the people and said, His blood be on us, and on our children" (Matt. 27:24–25).

What is the significance of this hand-washing act? Roman rulers in Palestine had to know the religious and cultural customs of those over whom they would reign. A notable example is King Agrippa's knowledge of the prophets (Acts 26:1–3, 26–27). Pilate knew God's law (Deut. 21:1–9). Where there was murder, and no criminal to blame, Israel's elders would gather where the body was, and, confident that there was no guilt upon the village, would wash their hands in token of the innocence of their people.

What a stinging rebuke this must have been to the accusers and instigators of Christ's death when Pilate called for water to wash his hands! They understood exactly what Pilate was saying—"This is murder—I am not guilty—I am innocent. If you have me crucify Him at your request, you are acknowledging your own law and are guilty of murder."

Every Jew in that crowd responded by saying, "His blood be on us and our children," implying their guilt of murder. Every Jew who did so was also familiar with Numbers 35:33. In no uncertain terms the Lord God Jehovah here states that He will bring retribution upon those who shed innocent blood. They were equally familiar with Moses' law where the God of justice and holiness implies "there is no haven for those who shed innocent blood" (Deut. 19:10–3). They knew the utterance of God in Joshua 2:19 that the blood of the innocent will surely fall upon the heads of those who slay such.

There was not a Jew in that throng who was not familiar with Samuel's teaching that it is death to the one who slays the Lord's anointed (2 Sam. 1:16). Yes, they knew He was the Messiah, God's anointed One, for Caiaphas, the high priest, had reminded them that Christ was to die for their nation (John 11:47–53).

With a knowledge of truth, and with an understanding of God's stern and righteous judgment, the Jews willfully lifted their voices in the face of an outraged heaven in that awful cry—"Crucify Him . . . release Barabbas . . . upon our heads and our children's heads will be this man's blood." And God heard! Their wish was granted and Jesus was led away to be crucified.

Roman Games at Christ's Trial

While the trial of Jesus was being conducted in Pilate's Judgment Hall, in a place called the Pavement (John 19:13), Roman soldiers were in adjacent rooms playing a game of chance called "The King," in which the winner would be crowned king. Pictured is an old "King" game carved on the pavement floor at Pilate's Judgment Hall (see fig. 68). Not only was this a mockery of Jesus as King before Pilate, but after Pilate condemned Him, the soldiers stripped Him, put on Him a scarlet robe, a crown of thorns, and a reed (scepter, symbol of rulership), and mocked Him, saying, "Hail, King of the Jews!" They spat upon Him, took the reed and smote Him on the head, took off the robe, put on His own raiment, and led Him away to Calvary (Matt. 27:27–31).

Figure 68. A Roman game

The Crucifixion of Christ

Crucifixion is known to have been practiced by the ancient Phoenicians. In 519 B.C. King Darius of Persia crucified 3,000 Babylonians. In ca. A.D. 66 the Romans crucified 3,600 Jews, igniting a Jewish revolt. By the time the revolt was settled, so many Jews had been crucified that the executioners ran out of wood for crosses! Among the countless thousands of Jews crucified over the years, the One who concerns us is God's only begotten Son, the Lord Jesus Christ (see fig. 69). Only artists' conceptions of His crucifixion are what we have seen, none of which were done earlier than A.D. 400. Each omits the true picture: "His appearance was so disfigured beyond that of any man and His form marred beyond human likeness" (Isa. 52:14 NIV).

What was crucifixion like? Many archaeological records have come to light which give us a vivid picture. Victims condemned to the cross first underwent the hideous torture of the scourge, and this was immediately inflicted on Jesus. He was seized by the soldiers, stripped to the waist, and bound in a stooping posture. His hands were tied behind His back to a post or block of wood near the tribunal. The Jews had a law limiting the scourging to forty stripes save one, but the Romans had no such law. As a result some victims were flogged so brutally that they died on the spot. The ends of the plaited leather strips of the whip had sharp pieces of lead or pointed bones which cut deep into the victim's back. Often the back of the person was cut open in all directions, eyes were torn out, teeth knocked out, and breasts

Figure 69. Calvary, the Place of the Skull

torn open. Sinews and bowels were exposed.

In addition to their scourging Jesus until His back was bloody, the soldiers plucked out His whiskers by the roots, and spat upon Him (Isa. 50:6). It was after this scourging that they laid the cross on His back. Giovanni Papini's *Life of Christ* describes the crucifixion.

> All else had been a prelude to this moment. For this cruel journey He had been born. Soon, instead of the cross being on Him, He would be on the cross, there to suffer the awful penalty of sin. From the time of His scourging and the cross being placed upon His back, from His being nailed to the cross until the time He gave up His spirit and was taken down and buried He suffered such as no mortal tongue could describe. What a tragic yet fruitful role this cross of the Redeemer was to play. It was upon this cross that we see man's unpredictable perverseness. Its weight was made heavy with the iniquities of the whole human race. Its coarse roughness was the leprous crust, the scaly hardness of men's hearts. Its sweating, slippery surface was the clammy coldness of man's sin-stained flesh. Its burdensome hulk was the clumsy effort of men made mad with the impression that they had become gods.

Christ found His cross a terrible burden, so great that He fell beneath its weight. But it drew out His strength, to preserve it, and to impart it to those who are yet without strength. He transformed it from a symbol of shame to one of glory, from a sign of death to one of immortality. At the crossroads of life it points to the *Way*. In the midst of uncertainty it shines with *Truth*. In the darkness of sorrow and sin and death, the Christ of the cross will illuminate a repentant heart and give eternal *Life*. [See "Christ, Wounds of" in Index.]

Discovery of a Crucified Victim

In 1970 Israeli archaeologists discovered in a hillside cave near Jerusalem the first remains of a crucified victim—the skeleton, including spike-pierced heel bones, of a man executed about 2,000 years ago. An inscription identified him as "Jehohannan Ben" (son of Jehohannan). The rest of the inscription was defaced.

Of interest to the archaeologists were the marks found on the crucified man's bones. They indicated the crucified position was not the erect, cruciform pose so commonly portrayed by artists. Jehohannan was probably held down by the Roman soldiers while his outstretched arms were fastened to the crossbar (see fig. 70). The spikes were not driven in the palms of his hands, but between the ulnar and radial bones just above the wrist. Once the hands were nailed, the legs were pressed together and twisted to one side (like a knee bend). A large spike, approximately 7 inches long, was driven through his heel bones and into the wood. To keep the victim from sagging, and possibly being torn loose from the cross as it was lifted and sunk into its hole, a small piece of wood, called a *sedecula*, was nailed to the upright post of the cross. This provided a support shelf for the crucified man's buttocks.

When Jehohannan was crucified, the spike through his heel bones had struck a knot. It had become so tightly imbedded that the executioner was unable to extract it from the cross. The feet were chopped off above the ankles. The body was placed in a 3 x 2 x 2 foot limestone ossuary, along with his amputated, but still pierced, feet.

Figure 70. An illustration of a crucified victim

The Nazareth Decree

Christ had predicted He would be raised from the grave the third day after His death (Matt. 16:21). The chief priests and Pharisees, always conniving, remembered this saying and asked Pilate that the sepulcher be made sure until the third day. They were given a watch (guards), and the tomb was sealed (Matt. 27:62–66).

An inscription, called the Nazareth Decree, or the "Tomb Robbers' Inscription," was discovered in Nazareth in 1878 (see fig. 71). It was a decree one of the Caesars had issued, which demanded a trial for anyone who "has in any way extracted the buried or maliciously transferred them to another place . . . or has displaced the sealing or moved other stones." If found guilty, they could be punished by death. This ordinance possibly explained one of the reasons why a watch was set at the tomb of Christ and why it was sealed.

Another reason, of course, was the ulterior motive of the Jews—to prove to their satisfaction that Christ would not come forth from the grave as He had predicted. They refused to believe that Jesus is God and that nothing could contain Him.

The guards' efforts were in vain, for God sent an earthquake and rolled away the stone from the tomb for Christ to come forth, thus fulfilling Christ's prediction. Although the soldiers were bribed by the chief priests to say His body had been stolen, His appearance to His disciples and to over 500 at one time proved the grave could not contain Him (Matt. 28:11–20; 1 Cor. 15:6). [See "Christ, Resurrection of" in Index.]

Historical Confirmation of Christ's Life

Christ Himself left very little, if any, material evidence of His earthly life and ministry. Critics claim because

Figure 71. The Nazareth Decree

of this, plus the fact that the New Testament alone contains the record of Christ, that we do not have sufficient evidence from secular history to prove His existence

But God has been pleased to use the pick and spade of the archaeologist to produce evidence confirming the reality of Christ as a historical figure and at the same time to silence the critics. Numerous discoveries of first-century historians have come to light to verify the New Testament of Christ's existence.

1. Flavius Josephus. He was born in A.D. 37, about four years after the death, burial, and resurrection of Christ. This Jewish historian not only mentioned John the Baptist as "a preacher of virtue who baptized his proselytes," and "James, the brother of him who is called Jesus," but spoke of Christ Himself.

> Now there was about this time Jesus, a wise man, if it be lawful to call him a man; for he was a doer of wonderful works, a teacher of such men as receive the truth with pleasure. He drew over to Him both many of the Jews and many of the Gentiles. He was [the] Christ, and when Pilate, at the suggestion of the principal men among them, had condemned Him to the cross, those who loved Him at the first did not forsake Him, for He appeared to them alive again the third day, as the divine prophets had foretold these and ten thousand other wonderful things concerning Him; and the tribe of Christians so named for Him are not extinct at this day.

2. Tacitus, a noted pagan Roman historian. He mentioned Nero's persecution of Christians at Rome in A.D. 64 and wrote the following in relation to his being blamed for setting fire to Rome: "To dispel the rumor, Nero substituted his culprits,' and treated with the most extreme punishments

some people, popularly known as Christians, whose disgraceful activities were notorious. The originator of that name, *Christus*, had been executed when Tiberius was emperor by order of the procurator Pontius Pilatus. But the deadly cult, though checked for a time, was now breaking out again not only in Judea, the birthplace of this evil, but even throughout Rome, where all the nasty and disgusting ideas from all over the world pour in and find a ready following."

In this one article alone Tacitus gives the "originator" of Christians as *Christus* (Christ), His home in Judea, His period of time (during the reign of Tiberius), and the name of Pontius Pilate, Christ's executioner. Christ was firmly fixed in contemporary history. Tacitus, elsewhere in his *Histories*, refers to Christianity when alluding to the burning of the temple and the destruction of Jerusalem in A.D. 70 by Titus.

3. Pliny the Younger. He was governor of Bithynia around A.D. 110. Pliny wrote numerous letters to Emperor Trajan about the problem of how to deal with the "disobedient" Christians in his jurisdiction. He insisted that they renounce their Christianity and would execute them if they persisted in confessing one Christus, unless they were Roman citizens, in which case they would be sent to Rome for trial.

One letter states that "many who were persuaded to invoke the pagan gods, to make an offering to the emperor's statue, and to 'curse Christus,' none of whom I am told, genuine Christians can be forced to do. Others, under interrogation said their alleged 'guilt of error' consisted of being in the habit of meeting before dawn on a fixed day when they would recite in turn a hymn to Christus as god, and would bind themselves by oath, not for any criminal act, but rather that they would not commit any theft, robbery or adultery, nor betray any trust nor refuse to restore a deposit on demand. This done, they would disperse, and then they would meet again later and eat together."

This was all the information Pliny could give to Trajan, and concludes that "it [Christianity] was a perverse religious cult carried to extremes." He then apologizes for troubling the emperor about it, but ended his letter by saying "it is affecting large numbers of all classes, and needs to be checked."

4. Suetonius, Roman historian. In his book, *The Twelve Caesars*, he said that Claudius, emperor from A.D. 41–54, "Drove the Jews out of Rome who were rioting because of Christus [Christ]." He said this expulsion took place in the ninth year of Claudius's reign, A.D. 49 (see Acts 18:1–2). This confirms that a Christian community was in Rome not more than sixteen years after the crucifixion of Christ.

There are many other sources that could be mentioned, all of which reveal that Christ and Christianity were well established on the pages of history, not only in Rome, but Greece, Asia Minor, Palestine, and Egypt. Both the sacred writings of Scripture and secular history confirm His existence. It is indeed difficult for the critic, or anyone else for that matter, to prove the nonexistence of Jesus Christ, the Son of God.

The Shroud of Turin

There has come to light in recent years a woven piece of burial material that Roman Catholics in particular claim to be the cloth that was used in the burial of Christ. The sheet is 14 feet, 3 inches long and 3 feet, 7 inches wide. It bears brownish-gray markings which when photographed appear as the negative picture of a bearded man. The face of the shroud is said to be the face of the crucified Christ.

The shroud has been kept in a cathedral in Turin, Italy, since the Middle Ages. It had become an object of worship, but there were some who were skeptical of its authenticity. For some time permission was not granted to test the cloth by the carbon 14 count method of dating to settle the issue.

The shroud may not relate to archaeology per se, but many times when an object comes to light bearing on Christian history, the carbon 14 count plays an important role in establishing the period of time of the item. In the summer of 1988 pieces of the shroud were finally tested by scientists at Oxford (England) University, the University of Arizona in Tucson, and the Federal Polytechnic in Zurich, Switzerland. Result: the dating tests proved the shroud was made about A.D. 1350.

In light of Gospel accounts of Christ's burial, one wonders if such a long piece of cloth bearing the image of a body would be possible. John's gospel tells us that Joseph of Arimathea and Nicodemus "took the body of Jesus and 'wound' [or wrapped] it in linen cloths . . ." (19:40; Matt. 27:59; Mark 15:46; Luke 23:53). They *wrapped* or *wound* the linen around His body. They did not lay the cloth on His body from head to foot; they wound it around His body as one would wrap gauze around an arm.

This would make it impossible for a full image of the person to be on a single piece of cloth. This was the custom used in wrapping the deceased.

The Archbishop of Turin, Cardinal Anastasio Ballestrero, the keeper of the shroud, confirmed the findings and determined the linen cloth was woven between A.D. 1260 and 1390. Such evidence proves that it is not an image of the crucified Christ, but the archbishop said Catholics may continue to venerate the shroud. It will be viewed as an icon, or picture of Christ, rather than a relic that came in contact with the body of Christ.

The Throne of St. Peter

An effective archaeological tool, the carbon 14 count, was used once again to prove that a particular relic was not what it had been thought to be. This time, carbon 14 proved that a chair or the "throne" upon which it was claimed that St. Peter sat was dated about A.D. 875. From the twelfth and thirteenth centuries popes sat in the chair for special ceremonies, and with its usage grew the tradition of its origin. Carbon 14 and other radiological tests confirmed the suspicions that had been raised about its authenticity.

A Sabbath Day's Journey

When the children of Israel returned from their seventy-year Babylonian captivity, their leaders reasoned that the holiness of the Law and the hardness of their hearts against it resulted in their exile. As a result, the rabbis devised a system of "oral laws" which, if obeyed, would be a measure of protection for them. These new laws were supposed to help preserve the original commandments. Here are a few examples that relate to "Remember the Sabbath day to keep it holy and do no work" (Exod. 20:8–11).

He who spills any liquid in a place where the soil is apt to produce something is guilty of violating the law against sowing.

If there be any dirt on a garment or the like, one may wipe it with a rag or the like, but he is not permitted to spill water on it, because of the putting of water is analogous to washing it.

Mud on one's garment may be scraped off with nail or with a knife if it be still moist, but if it be completely dry it must not be scraped off, for it is equivalent to the act of grinding.

It is forbidden to carry a covering as a protection from the sun or the rain, which commonly is known as an umbrella, because it is considered as making a tent.

What about a Sabbath day's journey recorded in Acts 1:12, where the distance is listed between the Mount of Olives and the city of Jerusalem? This distance was about 3,000 feet, based on the measurement the Israelites were allowed between themselves and the Ark of the Covenant (Josh. 3:4). This is how far the "oral" law would permit them to walk from one's house. The Rabbis, however, devised a loophole to increase the distance without breaking the law by depositing some food at the three-thousand-foot mark and declaring that spot as a temporary residence. The inscription on the pictured stone denotes the end of a "Sabbath Day's Journey" (see fig. 72).

A Famine in Judea

A prophet named Agabus warned of an impending famine in Judea which would occur during the reign of Claudius Caesar (Acts 11:27–30). There can be no doubt as to the historicity of such a famine as predicted

Figure 72. A boundary stone

by Agabus because ancient documents have been discovered which substantiate the biblical account. Already there were famines in the Roman Empire.

Suetonius, a first-century Roman historian, in his *Life of Caesars*, made mention of a series of famines and poor harvests during his reign. From about A.D. 41 to 54, this period was known as a time of great distress and scarcity over the whole then known world.

Two other first-century historians, Tacitus and Cassius, reported a famine so severe that it was esteemed a "divine judgment." They told of bad harvests in Greece, Asia Minor, and the Mediterranean (Judea) area, and that Claudius decreed famine prices for food at that time. The famine Agabus prophesied came to pass in Judea during the fourth year of Claudius's reign. Josephus said it was about A.D. 47, and the famine was so severe in Judea that the price of food was enormous and a great number perished. The church at Antioch sent relief to Judean believers.

John Mark Deserts
Paul and Barnabas

Scripture does not tell us why Mark left the missionary team of Paul and Barnabas as they were about to penetrate the region of Galatia (Acts 13:13). We could suggest several reasons.

1. Leaving the comforts of home and traveling in a foreign country causes many people to soon become homesick. Mark, no doubt, had been briefed on the ways and customs of the people of Galatia. Having arrived at Perga after crossing the Mediterranean from Paphos in Cyprus, perhaps he thought the journey inland to high mountains and endless stretches of bleak deserts would be suicidal. Then too, the people of Galatia spoke many dialects, making communication for him difficult. The Galatians were brutish and uncouth. Maybe Mark thought dealing with such people was beneath him. Possibly he had a desire to get back to the comforts of home.

2. He may have been jealous because Paul had taken over the leadership, which had been Barnabas's. Barnabas was either Mark's cousin or uncle, a relative on his mother's side (Col. 4:10). Perhaps this new position of Paul's over his relative offended him. It is quite possible Mark felt more comfortable under the leadership of Barnabas than of Paul, who was a very strict disciplinarian.

3. When Paul wrote to the Corinthians in his second letter, he made mention that in his journeys he had been in "perils of water and perils of robbers" (11:26). Archaeological findings in this region between Perga and Antioch of Pisidia show a number of inscriptions which refer to soldiers who had to keep order and peace, while other inscriptions refer to conflicts with robbers and drownings in streams.

This might give us the clue to Mark's desertion. Maybe he was frightened at the prospect of encountering robbers in Galatia—robbers who made travelers their prey as they passed through narrow mountain passes. Often robbed victims were slain. Melting snow from the mountains of Tarsus coursed its way through narrow passes, creating mighty rushing, overflowing streams, washing away bridges, and making traveling hazardous. This, too, would frighten anyone.

Whatever the reason, it incurred the displeasure of Paul, as we note in Acts 15:36–41, when Paul and Barnabas were about to embark on their second missionary journey. Barnabas wanted to take Mark; Paul didn't. An argument ensued and resulted in a split between them. Barnabas took Mark on his journey and Paul took Silas. Later Paul befriended Mark (2 Tim. 4:11).

Zeus (Jupiter) and Hermes (Mercurius), Grecian Gods

On Paul's first missionary journey with Barnabas they visited Lystra (Acts 14:7–13). The city was steeped in heathenism and mythology. It was not the superstition of an educated mind, nor the mythology of a refined and cultivated taste such as the Athenians, but the mythology and superstition of a rude and unsophisticated people.

Archaeological light on the worship of Zeus and Hermes in the region of Lystra was found on two inscriptions discovered there in 1909. They showed that the Lystrians believed two important gods had once visited the earth— Zeus, the father of gods and man, and Hermes, Zeus' son, the messenger and herald of the gods. The Roman name for Zeus was Jupiter, and Hermes was Mercury (or Mercurius). Lystra was under the tutelage of Jupiter, and tutelary divinities, though invisible, were imagined to live in and protect a city. The temple of Jupiter was a conspicuous object in front of the city gate, constantly reminding the Lystrians that someday, as Zeus/Jupiter and Hermes/Mercury (Mercurius) had appeared on earth before, they might return and visit Lystra.

When Paul and Barnabas visited the city, they immediately preached the Gospel (Acts 14:7). As Paul was preaching the Word, a certain man, impotent in feet and never having walked, listened intently. Paul perceived that he had faith to be healed, and the power of God through Paul enabled the man to leap and walk (Acts 14:7–10). As a result of this miracle, the people of Lystra thought Paul and Barnabas were gods—Jupiter and Mercurius.

Mercurius was the god of speech and eloquence, Jupiter's special messenger. Paul, because of his speech, was called Mercurius. Barnabas, probably because of his venerable appearance or the supposed likeness to their god, was named Jupiter. The priests of Jupiter who served in the temple at the city gate brought oxen and garlands and prepared to make a sacrifice before the people (Acts 14:11–13).

When Paul and Barnabas realized that the Lystrians thought their superstitious beliefs of gods appearing on earth had come to pass in Barnabas and himself, they ran among the people crying out, asking what they were doing. Paul reminded them that he and Barnabas were just humans the same as they, and that they had come to announce to them that they should turn from their futile religion to the true and living God, that this God is the One who gives rain from heaven and food for gladness. With difficulty, the crowds were restrained from offering sacrifices to this missionary pair (Acts 14:14–18).

In the midst of all this excitement, a group of opposing Jews from Antioch and Iconium came to Lystra and persuaded the Lystrians to denounce Paul for his preaching Christ. The Lystrians turned against Paul, stoned him, and dragged him outside the city, thinking he was dead. But God raised him up to continue on his missionary journey (Acts 14:19–20).

Converted Pagans at Thessalonica

Paul spent three Sabbaths in Thessalonica reasoning with the Jews concerning Christ as their Messiah. He must have stayed much longer in the city reasoning with the pagans, because his letter is written to those who had "turned from idols to serve the living and true God" (1 Thess. 1:9).

Archaeological discoveries reveal that the idolaters of Thessalonica believed that "After death no reviving or life; in the grave no meeting again or recognition." It is hard sometimes for babes in Christ to forget old things they were taught and believed as sinners, and Satan is anxious to capitalize on this. Possibly after conversion loved ones had passed away and there was concern about any future for the deceased who had trusted in Christ. "Will I ever see him/her again?" "If there is life beyond the grave, will I ever be able to recognize my loved one?" Word reached Paul concerning questions these new converts were asking, in particular the matter of what happens to a believer when death occurs (1 Thess. 4:13–18).

Paul's answer must have sent them into spiritual orbit when he said to them, "I would not have you to be ignorant, brethren, concerning them which are asleep [as your unsaved friends are with their pagan beliefs and as you used to be before you were saved], that ye sorrow not like your friends do who have no hope."

Paul then goes on to tell them about Christ's return for His own—the rapture, and not only will those who fell asleep in Christ but those who are alive and remain at His coming will be caught up *together* with Him and they shall ever be with the Lord! What comforting words these must have been to these babes in Christ. What a blessing this is to us having this background knowledge of these Thessalonicans.

The Areopagus, or Mars' Hill

Athens, Greece, furnishes much archaeological data from the ruins of the marketplace in the lowlands of the city to its temples, amphitheater, and in particular the Parthenon and temple ruins of Erechtheum on the Acropolis, all of which date back centuries before Christ (see fig. 73). There is no record of a church having been established there by Paul.

Adjacent to the Acropolis is a narrow, naked ridge of limestone. It rises some 370 feet above the valley and is separated from the Acropolis by a sixty-foot valley. This rocky knoll was consecrated to Ares, the god of war. Ares corresponds to the Roman god Mars, hence Mars' Hill.

When Paul arrived in Athens on his second missionary journey, he immediately began to preach the Gospel—the death, burial, and resurrection of Jesus Christ. Among the many groups of philosophers of that day were the Stoics and Epicureans.

They would generally sit in an amphitheater all day long, discussing various subjects, delving into the mysteries of life, the mind, and future life, ever seeking to learn some new thing. When they heard that Paul preached the resurrection of the dead, they took him to Mars' Hill to learn of this new doctrine.

Why the Areopagus, or Mars' Hill? There were any number of other places they could have taken Paul—many other more comfortable places to sit and listen rather than on a rocky hill.

Mars' Hill was the "judgment seat" of Athens. In Greek mythology, according to archaeological findings, this was the place where Athenian gods and goddesses descended to discuss matters, to make decisions, and to conduct trials requiring verdicts.

According to mythology, a famous trial was that of Orestes, who was charged with the murder of his mother. Orestus sought to bribe the gods to vote for his acquittal. He even tried to

"plea bargain" for a light sentence if found guilty. The vote was a tie, with Athena, the presiding judge, casting the deciding vote. The decision was "not guilty." Thus, Mars' Hill became the place where decisions were made.

Since the Epicureans and Stoics wanted to make a decision concerning Paul's new teachings about the resurrection of the body (and of Christ), he was taken to the centuries-old place of discussion and decision—Mars' Hill. Paul certainly had a background knowledge of the trial of Orestus—his bribing, plea bargaining, the politics of decisions and trials, and his sermon on Mars' Hill concluded with a most stinging rebuke of their beliefs.

In his sermon before these "learned" men (Acts 17:22–34), Paul said in effect in verses 30 and 31: "God has commanded all men everywhere to repent, for He has appointed a day in which He will judge the world in righteousness." He implied there would be no bribery, no plea bargaining, no arm twisting, no politics when each must stand before the God

Figure 73. A drawing of the Acropolis

who made heaven and earth. God will be presiding. There will be no voting. No decision will be made by a majority verdict. All your wrongs, your sins, will be judged by a righteous Judge, the Man God ordained to render a just verdict, the Man whom He raised from the dead—Jesus Christ (see Heb. 9:27).

Paul had brought them face-to-face with the living God, telling them that they were accountable to Him. There was no avenue of escape. Their philosophy could in no way be compared with Truth.

There is always conviction by the Holy Spirit when the Word of God is preached, resulting in a twofold reaction. Some believe and some do not. In the case of the "don'ts" on Mars' Hill, they interrupted Paul and mocked him because of his message on the Resurrection and Judgment by a righteous Judge. However, Paul's efforts were not in vain. One of the Mars' Hill judges, Dionyius the Areopogite, and others believed and followed Paul and his teachings of the Scriptures.

Altar to an Unknown God

While being taken to Mars' Hill, Paul observed their devotions and

Figure 74. The altar of an unknown god

noticed an altar with this inscription, TO THE UNKNOWN GOD (Acts 17:23; see fig. 74). The Greeks were polytheistic—having a god for any and everything. Paul told them "that in all things ye are too superstitious [very religious]." Not only did their many idols and temples prove this, but for fear of overlooking a god or goddess, they erected many altars to unknown divinities. The inscription on the pictured altar says, "Sacred, whether it be a god or goddess." Paul, who at one time did not know who the real God was, used their altar to tell them he now knew, as his Mars' Hill sermon shows.

Gallio, Proconsul of Corinth

Paul left Athens to begin a work in Corinth. There he became acquainted with Aquila and Priscilla and stayed with them while in the city, working at his trade as a tentmaker. Having reasoned every Sabbath with the Jews that Jesus was the Christ, opposition arose among certain Jews who accused Paul of preaching a religion contrary to Roman law. He was brought before Gallio, the proconsul of Achaia, the province in which Corinth was located (Acts 18:1–17). An inscription was found at Delphi in northern Greece in 1908 which bears the name of Gallio when he was in office in A.D. 51–53 (see fig. 75). This archaeological discovery gives us the definite date for Paul's visit to Corinth.

When Paul was charged by the Jews, he faced Gallio in his judgment seat or courthouse—*bema* in Greek. Evidently Gallio cared little about the accusation the Jews made against Paul and set him free. When Paul wrote to the Corinthians a few years later, remembering he had appeared before

Gallio's *bema* seat, he said in effect to the believers, "All might not have to appear before an earthly judge, but all must appear before the judgment seat of Christ, that everyone may receive the things done in his body, according to that he hath done, whether it be good or bad" (2 Cor. 5:10). The picture shows the ruins of Gallio's *bema* where Paul was tried. Ruins of the temple of Aphrodite, the goddess of love, are on top of the mountain in the background (see fig. 76).

Paul also used the sport-mindedness of Corinth to inform believers they should discipline themselves for their Christian walk as athletes do for their games. He referred to a technique in boxing: "So fight I, not as one who beateth the air."

If a boxer does not train, once in the ring he "beats the air," hoping to land a blow that gives victory. But if he has trained, he knows how to sidestep and duck, wearing his opponent out. He then knocks his opponent down. We too must train to keep our enemy, Satan, from gaining the victory.

Paul also used the example of an athlete who runs in a race, hoping to win a corruptible laurel wreath (crown; see fig. 77). Only one runner wins, but in our Christian race, *all* believers can be winners if they so train—winning an incorruptible crown (1 Cor. 9:24–27). By living a disciplined, dedicated life for Christ and remembering we must face His *bema,* we build upon the foundation that is Jesus Christ—gold, silver, precious stones, enduring rewards to lay at His feet in appreciation for all He has done for us. But if we are not living a disciplined, dedicated life, we are saved yet as by fire but suffer loss of rewards (1 Cor. 3:9–15).

Figure 75. Procounsul Gallio's inscription

Ephesus

The account of Paul's visit to Ephesus is in Acts 19:1–20:1. Archaeological excavations over a period of years have brought to light inscriptions and artifacts that not only give us a historical background of this once mighty city but relate to many significant items associated with Paul's three-year visit there (Acts 20:17, 31).

With the decay of Miletus in the south, Ephesus became the greatest city in Asia Minor—the gateway between Rome to the west and Asia Minor and Asia to the east. It was half oriental, half occidental. Ships from the then-known world sailed from the Mediterranean Sea into the Cayster River to Ephesus. It was united by great roads with commerce and markets from the interior, thus becoming the meeting place for various classes of people. It was here, possibly in the huge sports arena, that Paul fought with wild beasts (1 Cor. 15:32). It was here in the vast amphitheater seating 25,000 people, that the mob cried, "Great is Diana of the Ephesians" (Acts 19:28).

Paul's preaching in Ephesus produced a hearing of the Word of the

Figure 76. The ruins of Gallio's *Bema*

Figure 77. A relief of the winning of a corruptible crown

Lord Jesus throughout Asia, which resulted in many converts and a turning from idols to serve God (19:10, 17–20). It also resulted in loss of revenue for the idol makers and led to the uproar which exalted the goddess of Ephesus, Diana (19:23–41).

Evidence from excavations in Ephesus has produced much information about this religion. Many statues of Diana have been found, one as a multiple-breasted goddess of fertility. Coins minted in her honor show her head on the obverse side and the cult image of this lewd religion on the reverse.

Diana is the Roman name for the Greek goddess Artemis. Her honor is dated from remote antiquity. She was the patron goddess of Phoenician navigators long before Ephesus became important. She supposedly fell from heaven (19:35), and as the multiple-breasted goddess of fertility, she became the nursing mother of gods, people, animals, and was the patron goddess of sexual instinct.

The worship of Diana was more oriental than Greek in influence. Images of her remind us of idols of the Far East. Such multiple-breasted statues depict a religion in which all of life is fed and supported by many breasts of nature (see fig. 78). The lower part of the pictured statue depicts small-sized animals of Greek fables—bees, lambs, heads of lions, crabs, deer, and bulls. The image was the model on which the smaller images were formed to worship her.

The actual worship ceremonies of Diana at Ephesus were conducted by her priests and numerous priestesses. They were virgins when they offered themselves as slaves to Diana, afterward selling their bodies in the many brothels to help support the upkeep of her magnificent temple.

Figure 78. Statue and coins of "Diana the Great" of Ephesus

The Temple of Diana was considered one of the seven wonders of the ancient world. It was imposingly beautiful, a sight to behold. The temple was considered so holy that citizens of foreign countries brought gifts to her and deposited huge sums of money for safekeeping. One inscription mentions a man who gave twenty-nine gold and silver images of Diana to be used in public processions.

One month each year was dedicated to the worship of Diana. Her colossal temple was 425 feet long and 220 feet wide. There were 127 columns, each 60 feet high, some 16 inches in diameter, and each of them a gift of a king. Thirty-six columns were enriched with ornament and color. The staircase was formed with the wood of one single vine from the island of Cyprus. It is said that the sun saw nothing more magnificent than Diana's temple. Probably there were no two religious buildings in the world in which were concentrated a greater amount of admiration and enthusiasm than the temple of Diana and the Temple of Solomon.

The worship of Diana surpassed all pagan religious beliefs in superstition. Pillaged by the Goths in A.D. 111 and burned by a madman in A.D. 365, all that exists of the temple are a few pillars and statues in museums in Ephesus, Naples, and the Archaeological Museum in Istanbul. Its ruins were discovered after a series of excavations beginning in 1863.

Brothels

Although Ephesus was a very religious city, it was equally immoral. Tragically, sex was a highlight of its religion. Diana set the sordid example for virgins to become prostitute priestesses, selling their bodies in her honor.

Since Ephesus was the crossroad between Asian (oriental) and European (occidental) culture, commerce brought sailors from far and near. Making port here, many would immediately seek out prostitutes. This resulted in numerous brothels being conveniently located throughout the city. Pictured is a footprint carved in the marble sidewalk pointing to such a place (fig. 79).

This is the Ephesus which Paul came to visit and preach the Gospel. It is no wonder Paul told the Ephesians to "walk not as other Gentiles, put off your former manner of life, give no place to the devil, let no filthy words come from your mouth, grieve not the Holy Spirit" (Eph. 4).

Brothels were not limited to Ephesus, as Paul well knew. For example, as archaeology shows, the city of

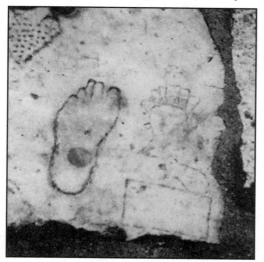

Figure 79. Footprint pointing to a brothel

Corinth had the reputation of moral corruption to the point where the expression "Corinthian girl" meant prostitute and the expression "to live like a Corinthian" signified the living of a loose, immoral life. Ritual prostitution in the temple of Aphrodite on the acropolis at Corinth was in part responsible for this reputation.

Soon after Corinth's restoration by the Romans in 44 B.C., there were about a thousand female temple slaves. It is little wonder that Paul, in writing to the Corinthians, emphasized the fact that the body of the born-again believer is the temple of the Holy Spirit, and that a member of Christ's body should not be joined to a harlot or defiled (1 Cor. 3:16–17; 6:14–19).

Rome was another city that had illicit places for sex-hungry men. Many wall paintings of sex orgies are still visible in Pompeii, which was covered by volcanic ash when Mount Vesuvius erupted in A.D. 79 (now excavated). Coins were minted with actual scenes of men and women in brothels. These coins or tokens were used to pay the women for their services and were called *spintrial*, a Latin word meaning unnatural lust or prostitution. One writer labeled them as "the famous brothel tokens of ancient Rome." It is no wonder that Paul gave such a vivid picture of sin in Romans 1:18–32, and why he made such an appeal to present one's body as a living sacrifice and be transformed to fulfill God's will in their lives (Rom. 12:1–2).

Footstools

Christ's resurrection was God's victory over Satan, sin, hell, and death (1 Cor. 15:17; Rev. 1:5, 18; Heb. 2:9, 14). His resurrection made possible His taking captive the one who formerly had held captive those in bondage of sin and in fear of death. "He [Christ] led captivity [Satan] captive" (Eph. 4:8). Through the mighty working of God's power in His resurrection, Christ is now above all principality and power and might and dominion, and every name that is named . . . and hath . . . all things under His feet—all these things as His footstool (Eph. 1:20–22; see also Judg. 5:12–13; Ps. 68:17–19).

Paul used the ancient custom of victorious monarchs who had images of their defeated foes carved on their footstools to illustrate this truth regarding Christ. The footstool of King Tut-ankh-amun of Egypt shows images of his defeated enemies on the top and sides (see fig. 80). Each time he sat on his throne each enemy was "under his feet." He even had pictures of his defeated foes painted on the soles of his shoes so that with each step, as he said, he "ground them in the dirt."

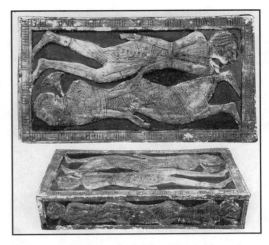

Figure 80. Footstool of King Tut-ankh-amun

The Armor of God

The New Testament speaks of the believer being in a spiritual warfare, hence a need to put on the armor of God (Eph. 6:11–18). Shown in figure 81 are Roman soldiers dressed in their armor, ready for battle at a moment's notice.

While Rome's battles were physical, the believer's is "against the wiles of the devil, for we wrestle not against flesh and blood, but against the prince of the power of the air, against principalities, against powers, against the rulers of darkness of this world, against spiritual wickedness in high places."

We fight the fight of faith by taking God's provision for this warfare—the "whole armor of God." No matter where the believer looked, he could always see a Roman soldier, and what a great illustration Paul used to remind them to be prepared for life's battles. By our putting on God's armor

1. Our loins are girt about with truth so that we might stand against the wiles of the Devil and resist him that he flee from us (Eph. 6:11; James 4:7).

2. We have the breastplate of righteousness to protect our hearts for daily praise and right living (Ps. 9:1; Prov. 4:23).

3. We have our feet shod (permanently fitted) with the preparation of the Gospel of peace to be on the move as His witnesses (Rom. 10:15).

4. We have the shield of faith to ward off the fiery darts (attacks) of Satan, who constantly seeks to get us to walk by sight and not by faith (Heb. 11:6).

5. We put on the helmet of salvation to protect our minds for Christ to do His thinking through us (1 Cor. 2:16; Phil. 4:8; Prov. 23:7a).

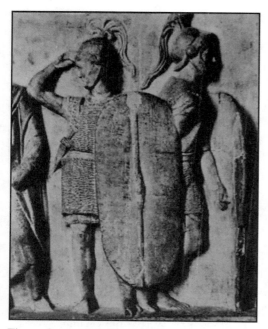

Figure 81. A depiction of Roman soldiers in full armor

6. We use the Sword of the Spirit—the Word of God—relying upon it for every victory in battle (Matt. 4:1–10; 2 Tim. 2:15).
7. We pray always that we enter not into temptation (Matt. 26:41).

Notice that this uniform is defensive. The weapons are defensive. There is no defense or protective armor for one's back. The true Christian soldier does not turn and run—this leaves them defenseless, with no protection against the enemy. There are no deserters, no defectors, and no cowards here. Clothed with God's whole armor, they "endure hardness as a good soldier of Jesus Christ" (2 Tim. 2:3) and can say with the apostle Paul, "I have fought a good fight, I have finished my course, I have kept the faith" (2 Tim. 4:7).

Roman Citizenship and Slavery

Roman citizenship was achieved in at least five ways: (1) born free, as was the case of Paul; (2) bestowed due to some favorable deed for Rome; (3) as an honor to a person of note, even to a slave who proved trustworthy; (4) to soldiers for bravery or upon their being honorably discharged; and (5) purchased, as noted in Acts 22:25–28. Figure 82 shows a military diploma, granting citizenship to soldiers who had been honorably discharged and their wives.

Since Paul was born free, this means his parents were Roman citizens. Sons usually followed their father's trade, and since Cilicia was heavily populated by Roman soldiers and in need of tents, possibly the high grade of craftsmanship in tentmaking by Paul's father merited citizenship.

To claim to be a citizen of Rome and not actually be one was punishable by death. Paul never would have made reference to his citizenship if he were not (Acts 22:25–28). No matter where a Roman citizen traveled throughout the empire, as a citizen he was entitled to all the rights and privileges the law provided. When Paul made his appeal to Caesar, this necessitated his going to Rome. Roman citizens were not crucified, as noncitizens were. When Paul met his fate, he was most likely beheaded, the capital punishment meted out to Rome's citizens.

Figure 83 shows Roman soldiers capturing a prisoner who will be sold as a slave. The dress on the prisoner shows that he came from the Parthian Empire. Throughout the Roman Empire it is reported that at least 30 percent of the population were slaves. They were not allowed to wear distinguishing marks lest it be discovered how numerous they were and so organize and revolt.

The New Testament Epistle to Philemon by Paul gives an interesting story of a runaway slave. Onesimus, one of Philemon's slaves, had apparently robbed his master (v. 18) and escaped to Rome. He heard Paul preach, was saved (v. 10), and became a faithful disciple (Col. 4:9).

Paul desired to use him as his own helper, but realized Onesimus had an obligation to his master, Philemon, and felt it his duty to send him back (vv. 13–14). Onesimus knew that to return meant he would be put to death, as the law required of a runaway slave, so Paul wrote a letter to his friend Philemon, first commending him for his stand in the Gospel, and then presenting his case in behalf of Onesimus. Paul requested that Philemon accept him as a brother in Christ since the slave had become a Christian. To ensure safe passage for Onesimus, Paul gave the letter to a fellow helper, Tychicus, who would vouch for Onesimus's return to his master should he be stopped by a Roman soldier.

Nero, Persecutor of Christians

Archaeology has given us much light on the Caesar, Nero, the "unrighteous judge" before whom Paul appeared. Born in A.D. 37, Nero was from a family of scoundrels. His father, a Roman government official with several murders to his credit, died when Nero was three. His mother poisoned his stepfather. She later married emperor Claudius, who adopted Nero.

After persuading the emperor to designate Nero heir to the throne in place of his own son, Nero's mother murdered Claudius before he could change his mind. At the age of sixteen

Nero became ruler of the Roman Empire (see fig. 84).

Nero had married his stepfather's daughter at the age of fifteen. He had his first wife slain and killed his second wife himself. To obtain his third wife, he had her husband killed. And to keep Claudius's own son Britannicus from claiming his father's throne, Nero had him poisoned.

His greed for publicity, especially in sports, drove Nero to gory acts of violence. Chariot races and bloody scenes with wild beasts and gladiators and prisoners became his delight.

When Rome burned for a week in

Figure 82. Certificate of Roman citizenship

Figure 83. A carving of the capture of a slave

from all sides things scandalous and shameful meet and become fashionable. Therefore, at the beginning, some were seized who made confessions; then on their information, a vast multitude was convicted, not so much for arson as of hatred for the human race. And they were not only put to death, but subjected to insults, in that they were either dressed up in the skins of wild animals and perished by the cruel mangling of dogs, or else put on crosses and set on fire, and, as day declined, to be burned, being used as light by night. Nero had thrown open his gardens for that spectacle, and gave a circus play, mingling with the people, dressed in a charioteer's costume and riding in a chariot. From this arose, however, toward men who were, indeed, criminals and deserving extreme penalties, sympathy, on the ground that they were destroyed not for the public good, but to gratify the savage instincts of one man.

By the time Nero was thirty-one years old, the Roman Empire was so weak that the Senate, officers, soldiers, and even the palace guards were defecting. Finally, the Senate declared Nero a public enemy and sentenced him to death by flogging. He escaped this sentence by committing suicide.

July, A.D. 64, it was rumored that he had set fire to the city to make room for a new palace. He made Christians, who refused to worship the emperor, the scapegoat, charging them with arson and "hatred of the human race."

The Roman historian Tacitus records the persecutions of Christians under Nero in A.D. 64 as follows:

> Nero put men in charge who knew how to punish with the most ingenious cruelty and wrought havoc with those the common people hated for their crimes and called "Christian." Christus [Christ], for whom the name was derived, had been put to death in the reign of Tiberius by the procurator Pontius Pilate. The deadly superstition, having been checked for awhile, began to break out again, not only throughout Judea, where this mischief first arose, but also in Rome, where

Figure 84. The profile of Nero

Emperor Worship and Citizenship Certificate

Thanks to archaeology, a decree issued by one of the Caesars was found, in which it was stated that Caesar was "god and savior" (see fig. 85). It indicates that Roman citizens had to affirm their allegiance to Caesar as such. This meant that emperor worship was common throughout the whole empire. In affirming allegiance before some magistrate or official, the citizen was given a certificate which had to be on his person as we must have a driver's permit when driving. Roman soldiers were at liberty to stop anyone and ask to see their credentials. If none could be shown, the individual was haled into court and questioned about his religious beliefs. Early New Testament saints could not produce any, and if one confessed that he was a follower of Jesus Christ, he was given opportunity twice to deny Christ and embrace emperor worship. Christians who refused were crucified, thrown to wild beasts, or became lighted torches.

An ancient bronze plaque states that in A.D. 37 the governor of Assos begged the favor of emperor Caligula, saying that "Every city and every nation is eager to behold the face of God, feeling that the most delightful age for mankind has now begun. We swear by the Savior and God, Caesar Augustus, and by our local deity, Athena, to be loyal to Gaius Caesar Augustus and all his house, to deem as friends those whom he favors and as enemies those whom he designates; with things to go well with us if we keep our oath, and the opposite if we break it."

The Catacombs

Persecution was so rampant throughout the Roman Empire, especially in the city of Rome, that no Christian was safe. Emperor worship was the rule of the day. Christians were well aware that their citizenship was in

Figure 85. Caesar's "God and Savior" decree and citizen's certificate

Figure 86. Catacomb paintings

Figure 87. Christian symbols found in catacombs

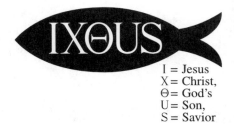

I = Jesus
X = Christ,
Θ = God's
U = Son,
S = Savior

Figure 88. Sign of the fish

heaven, and in escaping the Roman soldiers who questioned their Roman citizenship, they often fled to the catacombs.

Here the Christians felt safe. The soldiers were superstitious and would not enter these burial grounds. The first thing they would see, dimly lit by a candle, was a message carved in stone: "Take courage, O Christian, Caesar is not infallible." This was to let them know there were others just like them, and that together, in secret, they could worship the true God.

Over the years they left paintings and inscriptions which indicated their faith and trust in Christ as their Savior (see fig. 86). The earliest known inscription is dated A.D. 72. Other dates are inscribed through the fourth century when Christianity became the state religion.

Many scenes depict deliverance, such as Noah's survival of the flood, Jonah's escape from the great fish, Daniel's protection in the lion's den, and the raising of Lazarus. Other paintings reveal flowers and doves, symbolizing the loveliness and beauty of Christ in the midst of Rome's ugliness and God's peace and inner witness of His Holy Spirit in spite of tribulation in the world.

There are signs of an anchor, indicating their security in Christ (see fig. 87); a sword, which shows their trust was in the "Sword of the Spirit," the Word of God; the letter "X," symbolizing Christ Himself (*X* in Greek is the letter Chi, the first letter in the name *Christ*); and the sign of the fish (see fig. 88), denoting their trust in "Jesus Christ, God's Son, Savior." By taking the initial letters of this expression in Greek, the word *icthus* is spelled, which means *fish*. This sign of the fish let all Rome know that not everyone had bowed to Caesar as "god and savior."

There are no signs left by these early saints to indicate a belief in purgatory, confession of sins to a religious leader, a worshiping of Christ's earthly mother, Mary, or that Peter had anything to do with a Roman church. There is no evidence of formalism or of a political, socialistic gospel. There is one inscription which says, "Peter and Paul, pray for us," which the Roman Catholics use as their tradition to pray to saints, but it could well be an inscription to indicate these persecuted Christians wanted fellow believers to pray for them in their need, especially as we think of the admonition for believers to "pray one for another" (James 5:16; 1 Sam. 12:23).

A study has shown that the passageways of the various catacombs near Rome would total 550 miles if they were extended in a straight line. It is estimated that there are nearly 2 million graves in them. What a place to meet in secret to worship God and have fellowship, but here is where the Christians found freedom from their persecutors. These believers knew that salvation was in a Person—Jesus Christ Himself—and not in a church, a ritual, or a solemn sacrament. They knew that He, and He alone, was the Way, the Truth, and the Life (John 14:6).

Roman Prisons

We are primarily interested in these prisons because Paul was imprisoned first when he made his appeal to Caesar, and then later just before his death. There were three types of imprisonment throughout the Roman Empire:

1. Free custody (*custodia libera*), which was the mildest kind. Here the accused was committed to the

Figure 89. Interior of the Mamertine Prison (hole at arrow)

magistrate or senator, who became responsible for his appearance on the day of trial. This type of detention applied only to those of high rank. This was not a prison per se, and the person was released on his own recognizance.

2. Military custody (*custodia militaris*), which was introduced at the beginning of the imperial regime. In this form of custody the accused was given to a Roman soldier who was responsible with his own life for the safekeeping of his prisoner. This was further secured by chaining the prisoner's right hand to the soldier's left hand. The soldiers, of course, relieved one another in this duty. The prisoner was usually kept in the barracks, but sometimes was allowed to reside in a private house under the soldier's charge.

3. Public custody (*custodia publica*), the most severe kind of incarceration Rome inflicted on a prisoner. This type of prison was called the *tullianum*. One called the "Mamertine Prison" has been discovered in Rome. It had three distinct sections: (a) the *communiora*, where the prisoner had light and fresh air; (b) the *inteniora*, shut off by iron gates with strong bars and locks; and (3) the *tullianum*, or dungeon. Tullianum bred pestilences. They were cold, damp, filthy, smelly, and dimly lit. Excrement piled up; the odor was stifling. For one to enter such a dungeon, ropes were tied under his arms, and he was lowered through a hole cut in the rock. There were no doors or windows and absolutely no possibility of escape. Some prisoners had stayed so long their chains were rusted. Many died in such pits before coming to trial. The only time fresh air came into the dungeon was when the door to the hole was opened to either

let down a prisoner or take one out for trial or to take out a body.

When Paul was rescued by Roman soldiers after his temple experience in Acts 21:31–37, he was detained in the soldiers' barracks under *custodia militaris*. This was the same imprisonment he experienced under Felix in Caesarea (Acts 24:22–23) and during his two-year imprisonment in Rome when he wrote his four "Prison Epistles" (Acts 28:30–31). Shown is a first-century letter, sealed and ready to go (fig. 90).

There is sufficient biblical evidence to show that Paul had two imprisonments. His second imprisonment was likely in the Mamertine Prison, the *custodia publica*. This was also the type of prison in which Paul and Silas were confined when in Philippi. Notice here it was called the inner prison, containing stocks (Acts 16:19–24).

When Paul wrote to Timothy in his second epistle he said, "I am suffering to the point of being chained like a criminal" (2:9 ASV). This certainly was not his lot under *custodia militaris*. The picture in figure 89 shows the interior of the Mamertine Prison. The arrow points to the hole through which prisoners were let down. The plaque is in memory of Paul, showing him placing his hands on a new convert while other converts praise the Lord. No matter where Paul was—in prison, before kings and governors, in synagogues, in marketplaces, before Gentiles and philosophers—he always witnessed for his Savior, determined to know nothing among them save Jesus Christ and Him crucified (1 Cor. 2:2).

Paul's Trial

At this point of Paul's imprisonment it is wise to bring up archaeological evidence that reveals the type of trial Paul faced. Nero was very bitter against Christians. There were believers in his own household, whose presence no doubt agitated him (Phil. 4:22).

Jews also were bitter against Christians and Paul in particular. They could easily have let Caesar know their feelings, especially since they were still angry about his first arrest coming to nothing.

No matter where Paul went, his preaching the Gospel agitated the Jews, who could contact soldiers about his whereabouts. When he was re-arrested and taken to Rome, he requested Timothy to bring his cloak, books, and especially the parchments he had to leave behind in the home of Carpus in Troas (2 Tim. 4:13; see fig. 90). You can well imagine his desire for the cloak to help keep him warm in the cold, damp dungeon.

Figure 90. First-century letter and sealed parchment

Although Paul was innocent of all charges brought against him, in the eyes of Rome he had already been tried, found guilty, and condemned to die. Only the formality of a trial stood in the way of his execution. The original charge against him was one of a religious nature. Now, however, the stigma of being branded a Christian made it easy for the court to charge him with treason and sedition. Brought before the tribunal in fetters or chains under the custody of a military guard, the order of the court was as follows: (1) the speech of the prosecutor; (2) the examination and cross-examination of witnesses by the prosecutor; (3) the speech of the prisoner; and (4) examination and cross-examination of the witnesses for the defense.

Paul had been accused of being a "ringleader of the Nazarenes" and of sedition—preaching a different kingdom than Rome, the "kingdom of God" (Acts 19:8; 24:5). Preaching another kingdom than Rome was a most serious charge; it amounted to *majestas*, or treason against the commonwealth, and was punishable by death. When the parties on both sides were heard and all the witnesses examined, the judgment of the court was taken. No matter the opinion of the magistrates, the emperor would give sentence according to his pleasure, without any reference to the judgment of the majority. But doubtless the seared conscience made Nero immune to emotions, which must have shaken the nerves of those in judgment. Nero's verdict? Paul must die.

A date for Paul's execution would be set by the emperor, and soon the curtain would fall for the one man who probably did more to

Figure 91. The Roman emperor Titus

spread the Gospel than all other apostles combined.

On one occasion Paul said: "I labored more abundantly than they all" (1 Cor. 15:10). He had fought a good fight, he had finished his course, and he had endured to the end by keeping the faith. He resigned himself to Nero's sentence by saying, "I am now ready to be offered, and the time of my departure is at hand" (2 Tim. 4:6).

"To be offered" means "to be poured out in libation"—to be sacrificed in death. It is no wonder he could say, "For me to live is Christ and to die is gain" (Phil. 1:21). Paul was not crucified as were many other Christians. As a Roman citizen, he was beheaded, and his own epitaph is recorded in 2 Timothy 4:6–8. He is now absent from the body, present with the Lord!

Figure 92. Detail from the Arch of Titus showing the spoils of victory from the destruction of Jerusalem—Table of Showbread, Trumpets of Priests, and Candlestick of the Temple

Destruction of Jerusalem

When Christ foretold the destruction of Herod's temple in Jerusalem, He clearly had in mind the destruction of the city itself (Luke 21:5–6, 20–24). Because of Jewish rebellion against Rome's tyranny, armies were sent to and stationed in Palestine to keep order. During one such rebellion in A.D. 68, Vespasian's army had routed the Jews in Jericho and Qumran [see "Dead Sea Scrolls" in Index]. Called back to Rome to become emperor in A.D. 69, Vespasian was replaced by his son, Titus (see fig. 91), who fulfilled Christ's prophecy in A.D. 70 when he began the siege that led to the destruction of Jerusalem.

Titus ordered the city razed and the temple destroyed and was responsible for the slaughter of over 600,000 Jews. Thousands were taken captive. He celebrated his victory in Rome the following year, according to Josephus, accompanied by Jewish prisoners and the spoils of war, which included a copy of the Law, the golden table of showbread, and the golden lampstand.

Titus was made emperor of Rome in A.D. 79, and died two years later. His arch in Rome (see fig. 92), built to commemorate his victory over Jerusalem, was dedicated after his death in A.D. 81. On one side it depicts his soldiers making their triumphal entry into the city, and on the other side it depicts his soldiers crowned with laurel and carrying the seven-branched lampstand, the table of showbread, and the priests' trumpets from the temple.

Roman soldiers of the Tenth Roman Legion were stationed by Titus in Jerusalem to keep order. Many tiles bearing an inscription of this legion have been found, and some years ago a

Figure 93. Tenth Roman Legion monument

monument bearing this inscription, "Tenth Roman Legion," was excavated (see fig. 93). Further evidence of Jerusalem's destruction by Titus is seen on this "Judea Capta" coin (see fig. 94), which was minted in honor of Titus. The reverse side shows two Jews in utter defeat seated beneath a palm tree.

Figure 94. Judae Capta coin

Figure 95. Temple stones with grooves

Summary

From the beginning of our expedition in this section to its conclusion, we have encountered one proof after another in supplementing the records of the Bible with living messages from a buried past. Modern archaeological discoveries shed abundant light on ancient world history from God's point of view.

When God employed the science of archaeology in causing "truth to spring out of the earth" (Ps. 85:11a), He gave to the champions of Scripture a new weapon to attack the critics of the Word—those who question the authenticity and trustworthiness of the fundamental doctrines of Christianity.

Archaeology has shown that the events recorded in the Bible actually happened. It has further shown that names of kings, nations, and peoples did in fact exist, and that many customs, so unfamiliar to our Western minds, were factual practices.

Just as the "heavens declare the glory of God and the firmament showeth His handiwork," so the evidence triumphantly shows the Bible worthy of believing. What has come to light by the pick and spade of the archaeologist is by no means the end. It has whetted the appetite to keep on digging—to excavate sites yet buried, to glean more information about God's Book.

In war, it was unusual for a building to be completely destroyed. Many times stones at the base were left intact while walls crumbled. However, Jesus predicted that in the destruction of the temple, "There shall not be left here one stone upon another, that shall not be thrown down" (Matt. 24:2).

Precious metal fitted in grooves often held temple stones together (see fig. 95). Knowing this, the soldiers literally took the temple apart stone by stone [see "Temple, Destruction of" in Index]. The destruction of Jerusalem as predicted by Christ also fulfilled Moses' words that if Israel disobeyed the Lord, the result wold be worldwide dispersion (Deut. 28:15–65). [See "Dispersion of the Jews" in Index.]

God's Word

I paused last eve beside the
     blacksmith's door,
     And heard the anvil ring, the
          vesper's chime,
And looking in I saw upon the floor
     Old hammers, worn with beating
          years of time.

"How many anvils have you had?"
    said I,
    "To wear and batter these
        hammers so?"
"Just one," he answered. Then with
    twinkling eye:
    "The anvil wears the hammers
        out, you know."

And so, thought I, the anvil of God's
    Word
    For ages skeptics' blows have beat
        upon,
But though the noise of falling blows
    was heard
    The anvil is unchanged; the
        hammers gone.
                    —John Clifford

We have sought to show in this threefold book of Christian evidences that the Bible is divinely inspired. There is ample proof to substantiate its accuracy in scientific statements, its fulfilled prophecy, and archaeological discoveries as they relate to historical statements and customs in the Scriptures.

The Word of God *will* stand the tests of time, no matter how many hammers future critics may wield. The believer can rest in God's promises: "If men hold their peace [or become critical of the things of the Lord], God will make stones immediately cry out" (Luke 19:37–40); He will cause truth to spring out of the earth (Ps. 85:11a). Today it is the critic who is on the defensive and behind the times—not the Christian.

With all this evidence at hand, may God help us to hide His Word in our hearts that we might not sin against Him (Ps. 119:11). May we adopt the fourfold purpose of the Essenes [see "Essenes" in Index], testify as Paul did

(Acts 20:20–21), and contend for the faith as did the early New Testament saints (Jude 3). If we do this, we can say with Paul, "For to me to live is Christ." And when our time comes to be absent from the body, present with the Lord, we can complete Paul's statement—"and to die is gain" (Phil. 1:21; 2 Cor. 5:8).

Letter from Heaven

I'm interested in heaven because I have a clear title to a bit of property there ever since I placed my trust in Jesus Christ as my very own personal Savior, February 17, 1938. I did not buy it. It was given to me without money and without price. But the Donor purchased it for me at a tremendous price, a tremendous sacrifice, His very own precious blood. I am not holding it for speculation since the title is nontransferable. It is not a vacant lot.

All these years I have been sending up materials out of which the Master Architect and Builder of our vast universe has been building a mansion for me, a house which will never be remodeled or repaired because it will always suit me perfectly and individually. It will never grow old or deteriorate. Termites can never undermine its foundation, for it rests upon the Rock of Ages. Fire cannot destroy it, floods cannot wash it away, tornadoes cannot blow it away, nor can earthquakes bring it to rubble. No locks or bolts will ever be placed on any of its doors for no corrupt person can possibly enter that land where my dwelling stands—now nearer completion than when I first believed. When I go to meet my Savior and stand on the shores of heaven—absent from body, present with the Lord—my house will be ready for me to enter and abide in peace eternally, without any fear of ever being evicted!

There is a valley of deep shadows between the place where I now live in Pennsylvania and that to which I shall journey, maybe sooner than I think. I cannot reach that home in that city of gold without passing through this dark valley of shadows (unless, of course, I am raptured first), but I am not afraid, because the best Friend I ever had went through this same valley long, long ago and drove away all its gloom. Oftentimes when I looked at the single set of footprints, I thought I was all alone, but He was carrying me and the footprints were His. He has stuck by me through thick and thin since we first became acquainted, and I have His promise in printed form that He will never leave me nor forsake me, that He will be with me *always, never* to be left alone. He will be with me as I walk through the valley of the shadow of death, and there is no possibility of my losing my way because He is always present to guide me on the straight and narrow Way that leads to eternal life.

I have no assurance I will be here another day, that I will hear another sermon on "heaven." My ticket to this bright, glorious eternal abode has no date marked for the journey, no return coupon, no place for cancellation, and no permit for any baggage. Yes, I am ready to die, and I shall look forward to meeting all my saved loved ones and friends over there some day.

Surely His and truly yours,
Robert T. (Bob) Boyd

Appendix

Gods and Idols Mentioned in the Bible

Archaeologists have contributed greatly to our knowledge of pagan religions, the gods they worshiped, and their practices. The evidence shows that which the remnant of the children of Israel and early New Testaments saints had to contend as they sought to maintain their faith in the true and living God and His Son, Jesus Christ.

Adrammelech: 2 Kings 17:31. Assyrian sun deity; king of fire. Humans, especially children, were offered to this god. [See "Molech" in Index.]

Anammelech: 2 Kings 17:31. Assyrian moon deity; *queen of fire*. [See "Molech."]

Ashima: 2 Kings 17:30. Assyrian deity; a "goat" (four-footed beast: Rom. 1:23).

Ashtoroth (Astarte): 1 Kings 11:33. Plural of *Ashtoreth*. Canaanite fertility goddess; sexual love. [See "Queen of Heaven" in Index.]

Astrology/Divination: Deuteronomy 17:2–5; 2 Kings 21:5–6. [See Index.]

Athirat: Mother of Baal, patron goddess of love, fertility, and sex. She was glorified and honored with the usage of carved sex symbols of nude males and females on six-foot tree stumps with an altar placed between them. The Hebrew word for Athirat is *Asherah* (plural, Asherim), which is translated *grove* or *groves* in our King James Bible. Note 1 Kings 16:33; 2 Kings 17:9, 16. Israel was forbidden to build and worship at such an altar (Deut. 16:21–22. [See "Baal Worship" in Index.]

These "groves" or *Asherim* were for the purpose of Baal's priests and prostitute priestesses performing sex acts as patterns to induce the worshipers of Baal to satisfy their own lustful desires. All this led to what Moses described in Leviticus 18, which formed the foundation for the religious practices of the Canaanites. Paul indirectly referred to such behavior in Romans 1:18–32.

Athtar: [See "Molech."]

Baal: [See Index.] There are traces still

extant of customs in Ireland, Wales, and in parts of Scotland, which evidently show that Baal worship was practiced by some of our ancestors under the ancient Druids. In Perthshire, Wales, there is a town called Tillie-baltane—*the hill of fire of Baal.*

Baal-berith: Judges 8:33. *Lord of covenants*; worship of Baal by the Shechemites.

Baal-peor: Numbers 25:1–3. *Lord of the opening*; worship of Baal by the Moabites. Note Israel's sin with the Moabites.

Baal-zebub: 2 Kings 1:2. Ekron deity; *lord or god of flies*, who became the *Beelzebub* of the New Testament, and who supposedly had power of curing certain diseases (Matt. 10:25; 12:24). Baal was often designated "Zebul," meaning *Prince*. In devil, or demon worship, "Princely Baal" was the name for Satan, "Prince of the Demons." Demon worship was common even before the children of Israel entered the Promised Land (Deut. 32:17). During Christ's time the Pharisees referred to the Devil as "Beelzebub, prince of devils [demons]" (Matt. 12:22–27), which is a corruption of "Princely Baal."

In the worship of demons, it is not surprising to learn that the followers of Baal used *snakes*, which are symbols of Satan, as noted in Genesis 3:1–15 and Revelation 20:2. Near Dagon's temple in the ruins of Ugarit (Ras Shamra), archaeologists found an image which depicted a snake priestess with a large snake about her breast and hips. Among other objects found was a design of two sacred prostitute dancers with the headdress of a snake, a large number of silver snakes, resembling those used in sacrifices, and a serpent carved out of stone. [See "Nehushtan/Brazen Serpent" in Index.]

Bel: Jeremiah 50:2. Babylonian form of Baal.

Brazen Serpent: [See "Nehushtan."]

Chemosh: Numbers 21:29. Moabite deity; subduer. Human sacrifices were made to this god (2 Kings 3:27). [See "Moabite Stone" and "Molech" in Index.]

Chiun: Amos 5:26. A form of star worship; associated with *Rephan* in Acts 7:43.

Dagon: 1 Samuel 5:2. Philistine deity; part man and part fish, god of agriculture.

Diana the Great: [See Index.]

Gad: Joshua 11:17. God of fortune; a *troop*, a *number* (Isa. 65:11). Possibly a representative of Jupiter and Venus—stars of fortune.

Golden Calf: [See Index.]

Groves/High Places: [See "Athirat" in Index.]

Ishtar: Babylonian goddess of love and war, the goddess to whom Nebuchadnezzar gave praise for his victory over Jerusalem (2 Chron. 36). She had male and female prostitutes attached to her temples. As the goddess of war, she was often pictured with lions. Although the name *Ishtar* is not found in the Bible, the related plural form (translated Ashteroth) occurs many times. The expression "queen of heaven" used by Jeremiah (7:18) is probably a title of Ishtar. The Phoenicians referred to her as *Astarte*, and the Greek goddess Aphrodite owes much of her character to Ishtar. [See "Ashtoroth" in Index.]

Jupiter (Zeus): [See "Zeus" in Index.]

Meni: [See "Gad" in Index.]

Mercurius: [See "Hermes" in Index.]

Merodach: Jeremiah 50:2. Babylonian and Assyrian god of war, guardian of the people.

Milcom: 1 Kings 11:5. An Ammonite idol. Same as *Molech*.

Molech: 2 Kings 23:10. Moabite god of fire. Human sacrifices were made not only to the chief god, Baal, but to many lesser gods. Athtar, a god who attempted to occupy Baal's throne while he was on a journey or asleep in the nether world, was branded in the Baal Epic as "Athtar the terrible." He reappears later as Chemosh, the national god of the Moabites, and later as Molech, the god Israel was forbidden to offer her sons and daughters as sacrifices (Lev. 18:21). Molech's idol was a hollow brass image, having the face of an ox with outstretched arms. Raging fires would heat the image red-hot, and as infants were placed in the arms, priests would beat drums to drown the noise of crying mothers, lest fathers would be moved with compassion to stop the rites. Some children were forced to pass through long rows of these idols. Many suffocated from the heat and died. When King Manasseh seduced Israel to do more evil than the surrounding Canaanite nations, he made his sons to "pass through the fire" [of Molech] (2 Kings 21:6). Note Psalm 106:37–39; Jeremiah 19:4–5.

When Jericho was rebuilt by a man named Heil (an act which God denounced in Josh. 6:26), he fulfilled God's Word in the offering of his two sons as human sacrifices in the wall and gate foundations of that city (1 Kings 16:34). This method of human sacrifice required the victim to be placed in the footing of the wall or gate foundation and have the stonecutters place heavy stones on their bodies, thus burying them alive. [See "Human Sacrifice" in Index.]

Nebo: Isaiah 46:1. Assyrian and Babylonian god of speech and learning. *Ne* was often incorporated in names of kings. Nebuchadnezzar means "Nebo protect my boundary."

Nehushtan/Brazen Serpent: 2 Kings 18:4. *Nehushtan* is a word of contempt, which means a "piece of brass," applied to the brazen serpent (Num. 21:8). Having preserved this object since their wilderness journey, Israel burnt incense to it in connection with her worshiping Baal and demons or the Devil.

Nergal: 2 Kings 17:30. Assyrian deity; a lion, who supposedly presided over the fortunes of war and hunting; associated with the planet Mars.

Nibhaz: 2 Kings 17:31. Assyrian deity; a dog. Worshiped by the Avvites when the Samaritan race was being formed. [See "Samaritans" in Index.]

Nisroch: 2 Kings 19:37. Assyrian deity; a great eagle. This god was worshiped by Sennacherib after his unsuccessful attempt to conquer Jerusalem from King Hezekiah. He was slain by his two sons while worshiping Nisroch.

Queen of Heaven: Jeremiah 7:18; 14:15–25. The moon was worshiped as the "queen of heaven" under the title "Ashtoreth," and was generally associated with Baal, the sun. In Roman Catholic circles today, Mary is called "queen of heaven." The sun was associated closely with the agricultural Canaanites, so they worshiped the sun, moon, and stars. Baal's subjects not only worshiped the heavenly bodies because of help derived from them, but for fear of their power also.

The sun, blazing in the heat of the day, especially in desert regions, could cause a sunstroke, resulting in a premature death. Its brightness would often weaken the eyes, causing ophthalmia. Superstitious beliefs prevailed regarding the moon. People thought a full moon could cause spoilage of meat, temporary or permanent blindness, distortion of features such as the mouth drawn to one side, death to newborn animals, and even temporary insanity, from which we get our word *lunacy*. Extreme coldness in the desert regions at night was attributed to the moon. Since the sun did smite them by day, superstition caused the people to think that the moon could smite them by night. Psalm 121 was probably written by an Israelite believer who asked a question in verse 1: "Shall I look to the high places like the worshipers of Baal for my help? Is this where I get my help?" His answer was an emphatic *no!* His help came from the Lord, who neither slumbered nor slept, who kept him safe from being smitten by Baal, Ashtoroth, and the queen of heaven, the moon (vv. 4–6).

One of the features of pagan temples was wall enclosures but no roof, which enabled worshipers to offer their sacrifices on the altars and look heavenward in the daytime to the sun and at night to the moon and stars. Such a practice was forbidden by God, first, because they were to have no other gods before them, and second, astrology and divination led to witchcraft and sorcery. [See "Astrology" in Index.]

Rephan: Acts 7:43. [See "Chiun" in Index.]

Rimmon: 2 Kings 5:15–19. A Syrian deity; representing the sun.

Succoth-benoth: 2 Kings 17:24–30. Probably refers to tents or booths erected by Assyrians sent to repeople Samaria after the Northern Kingdom fell and linked to the Babylonian god, Marduk, guardian deity.

Tammuz: Ezekiel 8:14. Syrian god of fertility, equivalent to Osirus in Egypt. His consort was the goddess Ishtar. His death (though he was supposedly later revived) was taken to represent the coming of winter and long dry seasons. Israelite women were engaged in mourning rites in the temple of Jerusalem, showing how far they had departed from God's commandments.

Tartak: 2 Kings 17:31. Assyrian deity; an ass (donkey).[See "Nibhaz" in Index.]

Terraphim: [See Index.]

Unknown god: [See Index.]

Recent Archaeological Discoveries

Archaeology is an ongoing science. There were over twenty expeditions scheduled in Israel alone for 1994. Others are also scheduled in the Near East. While there have been many major discoveries in the past, additional artifacts, both major and minor, are still coming to light to help give a background knowledge of times, customs, and events. Some even mention Bible characters. Sometimes a find comes to light in an actual dig, other times by accident or by an illegal find in an antiquity shop. Following are some examples:

Tomb of Caiaphas

Recently a tomb in a Jerusalem forest caved in and four boxes were found. The tomb had been plundered, but two boxes (ossuaries) were undisturbed. An ossuary is a large coffin or burial chamber in which several bodies are placed. After the skin dries, the skeletons are placed inside the ossuary. One ossuary had the name *QUFA— Caiaphas*—the Caiaphas family tomb. Inside were the bones of six people, one an elderly man who might have been Caiaphas, the high priest who illegally tried Jesus before sending Him to Pontius Pilate to be crucified (Matt. 26:57; 27:1–2).

Mosaics

Mosaic designs often show up among the ruins of houses or buildings, usually either on the floor or a wall.

Five Loaves and Two Fishes. A church built over the ruins of an ancient church, located above the Sea of Galilee, contains a beautiful mosaic of the five loaves and two fishes used by Jesus to feed almost 5,000 men plus women and children (John 6:8–10).

Map of Jerusalem and Vicinity. At Madaba, on the eastern side of the Dead Sea in Jordan, a large mosaic of this part of the Holy Land was discovered. It not only shows specific areas, but several important buildings, especially in the city of Jerusalem.

Philip Baptizing the Eunuch. In the desert between Jerusalem and Gaza, ruins in an excavated site revealed a beautiful colored mosaic of this event on a wall as recorded in Acts 8:26–38, which took place after Philip's successful evangelistic campaign in Samaria.

Jesus Calling His Disciples. Near the Sea of Galilee there was discovered a colorful mosaic of Jesus calling His fishermen disciples to come and follow Him.

A Synagogue Mosaic. Such a circular one was discovered in the ruins of a synagogue in Tiberius depicting a Torah shrine. It is flanked on each side by a Menorah and surrounded by several religious objects, a palm tree and fruit, both associated with the festival of the tabernacles, a shofar (ram's horn), and an incense shovel.

Coins

Coins are frequent discoveries. Silver coins of Alexander the Great are numerous and also of Roman emperors on the obverse side and the Roman eagle on the reverse. An unusual bronze medallion or coin is on display at the Israel Museum. It was struck over 1,700 years ago in Asia Minor (Turkey) near where it is said that Noah's ark rested on the mountains of Ararat. The obverse side depicts the Roman emperor Gallus. The reverse side gives a threefold picture of the flood story: (1) Noah and family in the ark sheltered from the rain, (2) a dove with an olive branch in its beak, and (3) Noah and his wife with arms upraised in an attitude of thankfulness for their salvation. [See "Judea Capta Coin" in Index.]

The Copper Scroll of Temple Treasure

This scroll was found with the many hidden Dead Sea Scrolls. It mentions the temple tax and its burial, listing sixty-four locations where huge amounts of treasure are said to be buried—26 tons of gold and 66 tons of silver. So far, none has been found.

The Place of the Trumpeting

Archaeologists have discovered some of the ruins of the city of Jerusalem dating to ca. A.D. 70, when Titus sacked the city. For the first time they found evidence of damage done by the Roman soldiers—including evidence of fire.

In the fall of 1970, a 6-foot protecting stone (parapet) believed to be a part of the tower of Herod's temple was found with this inscription: "To the house of the blowing of the ram's horn." This 8-ton stone is surmised to be a part of a tower above the priest's chambers in the southwest corner of the temple. Josephus's record of the Jewish wars describes this very spot: "Over the roof of the priests' chambers, where it was the custom for one of the priests to stand and proclaim by trumpet-blast the approach of the seventh day in the late afternoon and its close on the next evening, calling the people in the first case to cease work and the second to resume it." Trumpets were also blown for a fast and for people to sanctify themselves (Joel 2:15–17).

The Temple Mount Steps

While finding further evidence near the southwest corner of the Herodian temple platform, magnificent stones, some 30 feet long (Mark 13:1), a wide street, and a plaza with a broad staircase leading up to the temple area were unearthed. Up these same steps Jesus walked as He went to the temple.

A most striking discovery was the *Royal Portico* along the entire width of the southern side on top of the flattened mount. The main entrance to the temple and its courts was through two massive gates—the *Double Gate* and the *Triple Gate*, both called the *Huldah Gates* in ancient sources. Of these gates and the Royal Portico Josephus wrote, "This portico was more deserving of mention than any under the sun." When traces of this portico were found, there were four rows of monolithic pillars, 162 total, and each 30 feet high and 5 feet in diameter, each topped with Corinthian capitals. It was in these porticos that Rabbi Gamaliel taught Saul of Tarsus (Paul), and certainly one of the places where Jesus Himself preached. Also found in this same area were ruins of buildings dating back to Solomon's time.

The Synagogue at Capernaum

At the north end of the Sea of Galilee there are the ruins of a fourth-century A.D. synagogue revealing the interior where the Jews met on the Sabbath and an outer court where the Gentiles could attend for the Rabbi to teach them after the Jews' service. Beneath these ruins are the actual ruins of the synagogue in which Christ Himself preached (Matt. 4:13; Mark 1:21–25). So often visitors to the Holy Land are able to "walk where Jesus walked" and visit many sites He visited.

Recent archaeological discoveries

Discovery/Location	Discoverer/Year Found	Date/Language	Contents/Biblical Significance
Rosetta Stone, near village of Rosetta, Egypt. See Index	Capt. Broussard, Army of Napoleon, 1799 Translated by J. F. Champollion, 1822	Approx. 200 B.C. Greek, demotic, hieroglyphics (latter two, Egyptian)	Decree by priests of Memphis honoring Ptolemy V Epiphanes. Same decree in three languages (Greek at bottom). Champollion produced hieroglyphic grammar and dictionary, leading to deciphering other two.
Shishak (Sheshonk) Temple, Karnak (Thebes), Egypt. See Index	1825. Flinders Petrie able to decode, 1896	ca. 920 B.C. Egyptian hieroglyphics	Shishak's victories in Judah and Jerusalem (2 Chron. 12:1–9).
Sennacherib—Taylor Prism, Nineveh, Iraq. See Index	J. E. Taylor, 1830	ca. 685 B.C., cuneiform (Akkadian, Neo-Assyrian)	Annals of Sennacherib, including his siege of Jerusalem (Isa. 37) and his mention of Hezekiah.
Behistun Rock, Zagros Mountains, Iran. See Index	Henry Rawlinson, 1835	521–485 B.C. Persian, Elamite, and Cuneiform (Akkadian)	Trilingual inscription of Darius that opened door to translation of ancient cuneiform writing.
Sargon's Palace, near Nineveh at Khorsabad, Iraq. See Sargon in Index	Paul E. B. Place, 1851–1855. Excavated again 1851–1855, and 1932, 1933	722–705 B.C. Akkadian	Including many bas-reliefs and annals. He claimed to have captured Samaria and lists number of captives. Refers to commander Tartan (Isa. 20:1). Ashdod excavated; Tartan confirmed.
Black Obelisk of Shalmaneser, Calah, (ancient Nimrud) Iraq. See Index	Austin Henry Layard, 1846	850 B.C. Akkadian (Neo-Assyrian)	Military victories of Shalmaneser III of Assyria. Depicts King Jehu of Israel paying tribute, an event not recorded in the Bible.
Sennacherib's Palace, Nineveh, Iraq. See Lachish in Index	Layard, 1849–1851 H. Rassam, 1853–1877	ca. 700 B.C. Akkadian	Over 70 rooms lined with sculptured slabs of military fetes, including 13 showing siege of Lachish. Confirms 2 Kings 18:14–16 that Hezekiah paid tribute to Sennacherib.
Ashurbanipal's Palace, Nineveh, Iraq. See Creation Tablets and Flood in Index	Layard and Rassam, 1850–1854	Ashurbanipal reigned 668–626 B.C. Neo-Assyrian	Numerous clay tablets found in his library, including ancient copies of creation and the flood. Some tablets dated ca. 2300 B.C.
Susa, city of, in steppe country east of the Tigris River, Iran. See Susa (Shushan)	William K. Loftus, 1851	Sixth-century B.C. picturesque objects in early Elamite (script)	Biblical city of Shushan. Much information on Persian city of Queen Esther and Nehemiah, the king's cup bearer.
Ephesus, Asia Minor. See Ephesus in Index	John T. Wood, 1863, plus later excavations	ca. 2000 B.C. (?) Greek (koine)	Oriental/Occidental culture. Famous for temple of Diana.
Moabite Stone, Dibon in Jordan. See Index	Rev. F. Klein, 1868	ca. 840 B.C., Moabite	Mesha, king of Moab, rebelled against Omri, king of Israel. Stone confirms and supplements 2 Kings 1:1; 3:4–5.
Cyrus Cylinder (Decree) Babylon, Iraq. See Israel's Release in Index	Rassam, 1879–1882	539/7 B.C. cuneiform	Records his conquests and subsequent freeing of captured peoples, which included Israel's return (Ezra 1:1–4).
Siloam Inscription, Jerusalem. See Conduit of Hezekiah in Index	By young truant boy, 1880. Translated by A. H. Sayce	ca. 701 B.C., Hebrew	Gives details concerning Hezekiah's construction of conduit beneath city of Jerusalem (2 Kings 20:20). Shows length of ancient cubit.

Chart 3. Recent archaeological discoveries

Discovery/Location	Discoverer/Year Found	Date/Language	Contents/Biblical Significance
Nabonidus Chronicle, Babylon, Iraq. See Nabonidus and Balshazzar in Index	T. G. Pinches	555–539 B.C. cuneiform	Although Bible states Belshazzar was last king of Babylon, annals of king Nabonidus shows that in his absence he had placed Belshazzar in his stead, making him *second* ruler and Daniel *third* (Dan. 5:7, 29).
Amarna letters (300 letters), Tel el-Amarna, Egypt. See Amarna Letters in Index	By Egyptian woman in trash pile; excavated by Flinders Petrie, 1887	Fourteenth century B.C. Akkadian (Neo-Assyrian)	Correspondence between Pharaoh Akhenaton and kings of city-states in Palestine asking for help as Israel invades Canaan. Reveals political situation of Canaanite nations at that time.
Elephantine Papyri, Elephantine Island, Aswan, Egypt. See Index	Found by Arab woman. Bought by C. E. Wilbour, 1893	Fifth century B.C. Aramaic	Family archives and correspondence of Jews who fled to Egypt prior to Babylonian captivity. Relevant to Jeremiah's warning (42:18–22). Confirms historicity of Sanballat (Neh. 2:10).
Merneptah Stele, Thebes, Egypt. See Index	Flinders Petrie, 1896	1220 B.C., Egyptian hieroglyphics	Large black granite stele found at mortuary chapel of this pharaoh. Only mention of "Israel" on Egyptian inscriptions. Merneptah boasted he subjugated Israel in his fifth year, ca. 1220 B.C., indicating Israel was then in Canaan as established people.
Oxyrhynchus Papyri Oxyrhynchus, Egypt. See Greek Influence (language) in Index	B. P. Grenfell and A. S. Hunt, 1897–1900	During period of New Testament	Documents from trash cans of priests showing *koine* Greek language of common people (Mark 12:37).
Babylon, Iraq. See Babylon, Fall of, and Babylonian Chronicle in Index	Robert Koldewey, 1898–1914	600 B.C., cuneiform	Buildings, temples, Ishtar Gate, etc. Illuminates Daniel 4:30 and Isaiah 13:19. Clay tablet mentions king Jehoiachin and Nebuchadnezzar's coronation.
Hammurabi, Code of, Susa, Iran. See Index	M. J. de Morgan, 1901	ca. 1755 B.C., Akkadian	Codified Babylonian laws but the difference shows ethical superiority and spiritual uniqueness of Moses' law.
Weld-Blundell Prism, Kish, Iraq. See Index	Found 1906; published by Langdon in 1923	Between 2256 and 2000 B.C. during reign of Uruk. Cuneiform	Lists ruling kings before and after Noah's flood; naming Mesopotamian (Sumerian) cities.
Hittite Documents, Boghazkoy (ancient Hattusah), Turkey. See Hittites in Index	Hugo Winckler, 1906 Kurt Bittel, 1954–1963	Sixteenth century B.C. Hittite cuneiform	Light on Patriarchal times (Gen. 23). Over 10,000 documents found of legends, myths, covenant forms, and law codes.
Cyrenius, Syrian governor. See Census of Cyrenius in Index	Sir William Ramsey, 1912	10–6/5 B.C.	Shows Cyrenius was twice ruling Syrian official. Other writings on papyrus show his poll tax took place every fourteen years, beginning in reign of Caesar Augustus (Luke 2:1ff).
Ur of the Chaldees, Mesopotamia (Iraq). See Index	J. E. Taylor, 1854 Leonard Woolley, 1922–1934	2,500 B.C. cuneiform	Mathematical and medical documents, lyres, gold and silver jewelry, etc., showing advanced state of culture, but idolatrous (Josh. 24:2, 15).
Nuzi tablets, Nuzi, Iraq. See Index	Edward Chiera, 1925–1932 E. A. Speiser	Fifteenth century B.C. Hurrian dialect of Akkadian	Background of life during times of late Patriarchs. Records about marriage, inheritance rights, etc.

Discovery/Location	Discoverer/Year Found	Date/Language	Contents/Biblical Significance
Ras Shamra Tablets, Ugarit, Syria. See Baal Worship in Index; Baal in Appendix	C. F. A. Schaeffer, 1929–1937	Fifteenth century B.C. Ugarit (Semitic)	Revealed mythological background of Baalism, Canaanite religion. Literary epics, dictionaries, alphabet tablet. Language close to Hebrew.
Persepolis, city of, Iran. See Behistun Rock and Daniel in Lions' Den in Index	Ernst Herzfeld, 1931	ca. 500 B.C. cuneiform, Elamite, and Persian	City of Persian kings; common to Ezra 7:12. Confirms names of Persian kings: Darius, Artaxerxes, Cyrus (Ezra 4:5–7; Neh. 2:1).
Lachish Letters, Tell el Duweit, Israel. See Index	James L. Starkey, 1933–1936	588 B.C., cursive Phoenician	Twenty-one letters, written on broken pottery (ostraca), revealing political and military situation just before Nebuchadnezzar destroyed Jerusalem.
John Ryland Papyrus, Egypt. See Greek Influence (language) in Index	C. H. Roberts, 1935 B. P. Grenfell	ca. 125 A.D. Greek *(koine)*	Dated to first half of second century A.D. and circulated in Egypt about 130–150 A.D. One fragment revealed part of John 18:31–33 and the other side part of John 18:37–38, part of trial of Christ, proving that John's gospel written earlier than 125 A.D.
Dead Sea Scrolls, Qumran, Jordan. See Index	Bedouin boy, 1947	Second century B.C. into first century A.D.	Ancient Hebrew religious writings. Contains all books of Bible except Esther. No break between Isaiah 39–40.
Lipit-Ishtar, Law Code of King Isin, Nippur, Iraq. See Hammurabi, Code of in Index	University of Pennsylvania Pennsylvania 1889. Translated by Francis R. Steele, 1948	1864–1854 B.C. Sumerian	Legal text with thirty-eight regulations, many similar to Hammurabi's laws. Shows Moses' laws superior to lawgivers preceding him, and critical argument that Moses' law is "too early and advanced" for his time crumbles.
Babylonian Chronicle, Babylon, Iraq. See Fall of Jerusalem in Index	Donald Wiseman, 1956	626–594 B.C. Akkadian (Neo-Babylonian)	Confirms Nebuchadnezzar's capturing Promised Land territory from Egypt, taking captive king Jehoiakim and Jehioachin at Jerusalem, listing Jehoiachin's rations, and listing date of Jerusalem's defeat, 15/16 March, 586 B.C.
Megiddo, city of, Israel. See Index	C. S. Fisher, P. L. O. Guy, G. Loud, Yigael Yadin, 1960s	First millennium B.C.	Various buildings from times of Israelite kings. Solomonic blueprint (1 Kings 9:15). Was a store city and horse/chariot center.
Pontius Pilate Inscription, Theater at Caesarea. See Index	A. Frova, 1961	28–36 A.D. Greek	Mentions "Tiberium" temple, erected by Pilate, prefect of Judea, in honor of Caesar Tiberius.
Jerusalem, city of, area near Pool of Siloam, Israel. See Destruction of Jerusalem in Index	Kathleen Kenyon Roland de Vaux 1961–1967	About 1000 B.C.	Showed that Davidic city was larger area than thought. Wall excavated was Nehemiah's (Neh. 4:6; 6:15).
Ebla, city of Tell Mardikh, Syria. See Index	Paolo Matthiae 1974 to present	2300 B.C. Eblaite and N. W. Semitic cuneiform	Over 15,000 tablets reveal events of political and daily life, listing cities, many biblical, as well as many names of Bible characters. Earliest creation tablet, in some ways parallel to Genesis 1.

They learned what it must have been like when "He went about doing good, healing all who were oppressed of the devil, for God was with Him" (Acts 10:38).

Living Quarters—Houses—Implements

With all our sophisticated household goods and appliances today, we have a feeling of pity for the ancients who never had it as good as we do. When Solomon said "there is nothing new under the sun," he didn't necessarily have in mind such inventions that make life easy for us, but that people had what they needed, what was necessary to carry on daily life.

Excavations find that houses had adequate, comfortable furniture that would be the envy of antique collectors today. Cooking utensils were as "modern" as ours! Vegetables, fish, and most meat were cooked slowly in pots with tightly covered lids. Steam escaped through vent holes. They were made to stack neatly. Some frying pans were deep for deep-frying. Large jars were fired to cause *sweating*, which kept the water cool. Even a three-burner stove has been found. Hardware—nails, screws, spikes, washers—and tools of all sorts were plentiful.

Thanks to many archaeological discoveries, we now know that things weren't as bad for some of the "primitives" as we thought. Bath and toilet facilities were amazingly advanced even though we would call them "country outhouses."

Calf Worship

An excavation at the Old Testament site of Ashkelon in 1990 brought to light a small silver calf, symbolic of the calf worshipers of those in Canaan. This city was very popular in the days of Samson and Delilah (Judg. 14:19). The apostle Paul wrote about early man refusing to retain a knowledge of God in his heart and mind and turning from the Creator to the creature (man) and to four-footed beasts (Rom. 1:21–32). Such led to a vulgar, sensual, sexual, human-sacrificing religion. Israel in particular often substituted calf worship for worshiping the True and Living God. [See "Golden Calf Worship at Sinai" (Exod. 32:2–4).] Calf worship was instituted by King Jeroboam of the Northern Kingdom of Israel (1 Kings 11; 12:25–28). Hosea denounced Israel for worshiping Baal and offering their children as human sacrifices and worshiping calves (13:1–2; Jer. 19:4–5 NIV).

A discovery of such as this silver calf confirms that such idols were in vogue in Old Testament days. God's judgment for this sin brought about "Ashkelon becoming a desolation" (Zech. 2:4). Everything the archaeologists found at this site was confirmation of God's prediction—desolation.

Seals and Clay Bullae

Many seals and the bullae of individuals who are mentioned in Scripture have been discovered [see "Seals" in Index]. Many seals were like signets in rings, usually containing the name and position of the person. Bullae (plural) were individual clay objects containing the same information. Although many names are hard to pronounce and are meaningless to us when we read of them in the Scriptures, these people actually did exist and had a part in Bible history. These bullae were used as signatures and pressed into soft clay to make a document legal. Those like the one in figure 96 were sometimes affixed to the knot of a string used to bind scrolls. This permitted only authorized persons to open these documents.

Listed are several Bible characters. While some have been found at various sites, in October 1975, over 250 were discovered in antique shops. The hoard had been found in all probability by Arab villagers and illegally sold to dealers. Many seals are from Jeremiah's time prior to Israel's Babylonian captivity (586 B.C.).

Belonging to Berekayahu, son of Neriyahu, the Scribe. Translation of seal: "Baruch, the son of Neriah," secretary and faithful associate of Jeremiah (36:4). The full meaning of "Baruch" was not known until the discovery of this bulla. His name means "blessed of Yahweh" (God).

Gemaryahu, son of Shapan. Gemaryahu is "Gemariah," who was a scribe to king Jehoiakim in Jeremiah's day. Baruch read the words of Jeremiah from the scroll in the house of the Lord in the chamber of Gemariah, the son of Shapan (Jer. 36:10–12, 25). Gemaryahu is to Gemariah what Neriyahu is to Neriah in Baruch's seal, the same as Hiliyahu is to Hilliah on Azaryahu's seal.

Belonging to Azaryahu, son of the high priest, Hilkiyahu. Translated, this seal reads: "Belonging to Azariah, son of Hilkiah, the high priest (1 Chron. 9:11). Hilkiah and Azariah were the grandfather and great-grandfather of Ezra (Ezra 7:1).

Belonging to Seriahu, son of Neriyahu. He was Baruch's brother (Jer. 32:12; 51:59). Seriah served as quartermaster when he went with king Zedekiah of Judah as prisoner to

Figure 96. Illustration of a clay seal or bulla

Babylon. Jeremiah had written a book in which he told all the evil that would come upon Babylon and instructed Seriahu to take it with him. Upon completion of reading it to the people, he was to bind a stone to it and cast it in the Euphrates River (Jer. 51:60–64).

Haman, son of Hilkiyahu (Hilkiah) *the priest.* This is a seal in a ring. It was discovered somewhere in northeast Palestine (place unknown) and was taken to Paris, France, in 1980. It is over 2,500 years old. Hilkiah is the priest who found the scroll (Torah, Moses' writings) in the temple during the reign of King Josiah of Judah (2 Kings 22:8).

The seal of *Yerame'el* (Jerahmeel), *son of King Jehoiakim.* He was sent by the king with two officers to arrest Jeremiah and Baruch due to Jeremiah's unpopular prophecies (chap. 36). Another seal contains both the names of Baruch and Yerame'el.

Elishama's bulla was also included in this hoard. He was a scribe and servant of King Jehoiakim (Jer. 36:12).

Jezebel. It is possible that a recently discovered seal belonged to Jezebel, the pagan, wicked wife of King Ahab (874–853 B.C.). She was the daughter of Ethba'al, king of Sidon. She was condemned for promoting Baal worship in the Northern Kingdom of Israel. She also used her husband's seal to have Naboth put to death so Ahab could possess his vineyard (1 Kings 21). This seal which may be hers is in Phoenician style but also has some images of Egyptian signs. Four paleo-Hebrew letters spell YZRL, which is *Jezebel.*

Amotz. Several seals have been discovered in Dan during the past twenty-seven years. One belongs to an unidentified "Amotz" of the eighth century B.C. Amotz is "Amoz," the name of Isaiah's father (Isa. 1:1). It is not certain if this was the seal of his father.

Zkryo's seal is translated Zechariah, meaning "God [Yahweh] remembers." Since there are twenty-seven Zechariahs mentioned in the Bible, it is difficult to say who this might be.

Silver Amulet

A small rolled silver amulet, dating from the seventh/sixth century B.C. was found to contain four Hebrew letters—*yod, he, waw, he*—the form of the unpronounceable name of God—*Yahweh* or *Jehovah*. This amulet was discovered in an archaeological excavation in Jerusalem and is the first time God's name has been found on an artifact.

Pomegranate Artifacts—Stand and Scepters

The pomegranate fruit was a symbol of fruitfulness in Canaan (Num. 13:23; Deut. 8:8). It was designed as a decorative motif ornament on the priests' garments (Exod. 28:33–35). The design was hammered into brass works in Solomon's temple (1 Kings 7:18–20). Pomegranate earrings have also been found.

There surfaced in Jerusalem recently a rare find, a small temple ornament carved from a piece of ivory representing a pomegranate. It is very small, about 1 ¾ inches high, about 1 inch in diameter, and shaped like a vase. It is not known if it topped a scepter or decorated a box top. It is round with a flat bottom and a thin neck that blossoms out into six petals, four of which are intact. At the bottom of the petals a small hole goes into the neck in which a scepter was placed.

An inscription just below the petals reads: "Belonging to the Temple of Yahweh, holy to the Priests." This inscription, along with the silver amulet, are the only two discoveries that contain the divine name of God. This ivory pomegranate was found in a dealer's shop; its place of discovery is unknown.

To add further information to the use of the small pomegranate ornament, a recent discovery brought to light two pomegranate scepters and an incense stand found in a gravesite on the Mediterranean coast just south of Haifa. They date from the period of the Judges. Also found was an incense burner.

Incense was a mixture of spices (Exod. 30:34–35). It was burned each morning with fire taken from the altar of a burnt offering sacrifice as the priests dressed the lamps. On the Day of Pentecost the priests brought the incense into the Most Holy Place so that the Ark was engulfed in a huge cloud of smoke (Lev. 16:12–13). The sons of Aaron and the Korahites were punished with death for using it improperly (Lev. 10; Num. 16).

In Christ's day this procedure was done by ordinary priests and it was also a time of prayer for the people (Luke 1:9–10).

House of David; David, King of Israel

In the summer of 1993 there was a discovery in ancient Dan of a tablet of the ninth century B.C., referring to both the "House of David" and to the "King of Israel." As the discoverer said: "This is the first time the name of David has been found outside the Bible. This inscription refers not only to David but to the 'House of David,' the dynasty of the great Israelite King. If this proves anything, it shows that both Israel and Judah, contrary to the claims of some scholarly biblical minimizers, were important kingdoms at this time [during the events mentioned]."

Other artifacts found at Dan contained inscriptions referring to the god Baal. Several inscriptions referred to the "god of Dan" and to the "gods of the Danites," which helped to identify the excavated site as Dan.

Fragments of Matthew's Gospel

Recently (in early 1995), three small papyrus fragments of Matthew, stored in a library in England for decades, were reexamined. It was determined that they date to the latter part of the first century A.D. From a scholarly perspective, this is a sensational conclusion since the majority of New Testament scholars believe the Gospels were written much later, after the stories of Jesus had time to "develop." Such an early dating of a copy of Matthew circulating in Egypt means the original was written within the lifetime of those who witnessed the events described in the Gospels.

Summary

In our consideration of biblical archaeology, it is interesting to note how it has given us confirmation of its historical accuracy, illuminated many Bible customs, and illustrated many truths. In closing, I would like to compare one biblical truth to one of ancient Egypt's tenets, a religious belief based on mythology.

The picture (see fig. 97) reveals what is taught in the Egyptian "Book of the Dead" concerning judgment and eternity. Osiris was the god of the underworld and symbolized the creative forces of nature and eternity. The picture depicts the god Anubis, the god of the dead, acting in behalf of the god Osiris, who is examining the tongue (spoken words) of an individual with his right hand and balancing the scales with the symbol of eternity in the right side of the scales and the person's heart in the left. The baboon sitting on top of the scales is the god of intelligence—all knowledge. He is recording the deeds of the individual whose heart is being weighed. This whole action denotes a belief in "good works outweighing bad deeds," a centuries-old philosophy that is a common belief held by multitudes today, even good religious people.

The prophet Daniel gives an illustration of this philosophy of the pagan king of Babylon. No one would dare question his "goodness" or the "good works" he was displaying at the banquet he was giving for a thousand of his guests. Suddenly, during the festivities while entertaining royalty, he saw some foreign words being written on the wall of the palace by a hand. Not knowing what it meant, he sought an interpretation from his so-called wise men, but to no avail. Seeking Daniel's help, he was told by this man of God that "You are found weighed in the balance [of God's scales] and are found wanting" (5:1–6, 25–27).

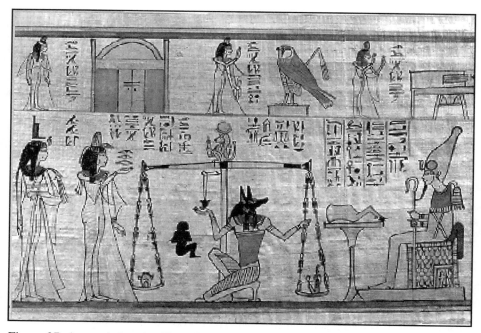

Figure 97. A mural showing Egyptian beliefs of judgment and eternity

How true of countless numbers who have never tasted and found "that the Lord is good; blessed is the man who trusts in Him" (Ps. 34:8). No one can go wrong in believing what the Bible says about man's need for something that will give him the needed "weight" to balance God's scales in his favor. "We have all sinned and come short of the glory of God" (Rom. 3:23). Our God is the God of intelligence—He is all-knowing (omniscient). "The eyes of the Lord are in every place beholding the evil and the good" (Prov. 15:3). "It is appointed unto [every] man once to die, and after that the judgment" (Heb. 9:27). He will then find that his good deeds do not weigh enough for God's favor, and Jesus will say to him, "Depart from Me, I never knew you" (Matt. 7:21–23). However, if there is true repentance and a belief in and an acceptance of Jesus Christ as his/her own personal Savior, there will be a change of heart and God will provide eternal life, giving an eternity with Him in heaven when life on earth ends (John 1:12; 10:28). "For by grace are you saved by faith, and that not of yourselves, it is the gift of God, *not of works, lest any man should boast*" (Eph. 2:8–9).

Illustration Acknowledgments

Alinari, F., Rome, Italy, Fig. 92

American Baptist Publications, Philadelphia, Fig. 54

American Numismatic Society, New York, Figs. 67 (coins), 78 (coins), 84

American School, Classical Studies, Athens, Greece, Fig. 76

Ashmolean Museum, Oxford, England, Fig. 17

Boyd, Robert, Figs. 2–3, 5, 8, 11–12, 18, 21, 23, 27, 32, 34–35, 38–39, 46–47, 51–52, 59–60, 62–63, 65–66, 68–71, 77, 79, 87–88, 90, 94–96

British Museum, London, England, Figs. 7, 13–16, 26, 29, 43–45, 48–49, 53, 55, 57, 83, 91

Cairo (Egypt) Museum, Figs. 22, 30, 80

Cameron, George, Ann Arbor, Mich., Fig. 9

Delachuax & Niestle, Neuchatel, Switzerland, Fig. 56

Felbermeyer, Johannas, Rome, Italy, Fig. 75

Israel Museum, Jerusalem, Fig. 4

John Ryland Library, Manchester, England, Figs. 85, 89

Livingston, David, Archaeology and Biblical Research, Ephrata, Penn., Fig. 6

Louvre, Paris, France, Figs. 28, 31, 36, 41, 81

Matson Photo Service, Los Angeles, Calif., Figs. 58, 93

Metropolitan Museum of Art, New York, Figs. 25, 82, 97

Naples (Italy) Museum, Fig. 78

NASA Photography, Houston, Fig. 1

Oriental Institute, University of
Chicago Museum, Figs. 10, 21,
37, 50

Palestine Archaeological Museum,
Amman, Jordan, Fig. 42

Pontifical Biblique Institute,
Jerusalem, Israel, Figs. 64, 72, 86

Rubinger, David, Fig. 67

Smithsonian Institution, Washington,
D.C., Fig. 40

Trever, John, Berea, Ohio, Fig. 61

University of Pennsylvania Museum,
Philadelphia, Figs. 19, 24

Bibliography

Aling, Charles F. *Egypt and Bible History*. Grand Rapids: Baker Book House, 1981.

Bergman, Jerry. "The Pinnacle of God's Creation." *Impact* #133. El Cajon, Calif.: Institute for Creation Research.

Boyd, Robert T. *World's Bible Handbook*. Iowa Falls: World Bible Publishers, 1992.

Biblical Archaeology Review. Vols. 1981–93. Washington, D.C.

Brown, Arthur I. *Wonderfully Made*. Westchester, Ill.: Christian Readers Club.

_____. *God and You: Wonders of the Human Body*. Findlay, Ohio: Fundamental Truth.

Budge, E. A. Wallis. *The Gods of the Egyptians*. New York: Dover Publications, 1969.

Caesar, Julius. *The Civil War*. New York: Dorset Press, 1976.

Chadwick, Henry. *The Early Church*. New York: Dorset Press, 1976.

Clayton, P. and M. Price Jr. *Seven Wonders of the Ancient World*. New York: Dorset Press, 1988.

Conybeare, William John and John Saul Howson. *Life and Epistles of St. Paul*. Grand Rapids: Wm. B. Eerdman's Publishing Co., 1953.

Cook, William J. "Revisiting the Big Bang." *U.S. News & World Report*, January 29, 1990.

Curtis, Adrian. *Ugarit, Ras Shamra*. Grand Rapids: Eerdmans, 1985.

Davidson, Michael. *The Splendors of Egypt*. New York: Crown, 1979.

DeHaan, M. R. *The Chemistry of the Blood*. Grand Rapids: Zondervan, 1953.

_____. *Evolution and Creation*. Grand Rapids: RBC Ministries.

Dehan, Emmanuel. *Megiddo—Armageddon*. Tel Aviv, Israel, 1976.

Dick, Lois Hadley. *From the Wastelands of Egypt*. Chicago: Moody Press, 1983.

Edersheim, Alfred. *The Temple*: Grand Rapids, Kregel Publications, 1997.

Ephesus. Istanbul: Nici Keskin Press.

Everest, F. Allen. *Hidden Treasure*. Chicago: Moody Press, 1955.

Fagan, Brian M. *The Adventures of Archaeology*. Washington, D.C.: National Geographic Society, 1985.

France, R. T. *The Evidence for Jesus*. Downers Grove, Ill.: InterVarsity Press, 1986.

Free, Joseph P. *Archaeology and Bible History*. Wheaton, Ill.: Van Kampen, 1950.

Gilbert, Martin. *Atlas of Jewish History*. New York: Dorset Press, 1976.

Gish, Duane T. and Donald H. Rohrer. *Up with Creation*. San Diego: Creation Life, 1978.

Glueck, Nelson. *The Other Side of Jordan*. Jerusalem: American School of Oriental Research, 1970.

Gordon, Cyrus H. *Hammurabi's Code*. New York: Holt, Rinehart and Winston, 1963.

Gordon, Maurice Bear. *Medicine Among the Ancient Hebrews*. 1941.

Ham, Ken. *Were You There?* El Cajon, Calif.: Institute for Creation Research, 1989.

_____. *About Dinosaurs*. 1989.

_____. *Is God an Evolutionist?*

Hand, John Raymond. *Why I Accept the Genesis Record*. Lincoln, Nebr.: Back to the Bible, 1972.

Hislop, Alexander. *The Two Babylons*. Neptune, N.J.: Loizeaux Brothers, 1959.

Howe, George F. *God Created*. Chicago: Moody Press, 1964.

Ironside, Harry. *Minor Prophets*. Neptune, N.J.: Loizeaux Brothers, 1909.

Ishak, Amran. *The History of the Samaritans*. Jerusalem: Greek Covenant Press.

Israel Archaeology. Jerusalem, 1974.

Josephus, Flavius. *The Complete Works of Josephus,* translated by William Whiston. Grand Rapids: Kregel Publications, 1960.

Keller, Werner. *The Bible as History*. New York: William Morrow, 1963.

Kenyon, Kathleen M. *Ancient Jericho*. Jerusalem: Covenant Press, 1957.

Lewis, Jack P. *Historical Background of Bible History*. Grand Rapids: Baker Book House, 1971.

Ludwig, Charles. *Ludwig's Handbook on New Testament Rulers and Cities*. Denver, Colo.: Accent Books, 1983.

_____. *Ludwig's Handbook on Old Testament Rulers and Cities*. Denver, Colo.: Accent Books, 1984.

Maier, Paul. *Pontius Pilate*. Grand Rapids: Kregel Publications, 1967.

Masters, Peter. *A Tour of Biblical Evidence in the British Museum*. London: Sword and Trowel Publishers, 1984.

Matson, C. Eric. *Babylon*. Los Angeles: Matson Photo Service.

Morris, Henry M. and Duane T. Gish. *The Battle for Creation*. El Cajon, Calif.: Institute for Creation Research, 1976.

Morris, Henry M. *Creation and the Modern Christian*. 1985.

_____. *Decade of Creation*. 1981.

_____. *Did the Flood Cover the Earth?* 1989.

_____. *The God Who Is Real*. Grand Rapids: Baker Book House, 1988.

_____. *Remarkable Record of Job*. Santee, Calif.: Morten Books, 1988.

_____. "The Splendid Faith of the Evolutionist." *Impact* #111, 1982.

_____. "The Vanishing Case for Evolution." *Impact* #156, 1986.

_____. "The Logic of Biblical Creation." *Impact* #205, 1990.

McBirnie, William Stewart. *The Search for the Tomb of Jesus*. 1975.

McCrossan, T. J. *The Bible, Its Christ*. Seattle: 1947.

_____. *The Bible and Its Eternal Facts*. 1947.

Nadler, Sam. "A Fence Around the Law." *The Chosen People*, vol. 97, no. 113, November 1990.

Negen, Avraham. *Archaeology in the Land of the Bible*. Tel Aviv, Israel: Sadan Pub. House.

Newell, Philip R. *Six Days of Creation*. Chicago: Moody Bible Institute.

Owen, Frederick G. *Jerusalem*. Grand Rapids: Baker Book House, 1972.

Packer, J. I., Merrill C. Tenney, and William White Jr. *The Bible Almanac*. Nashville: Thomas Nelson Publishers, 1980.

Papini, Giovanni. *Life of Christ*. New York: Harcourt, Brace and Co., 1923.

Patrick, Richard. *Greek Mythology*. New York: Crown, 1972.

_____. *Egyptian Mythology*. 1972.

Patten, Donald W., Ronald R. Hatch, and Steinhauer. *The Long Day of Joshua and Six Other Catastrophes*. Grand Rapids: Baker Book House, 1973.

Pax, W. E. *In the Footsteps of Jesus*. New York: George P. Putman's Sons, 1970.

Pfeiffer, Charles F. *The Biblical World*. Grand Rapids: Baker Book House, 1966.

_____. *The Dead Sea Scrolls and the Bible*. Rev. ed. Grand Rapids: Baker Book House, 1969.

Pritchard, James B. *The Ancient Near East in Pictures*. Princeton: Princeton University Press, 1954.

Reade, Julian. *Assyrian Sculpture*. London: British Museum Pub., Ltd., 1983.

Revell Bible Dictionary. Grand Rapids: Fleming H. Revell Co., 1990.

Rimmer, Harry. *The Crucible of Calvary*. Grand Rapids: Eerdmans, 1938.

_____. *Crying Stones*. Berne Witness Company, 1941.

_____. *Dead Men Tell Tales*. Berne Witness Company, 1939.

_____. *The Golden Text for Today*. Wheaton, Ill.: Van Kampen Press, 1951.

_____. *Harmony of Science and Scripture*. Grand Rapids: Eerdmans, 1936.

_____. *Lot's Wife and the Science of Physics*. Grand Rapids: Eerdmans, 1947.

_____. *Modern Science and the Genesis Record*. Grand Rapids: Eerdmans, 1937.

_____. *The Shadow of Coming Events*. Grand Rapids: Eerdmans, 1946.

_____. *The Theory of Evolution and Facts of Science*. Grand Rapids: Wm. B. Eerdmans, 1935.

_____. *Voices from the Silent Centuries*. Grand Rapids: Wm. B. Eerdmans, 1935.

Rosetta Stone. London: The British Museum, 1971.

Roux, George. *Ancient Iraq (Assyria)*. Baltimore: Penguin Books, 1964.

Sanden, O. E. *Twelve Bridges No Evolutionist Has Ever Crossed*. Lincoln, Nebr.: Back to the Bible, 1961.

Schoville, Keith N. *Biblical Archaeology in Focus*. Grand Rapids: Baker Book House, 1975.

Science Is Discovering. Chicago: Scott, Foreman and Co., 1964.

Seiss, Joseph A. *A Miracle in Stone*. Philadelphia: Porter & Coats, 1877.

Shanks, Hershel. *The City of David*. Washington, D.C.: Biblical Archaeology Society, 1975.

Stalker, James. *Life of Paul*. Atlanta: Jermigan Press, 1981.

Strauss, Lehman. *The Rise and Fall of Babylon*. Levittown, Penn.: Lifeline Publishers.

Tacitus. *The Annals of Imperial Rome*. New York: Dorset Press.

Tenney, Merrill C., and I. D. Douglas. *The New International Dictionary of the Bible*. Grand Rapids: Zondervan Publishing House, 1987.

Totten, C. A. *Joshua's Long Day and the Sun Dial*. New Haven, Conn.: Yale University Press, 1880.

Trever, John C. *The Dead Sea Scrolls*. Grand Rapids: Eerdmans, 1968.

Uris, J. Hand and Leon Uris. *Jerusalem, Song of Songs*. Garden City, N.Y.: Doubleday and Co., 1981.

Vilnay, Zel. *The Guide to Israel*. Jerusalem: Hamokor Press, 1970.

Wilson, Clifford. *Ebla Tablets, Secrets of a Forgotten City*. San Diego: Master Books, 1977.

_____. *In the Beginning God*. Mount Waverly, Vict., Australia: Word of Truth, 1970.

_____. *Major Archaeological Discoveries*. Ephrata, Penn.: Associates for Biblical Archaeology.

_____. *New Light on New Testament Letters*. London: Lakeland Blundell House, 1971.

_____. *Rocks, Relics, and Biblical Reliability*. Grand Rapids: Zondervan Publishing House, 1977.

Zimmerman, Paul A. *Darwin, Evolution and Creation*. St. Louis: Concordia Publishing House, 1959.

Zuck, Roy. *Biblical Archaeology*. Wheaton, Ill.: Scripture Press, 1963.

Index

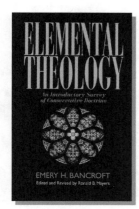

Elemental Theology:
An Introductory Survey
of Conservative Doctrine

E. H. Bancroft

B ancroft covers the basics of systematic theology in brief, easy-to-follow outline form that will be appreciated by students, teachers, pastors, and laypersons. His thorough survey of doctrine includes numerous quotations from well-known biblical commentators and study questions at the end of each chapter for personal or class review. Some of the specific doctrines discussed are:

The Doctrine of Jesus Christ
The Doctrine of the Holy Spirit
The Doctrine of Man
The Doctrine of Sin
The Doctrine of Angels

0-8254-2152-7   paperback   400 pp.

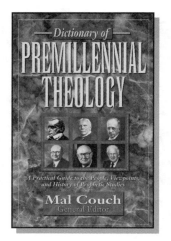

Dictionary of Premillennial Theology: A Practical Guide to the People, Viewpoints, and History of Prophetic Studies

Mal Couch, General Editor

More than fifty scholars, authors, and Bible teachers combine their expertise to compile this new concise dictionary of premillennial and dispensational theology. Entries cover major theological terms and concepts in prophetic studies as well as the eschatology of each book of the Bible, individual Scripture passages, and various extra-canonical writings. Also included are articles on the major figures in prophetic studies such as Scofield, Chafer, Ladd, Pentecost, Ryrie, and Walvoord, as well as historical figures such as the church fathers, Augustine, Jonathan Edwards, and John Nelson Darby.

0-8254-2351-1   paperback   448 pp.

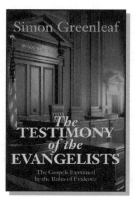

Testimony of the Evangelists: The Gospels Examined by the Rules of Evidence

Simon Greenleaf

How would the Gospels be regarded if they were submitted as evidence in a court of law? This fascinating question forms the basis for this time-honored work in substantiating the relevance and reliability of the Gospel records. Also includes an examination of the legal procedures in the trial of Jesus.

"The greatest single authority on evidence in the entire literature of legal procedure."   —*The Dictionary of American Biography*

0-8254-2747-9   paperback   128 pp.

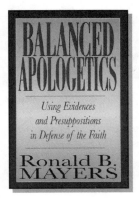

Balanced Apologetics: Using Evidences and Presuppositions in Defense of the Faith

Ronald B. Mayers

A systematic study demonstrating that a biblical and thoroughly balanced apologetic is possible—combining the best of both presuppositionalism and evidentialism. Mayers' careful argumentation, total commitment to Scripture, and practical focus provide a solid, biblical foundation upon which to understand and defend the Christian faith.

"Professor Mayers displays a mastery of the history of apolgetic thought. . . . Throughout he hews rigorously to the biblical data."
—Kenneth Kantzer

0-8254-3265-0   paperback   256 pp.

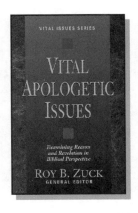

Vital Apologetic Issues: Examining Reason and Revelation in Biblical Perspective

Roy B. Zuck

When it comes to giving a reasoned defense of one's faith, just knowing definitions isn't enough. It helps to have reliable guidance through the critical issues of apologetics. Zuck draws upon the insights and study of numerous evangelical scholars and writers to address crucial questions in the field of Christian apologetics. Some of the chapters included are:

"The Nature and Origin of Evil" by Robert Culver
"Biblical Naturalism and Modern Science" by Henry M. Morris
"Ebla and Biblical Historical Inerrancy" by Eugene H. Merrill

0-8254-4070-x   paperback   264 pp.